W9-BLD-375

PEOPLE, PRIDE AND PROGRESS

125 YEARS OF THE GRANGE IN AMERICA

PEOPLE, PRIDE AND PROGRESS

125 YEARS OF THE GRANGE IN AMERICA

By David H. Howard

Foreword by
the Honorable Thomas S. Foley
Speaker of the U.S. House
of Representatives

Afterword by
Robert E. Barrow
Master of the National Grange

National Grange • Washington, D.C.

National Grange
1616 H. Street NW
Washington, D.C. 20006

Unless otherwise noted, all photographs in this book are from the National Grange collection.

First Edition
First printing
98 97 96 95 94 93 92 5 4 3 2 1

Library of Congress Cataloging-in-Publication Data

Howard, David H., 1944-
People, pride and progress : 125 years of the Grange in America / by David H. Howard ; foreword by Thomas S. Foley.
p. cm.
Includes bibliographical references and index.
1. National Grange--History. I. Title.
HD 1485.N39H68 1992
338.1'06'073--dc20 92-397

Contents

Foreword

I WAS PLEASED to accept the invitation of David H. Howard and the National Grange to write the foreword to *People, Pride and Progress: 125 Years of the Grange in America,* commemorating the 125th anniversary of this important organization. Throughout its history, the Grange has been an important voice for the citizens of rural America.

The list of the organization's accomplishments is long and varied, as the organization has successfully represented the interests of rural America during the last 125 years. Emerging as our nation began shifting from a largely agrarian economy to an urban one, the Grange has continued to adapt to the changing nature of rural America. When the Grange began, agriculture was shifting from self-contained farming operations to interdependent ones that had to look outward to survive. Over the course of its history, the Grange has sought to address the shifting nature of agriculture in this country with creative solutions. Its participation in cooperatives and insurance are just two examples of such innovation.

The Grange has also sought to improve the lives of Americans through participation in many of the public policy debates that have occurred throughout its history. This involvement in legislation at the local, state, and national level has forever changed the nature of America. The Sherman Anti-Trust Act, the direct election of senators, and the initiative process (widely used in my home state of Washington) are examples of the continuing influence of past Grange legislative efforts.

Not content to rest on its laurels, the Grange continues its active involvement on behalf of American agriculture and our nation's rural residents. The Grange continues with its educational and public policy efforts as agriculture faces new and increasingly complicated challenges.

As a longtime member of the Grange, this anniversary milestone has some personal importance for me. From a very early age, the contributions of the Grange were apparent to me during my visits to my family's farm. My forebearers came to Washington state as farmers and, for me, American agriculture and rural life exemplify the values that form the best part of the American character. Hard work, honesty, patriotism, and charity toward others have led to our success as a nation and those values are rooted in the agrarian nature of our history. The Grange has continued to nurture these values and maintain the quality of life for rural Americans that is so essential to the nation.

— *The Honorable Thomas S. Foley*
Speaker of the
U.S. House of Representatives

Preface

PUBLICATION OF A HISTORY such as this carries with it the risk that it will cement people's views of the past. In an organization with as many notable accomplishments as the Order of Patrons of Husbandry, the temptation is to glory in our historical achievements and let present challenges remained unfulfilled.

When delegates assembled in Greensboro, North Carolina, for the 1989 National Grange convention, they listened to National Lecturer Mary Buffington's words of caution about this tendency. "Where the Grange will be in five years or 10 does not rely on the past," Buffington said. "It depends entirely upon the directions today's members and leaders are taking it.... We can't continue to talk about [the] Grange helping to bring electricity and free mail delivery into rural areas and expect people of today to be impressed. But we can remember the basic idea that Grange was meant to be a leader, the organization that would tackle anything, and set our course to do those very things today."

The Honorable Thomas S. Foley, in his foreword to this book, sounds a note of agreement with Buffington when he says the Grange has never been content to "rest on its laurels." The accomplishments of the past, while interesting to students of history and important to record, can do no more than point the way for today's activists.

This history, like any book detailing the past, dutifully records the facts. But the goal has been to present a usable history which will provide inspiration and ammunition for Grange leaders and workers as they build their organization and continue community service and legislative efforts on behalf of rural Americans. The author has attempted to arrange the material and tell the story in a fashion which will be enjoyable to read, thereby ensuring widespread use.

Although the book can provide inspiration for today's Grange leaders, it must not do so by sacrificing the truth. A history which is totally self-serving, glossing over events which could, in retrospect, be construed as not entirely positive, would be a disservice to scholarship and to members who deserve an honest presentation. This book includes both the victories and the defeats.

The most notable lesson this Grange history teaches is that every great achievement resulted from leaders taking the initiative to fight for what they felt was right. The surprising element of this process is that, for the most part, those leaders were self-taught in the Grange halls which dotted the nation. Until recent years, the masters and other officers of the state Granges and the national organization were farmers, several of them without the benefit of advanced education. They rose through the ranks, gaining knowledge and experience at each step. Success reinforced their belief in the power of organized action and what it could accomplish. Without exception, their motives were for the improvement of an entire class of the American population, not simply those who paid dues to the Grange. This book shows what such character and dedication can accomplish.

Today, National Grange officers are convinced the social and economic problems which still plague rural residents can be solved by the same empowerment of leadership that kept the Grange a powerful force for 125 years. They have attempted to keep their organization receptive to new ideas so it can remain a potent instrument of progressive reform for generations to come.

America has few organizations which can match the grass-roots structure and proven effectiveness of the Grange. Unfortunately, it is unclear if today's members fully recognize the powerful tool they have in their grasp. When they do, there can be no doubt the victories of rural free delivery and farm electrification will seem minor in comparison with what they will ultimately achieve.

—Lebanon, Oregon
June 1992

Acknowledgements

THE AUTHOR'S NAME goes on the cover of a book, but seldom is that individual totally deserving of all the credit. This is certainly the case with *People, Pride and Progress.*

My initial motivation for tackling this intimidating project flowed from personal association with the Grange over the years, and involvement of family members dating into the nineteenth century. Despite grandparents and other relatives who seldom missed meetings at their Charity Grange hall (Linn County, Oregon), Georgetta and I would never have become members had it not been for Virginia Bohles Sims. Virginia signed us up at a quilt show in Fairmount Grange No. 252, Albany, Oregon, and spent the next year calling several times monthly to remind us of upcoming Grange events. We felt loved and wanted, and that prompted our willingness to participate. Virginia is the widow of former Oregon State Master Ted Sims, a man who also provided quiet but sincere encouragement as we became increasingly involved in the Grange. It was Virginia and Ted who gave us a copy of Gardner's *The Grange, Friend of the Farmer,* the book which provided the groundwork for this present volume.

There have been many others who gave invaluable assistance and encouragement. Leading the list was National Master Robert Barrow. He always has been helpful and supportive. My old friend and former boss Jack Silvers, chairman of the National Grange executive committee, was especially encouraging in that he expressed unwavering confidence in my ability to do the job well. Other executive committee members have given valuable support and comments while reading various drafts of the manuscript.

Many state masters and state Grange staff members have assisted in securing information and some of the photographs seen in the book. I especially have to thank the Oregon State Grange which provided me with a set of national *Journal of Proceedings* to use throughout the research and writing of this book. Several National Grange officers and department heads gave important direction.

Past Masters John Scott and Edward Andersen provided much input, making chapters on their administrations fun to write. Former National Lecturer Bill Brake provided a great deal of insight and information during a delightful day together in Traverse City, Michigan. His subsequent death is a loss to all who knew him.

National Grange staff members were always willing to answer my questions, search out materials and give valuable critical advice at each stage of the process. I need to single out each of them: Bob Frederick, legislative director; Judy Massabny, director of information; Harry Massey, director of membership development; and Leroy Watson, legislative representative.

A great deal of credit belongs to a group of individuals who served as readers while the manuscript was being developed. In addition to National Master Barrow and members of the executive committee, I was pleased to have a broad range of critics, people who had tremendous insight into the organization. Readers included C. Jerome Davis, high priest of Demeter, emeritus, and author of two outstanding books on the early history of the Grange; George Spies, a member from Massachusetts with an inexhaustible depth of knowledge about Grange history; Dr. Lowell K. Dyson, an historian with the U.S. Department of Agriculture who has written about the Grange in his book on farm organizations; Sister Thomas More Bertels, an insightful woman who has not only participated in, lectured and written about the Grange for many years, but has done much to convince Americans of the necessity of farm organizations in general; and Wib Justi, former National Grange youth director who worked for the organization during many of its most exciting years. Dr. William Barns, a retired member from the West Virginia University history department and author of an excellent history of the Grange in his state, had agreed to be a reader as well. His untimely death occurred as the first draft was being written. Joseph C. Goulden, one of America's best known writers of history and biography, gave needed inspiration and encouragement toward the end of the project.

I reserve special acclaim for the last reader. Bill Thorness, of Seattle, came to work in 1985 as my assistant editor at *The Grange News* and quickly became a trusted friend. When I went on to other pursuits, he assumed my job at the Washington State Grange and performed it well. Now the editor of a national trade magazine, he has been untiring in his technical editing of the manuscript and has my utmost appreciation for the hard work.

Tom Woods, whose excellent book on O.H. Kelley is listed in the bibliography, was our able guide and interpreter at the Kelley Farm. Donald Marti, whose interesting book about Grange women is also mentioned in the bibliography, provided the information which made Chapter 7 possible. A.R. Riggs and Tom Velk, of McGill University in Montreal, unselfishly shared their research, making possible the section in this book on the Bachelder administration. Alfreda Irwin, historian at the Chautauqua Institution, was our delightful host for a day and her help with the Grange-Chautauqua connection was cheerfully given.

Assistance also was received from the staff at the Cornell University library in Ithaca, New York, during examination of Grange archives there. Dr. Alan Fusonie, historian and chief of special collections at the National Agricultural Library in Beltsville, Maryland, helped unlock his institution's amazing resources. Oregon State University library personnel also have been helpful. Present leaders in several other fraternities generously gave their time answering my questionnaires, making possible the comments on fraternalism's future in Chapter 15.

Two special women complete my list of those who made special contributions to this effort. The first is no longer with us, but I thought of her often while working on this book. Avis Beam was longtime assistant editor of *The Grange News* and she completed her career there during my tenure as editor. A student of Grange history, she imparted to me the desire to uncover the fascinating stories of past accomplishments, legislative struggles and an occasional scandal. I wish she had been here to read the manuscript; she would have had numerous suggestions for its improvement.

Final praise goes to my loving wife and fellow Granger, Georgetta. Her assistance on research trips allowed me to cover twice the amount of material and her patience in subsequent months made completion of the manuscript possible.

1

Farmers Shaping America

LIKE AN ARCHEOLOGIST searches for telltale traces of ancient civilizations, someone interested in piecing together the story of America can use names on a map for clues to finding people and events which shaped our past. We tend to name our towns and landmarks for early citizens or choose names representing important milestones in our lives.

Communities around the nation are wearing the name of a fraternal organization tracing its story to the struggle of frontier farmers for equity and economic security. From Grangeville, Idaho, to Granger, Indiana, villages and towns where these early farmers lived and traded still refer to themselves with the name of the Grange. More than any other organization, the Grange has a permanent place on our American map.

There are communities called Granger in Iowa, Missouri, Ohio, Oregon, Texas, Washington and Wyoming as well as Indiana. Towns called La Grange are found in Arkansas, Tennessee, Texas, Georgia, Wyoming, North Carolina, Missouri, Kentucky, Illinois, and, with a small difference in spelling, in Ohio, Maine and Indiana. La Grange Park, Illinois, wraps up the list. Although some of these communities trace their name to an individual named Granger or some other source, most of them were named for the group that was so popular when the towns were formed.

When a sightseer looks up from the map and drives down some of the countless rural roads crisscrossing America, the reason for the popularity of Grange as a placename becomes more apparent. In many states it is impossible to travel very far without passing one of the thousands of Grange halls which dot our countryside.

Although Oliver Hudson Kelley, the recognized founder of the Grange, confessed that he took the name "Grange" from the title of a popular novel of the 1860s, the label has a more profound history. Many of the large farming estates in England and Ireland have been referred to as Granges for centuries. The word is still used in this fashion in the British Isles and its appearance on the Hamilton Grange Branch Library in New York's Harlem district, named for the original homesite of Alexander Hamilton, can also claim this meaning.

The word grange apparently comes from a Latin word meaning grain. A similar word in Spanish and Portuguese languages means a barn or farm, while others use the word to refer to a granary. Chaucer, Shakespeare and Milton employed the word in their writings.

There is an impressive organization behind the name. It is a fraternity which has left an imprint upon America that goes far beyond the pages of the road atlas. In the rural Grange halls as well as in the halls of Congress and many state capitols, this group has represented the needs and wishes of its members. The benefits of their accomplishments have enriched the lives of everyone.

The official name of the group commonly known as the Grange is the Order of the Patrons of Husbandry. The heart of the movement is in the local "subordinate" Grange—that hall down the road where members meet on a regular basis. Subordinate Granges in a county or somewhat larger region band together to work on joint projects and for occasional common meetings. The organization at

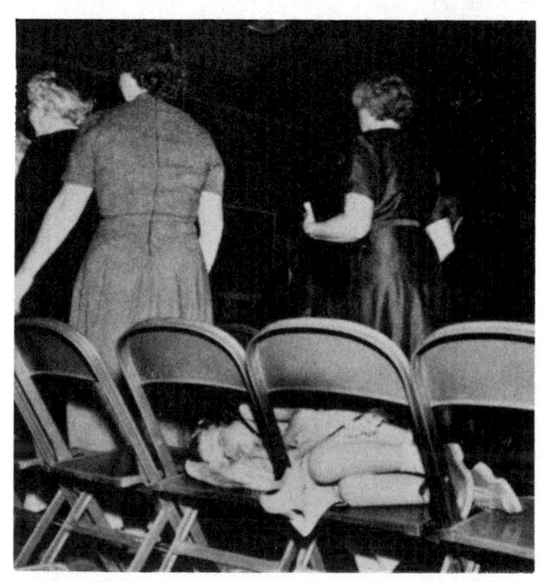

Many current Grange members grew up in the organization. In subordinate Granges with many younger members, the sight of children catching a snooze during a meeting is not unusual. Photos in this chapter, such as this one taken in 1957 at Oregon's Poison Creek Grange, are historical but representative of activities still popular in Granges of the 1990s.

that county or regional level is known as the Pomona Grange and it is a separate, independent structural entity within the Patrons of Husbandry. All the Granges, subordinate and Pomona, organize on the statewide level as a state Grange or Grange council. The difference between a state Grange and a council is the number of subordinate Granges within the state; states with a small number of Granges are designated as councils. State Granges and councils, with all their subordinate and Pomona Granges, are represented on a national level by the National Grange, headquartered in downtown Washington, D.C.

Local Granges, like all other organizations, hold regular meetings, elect officers and engage in a wide variety of other events. Although the Grange has roots in agriculture and at times in its history one needed to be a farmer to belong, nowadays members come from agriculture and a host of other occupations. Most members reside in small towns or rural areas, but Granges also exist and prosper in large cities like Washington, D.C., and Seattle.

Typical Grange meetings across the country have certain elements in common. There is an official opening exercise which includes a short prayer, salute to the flag and opening of a Bible on a stand in the middle of the hall. The business meeting is structured like those of most other groups and there is a special time set aside for a short program of an educational or entertaining nature. The meeting concludes with a brief closing exercise. Many Granges weave in a potluck dinner prior to the meeting or refreshments following in order to increase opportunities to socialize.

Sixteen officers lead a Grange

The officer slate for the Grange at each level is led by a master. This title, which refers to the position functioning as the organization's president or chairperson, is one of several officer names also dating back to the feudal English estates. The Grange's vice president is called the overseer and there are people assuming the duties of secretary, treasurer, chaplain and an executive committee. A lecturer is responsible for the short programs at each meeting. A chairperson for women's activities is appointed in some states and elected in others. A musician, almost always a pianist, adds his or her talent to create a warm and cheerful ambiance for each meeting.

Grange events provide opportunities for neighbors to work and play together. These women were obviously proud of their baking when photographed at Flowing Well Grange, Beaver Crossing, Nebraska, in 1956.

There are several other elected officers, however, who have no parallels in other groups with the exception of some fraternal orders. The Grange, like the Masons, Odd Fellows, Elks and Moose, is a fraternity. One distinctive feature of fraternal orders is their emphasis upon traditional procedures for conducting their meetings. These procedures, often called rituals, employ members who have specific parts to play in opening and closing ceremonies. The steward, assistant steward and lady assistant steward are Grange officers who present the flag, open the Bible, escort guests and new members. A gatekeeper "guards" the main entrance into the hall during the meeting. These titles date from old English manors and they originally designated jobs performed on the farm by its employees.

Three other officers, each required to be a woman member, have differing duties at various levels of the Grange. These officers, named Ceres, Pomona and Flora after Roman goddesses important to agriculture, are strictly ceremonial and their primary assignment is to join with other officers in offering instruction within a ritual format to new members.

The Grange, like other fraternities, has levels or degrees of membership and a member advances from one level to the next by participating in or observing the rituals for that level. Each level is called a degree and all regular members of the local subordinate Grange receive their initiation into the Grange by participating in the first four degree rituals. Each degree ritual is a collection of short speeches given by officers, intermixed with music and explanation of various symbolic "tools," such as the plow and hoe, seen in the Grange hall. The instruction makes numerous references to farming, the crops, seasons, seeds and soil, in order to teach lessons of brotherhood, duty to God, morality and the importance of hard work ("faith, hope, charity and fidelity").

New members often witness the first four degrees all in one day by seeing the first two on a Saturday or Sunday afternoon, breaking for a famous Grange potluck dinner, and then enjoying the third and fourth degrees following the meal. In some states, degree

Many Granges begin meetings with with a sumptuous potluck dinner or finish with refreshments. A committee, nowadays usually including male members as well, has charge of preparations. These ladies were busy in 1955 at Tobacco Valley Grange in Eureka, Montana.

teams (groups of members who have memorized their parts and who work together regularly to put on the degrees) are organized on a county or regional basis with the teams putting on several performances a year at selected Granges in their area.

Subordinate (fourth degree) members who wish to join in the Pomona Grange activities need to witness the fifth degree. Similarly, state Granges—usually on an annual basis at their state convention—perform the sixth degree for the benefit of members who wish to work at that level of the organization. Also annually, at the National Grange convention, the assembly of Demeter, the national ritualistic leadership, performs the seventh and highest degree of the order. This event always draws crowds of members, with the record attendance being 18,374 who traveled to Columbus, Ohio, for the 1947 conferral.

Since 1983, state Granges have been permitted to offer two classifications of membership. There are regular members who participate in degree work and are entitled to attend meetings and hold offices. An associate member classification, not yet recognized by all state Granges, is for individuals who want affiliation with the Grange organization but have no desire at the time of application to participate in its activities. These members qualify for certain member benefits such as insurance programs and they receive regular publications but cannot attend meetings or see the degree work.

Members are continually being asked about the Grange's reputation as a "secret" organization. Simply stated, the Grange, like other fraternities and many other groups, restricts attendance at business meetings and degree conferrals to its regular members of record. There are a few elements of the degree work which, in order to be properly understood, need to be appreciated in the context of the entire ceremony. Because of this, members generally do not talk openly about these aspects of the Grange ritual with nonmembers. Other signs and signals, such as an annual password and a unique Grange handshake, are remnants of early days before the advent of membership cards. Tradition within the organization dictates that these signs of membership be shared only with other members. The label of "secret organization" is exaggerated; nothing within the Grange is secret according to the negative meaning of that term.

Joining a local Grange is a positive step which can bring many personal rewards. Prospective members are recommended by existing members but, in actuality, anyone interested in joining merely needs to approach a member and ask for an application. Each new application is presented at a meeting and a confirmation vote on the application is held. The applicant is scheduled for the degree work or, in some states, an obligation ceremony, so they can become active as soon as possible. After successful completion of the initiation process, the new member is known as a Matron or Husbandman in the Patrons of Husbandry and often addressed as "sister" or "brother" by other members. This practice emphasizes the fraternal tradition of recognizing members as "family."

The Grange has an historical distinction as one of the first major national organizations besides the church and the now defunct temperance group known as the Independent Order of Good Templars which sought the membership and involvement of everyone in the family. Grange members have an equal voice and an equal vote at meetings regardless of their age, sex or position within the Grange. Children ages five through 14 are eligible to belong to a junior Grange, whether or not they come from a Grange family. In those subordinate Granges maintaining a junior Grange,

Sharing meals together has been a traditional method for promoting the sense of community and brotherhood. Granges have utilized potlucks since the early days of the organization. This group was at Geneva (New York) Community Grange in 1955.

young members conduct their own meetings, elect their own officers, have their unique ceremonial work and orchestrate a wide variety of activities under the guidance of adult advisers. Activities range from craft projects to community service endeavors involving hundreds of area youngsters. Many state Granges sponsor a series of summer camps for junior Grange members.

Individuals are eligible for full subordinate Grange membership upon their fourteenth birthday. In addition to their participation with adults, high school and college age members have, since the 1940s, opted in most Granges to host an additional slate of activities specifically designed for their interests. There are social functions, athletic events, group and individual competitions which capture their imagination. Granges are asked to appoint one of their members as a youth chairperson, an individual or couple to coordinate these activities and help enlist additional young people as members.

Unique programs are a Grange hallmark

The function of the committee for women's activities within the local Grange is an extensive one. The interesting development of this committee's role within the Grange will be covered in Chapter 7, but for now it should be noted that this group oversees the numerous dinner functions, much of the local fundraising, and administers a series of competitions in traditional homemaking arts such as needlework, quilt making and creating stuffed toys. The stuffed toy contest, inaugurated in 1976, is one of the Grange's most visible and touching outreach efforts. Tens of thousands of toys are made each year nationwide, judged for minor prizes and then donated by the box-full to childrens' wards of hospitals. The toys are claimed, one by one, by the young patients who take them home when they leave the hospital.

Another highly noticeable outreach program which originated within the women's activities department is the service provided to the nation's hearing impaired. Aside from educational work which will be described later, this endeavor (separate from the women's activities department since 1979) coordinates fundraising for various projects benefitting the hearing impaired.

Most members like to describe their local Grange as a community service organization and they view themselves in much the same manner as do members of other service groups such as the Lions and Kiwanis. In smaller towns the Grange is often the only community organization and the hall is in use nearly every evening for activities sponsored by the Grange and others. Dances, lectures, educational programs, concerts, neighborhood fairs, community meetings and debates all find a home in these halls. Blood pressure clinics, Red Cross blood donation sites, bookmobiles and food banks frequently operate from Grange halls. In many localities, residents visit the Grange hall on election days to vote. More often than not, Grange members are in the center of the action doing the volunteer jobs that have to be done.

In the fall Grange members in most communities assume the traditional agricultural role expected of them and descend en masse on the fairgrounds. The Grange and the county fair have been synonymous for generations, and it is with the delicately decorated displays of farm produce that Grange members advertise themselves as the custodians of agricultural interests. Some Grange members staff the livestock judging arenas while others supervise 4-H displays and demonstrations. There is often a Grange chuckwagon—a fundraising food booth that attracts fair-goers.

The Grange began as a family organization. Husbands and wives participate together—in housekeeping as well as recreational activities—unlike many other fraternal groups. This couple faced a counter full of dirty dishes at Harmony Grange, Westover, Pennsylvania, in 1956.

Part of the Grange responsibility as a family, community service organization is providing activities which help young people develop into responsible citizens. Many subordinate Granges sponsor junior Granges, scout, Camp Fire or 4-H groups.

Much of the monthly or twice-monthly Grange business meeting is taken up with planning and preparation for these events and community service programs. Occasionally there is a recognition night where the volunteers can parade the outstanding accomplishments of some of their fellow members. Mentioned, too, are the economic benefits to members achieved through cooperative efforts. Nonprofit Grange cooperative mutual insurance companies have been offering quality insurance products to members at extremely competitive rates for generations. In many communities the Grange was also responsible for organizing the local cooperative farm supply store or a popular credit union. Some state Granges manage buying clubs which offer participating members the opportunity to purchase needed goods at reduced group prices. Several states also have Grange-sponsored low-cost retirement homes.

The National Grange has embarked on a member benefits program called Grange Advantage and is offering a National Grange credit card through one of the major credit card companies. Through cooperation with a college selection service, the National

Grange is offering a program for college-bound students to assist them in selecting an appropriate college and directing them to financial assistance if needed.

A great benefit: a voice in government

But perhaps more than anything else, the Grange's interest in legislative action sets it apart from all other fraternities, service and family organizations. Since its earliest years, the Grange has included legislative involvement as one of its distinctive characteristics, an endeavor which at times has almost overshadowed its other functions. In this governmental relations undertaking one can most easily see the concept of "grass-roots" in action.

The Grange's legislative program, like so many of its functions, begins at the local Grange hall. During part of the meeting dedicated to a report from the legislative committee chairperson, lively debate often erupts on topics of mutual concern. Those topics could range from the need for a stop sign near the school to national issues such as tax laws or the upcoming farm bill in Congress. A resolution will be offered and discussed; if the resulting vote is affirmative, the resolution will become the policy of that Grange. In matters of strictly local consequence, like the stop sign issue above, the policy enactment empowers the Grange to use its collective strength to resolve the problem. Members of the legislative committee and often the master and executive committee members prepare strategy to ensure success for the Grange's position. They may appear and testify at a city council meeting, write letters to the editor, conduct an open forum or lobby county commissioners.

If the resolution adopted by the local Grange relates to an issue of regional, statewide or national interest, then the resolution goes on to other levels within the organization. County-wide or regional problems are discussed and resolved at the Pomona Grange level; statewide concerns advance to the state Grange convention.

State Granges are an important subdivision of the organization's work. Since the state Grange receives part of each member's low annual dues, it has resources to act upon resolutions which are accepted for Grange policy at the state session. Many state Granges maintain an office and lobbyists as well as other personnel to administer the far-reaching programs of the organization.

Resolutions adopted at the state level which are national in nature are taken by the master of the state Grange to the next National Grange convention. The master and spouse are delegates from the state Grange to the annual national session; they spend a week debating and rewriting several hundred resolutions which have grown from the grass-roots which are firmly anchored in the subordinate Grange.

Besides resolution work and the seventh degree, the annual National Grange convention features large displays of art, crafts, needlework, photography and stuffed toys—winners in numerous state contests advancing for national judging. There are talent competitions, speaking contests and numerous special activities for youth and junior members. Many of these events also occur at state Grange conventions.

The National Grange maintains an 11-story office building within two blocks of the White House. The top level of the Grange organization, like all other levels, has a separate set of elected officers with the same titles and similar duties. A legislative staff works on a daily basis with members of Congress and various departments of the federal government. Other elected or appointed Grange leaders ensure smooth sailing for all the contests, publications and activities within the organization. Additionally, there are several officers who compose the Assembly of Demeter, a body overseeing the fraternity's ritualistic activities. These positions include the high priest of Demeter, priest archon, and priest annalist (president, vice president and secretary, respectively). If a woman

The Grange offers the arena for members to discuss community concerns in an atmosphere of openness and tolerance. This member spoke out on an issue at Sodus (New York) Grange in 1955.

holds the position, the title is changed to "priestess."

Throughout the Grange, the tone has always been one of mutual helpfulness. The organizational mission statement, adopted in 1990, says the National Grange will "provide national representation for its members on rural and agricultural issues; provide economic services for its members; [and] provide organization promotion and expansion." This accurately conveys the focus of the Grange since its inception. However, the goals of the National Grange, immediately following its mission statement, suggest some of the changes brought about by 125 years of hard work by the organization. The goals are "to increase interest in the Grange to stabilize membership; [and] to strengthen the image of the Grange through increased participation."

Present day Grange leaders sometimes show their frustration as they examine the new resolutions which show up at state and national sessions. Many of them deal with internal organizational matters and have relatively little importance outside the Grange. Some of the other resolutions cover substantive issues but, more often than not, the easily understood legislative battles are over and new policies adopted at the conventions tend to be concerned with arcane fine points of the law. Leaders long for a couple of strong, positive issues to mobilize members—issues to make members' blood boil like earlier fights for rural electrification, for the Rural Free Delivery service, or Social Security coverage for farmers. One could almost suspect that the Grange had done too good of a job during its first 125 years. To some, the big battles appear to be over and it takes a lot of work to motivate people to get excited over today's challenges.

But that wasn't always the case. The environment into which the Grange was born perhaps offered too many challenges.

2

Seeking to Elevate Farm Culture

SINCE COLONIAL TIMES, Americans have considered theirs an agricultural nation. Our first census, taken in 1790, showed 96 percent of the population living in rural areas, most on their own farms. By 1860, on the eve of the Civil War, the rural population—people living on farms or in very small towns—had dropped to around 80 percent. Although the two million plus farms in America varied greatly in size and organization, the average size was 199 acres. Those farms supplied over 30 percent of the national income in 1860 and jobs for nearly 60 percent of the people.

There were problems in rural America, however, as the nation prepared for its four-year struggle with itself. Even though most non-farmers philosophically viewed farming as mankind's most hallowed occupation, the welfare of the farmer was woefully neglected by these admirers. In 1846 Congress heard from President James K. Polk that although farmers constituted "a large majority of our population," they "have heretofore not only received none of the bounties or favors of Government" but "had endured burdens that enriched others." Shortly thereafter Congress was told by President Millard Fillmore that "justice and sound policy" dictated the federal government do everything possible "to promote the interests and welfare" of the early farmers.

Although farmers were a majority of the population, they had no collective voice. Prior to 1800, when 90 percent of the people were engaged in agriculture, less than 13 percent of the members of the U.S. House of Representatives were farmers. By the 1840s that number had declined to 8.6 percent. Agricultural historian Gilbert C. Fite reports, "the main reasons politicians paid relatively little heed to agricultural interests were that farmers were not organized or united, they were widely scattered, and their interests often conflicted."

Most farms before the mid-nineteenth century were family-owned diversified operations which primarily met the needs of the family. Almost all of the family's food and fiber was produced at home and marketing of any excess production was done locally, with the general store merchant in the nearest town.

The growth of industry-based cities on the Eastern Seaboard created new tensions within American agriculture. Population shifts began to occur and residents of the cities, working in the new factories and shops, needed to buy their food. Marketing systems began to emerge for moving the increasingly abundant foodstuffs from the recently settled Midwest to the cities in the East.

Concurrently, farmers were given the benefits of a burgeoning technology in the form of implements which greatly expanded their production capability. The catch-22 situation which is familiar territory to today's farmer began to develop: The farmer needed to produce more in order to have excess to trade for equipment which would allow him to grow even greater crops. Along with the new equipment also came the need for agricultural credit. American farmers were beginning to move from a subsistence way of life to an industrial one.

In 1862 President Lincoln approved three pieces of legislation which began to partially fulfill the hopes of his predecessors Polk and Fillmore. On May 15 he signed the bill establishing the Department of Agriculture. Five days later the Homestead Act crossed his desk and then, in July, the Morrill Land-Grant College Act was signed, paving the way for our present network of colleges specializing in agriculture and engineering.

The Homestead Act has been championed as America's most noble effort to help its poor, hardworking citizens attain the good life of farming their own land. Under the act, settlers could claim a parcel of land—up to 160 acres—and, after five years of cultivation and improvements, they could receive full title at no cost. However, it was an honorable idea which came almost too late. By 1862, land speculators had already bought most of the best available farmland and the Homestead Act land was also offered for sale. Speculators bought the best pieces and resold them at inflated prices to settlers. There also were instances of graft on the part of government officials administering the frontier lands. Subsequent

Oliver Hudson Kelley (1826-1913) is recognized as the individual who originated the idea of the Grange and his efforts brought it into being.

accounting showed that only one out of every six acres of Homestead Act land went directly from the government to the settlers.

Between 1850 and 1870 railroad companies were the recipients of governmental largess when ownership of 150 million acres (an area larger than New England) was given to them. For example, 20 percent of the state of Kansas and 15 percent of Nebraska were handed over to railroads in an effort to stimulate rail construction. It was evident that the potential crops of the Midwest had to be moved to the East and apparently railroads at any cost were seen to be the answer. Would-be farmers, nonetheless, again ended up "enduring burdens which enriched others" by being charged outrageous prices for farmland the rail companies received as a gift.

There was ample dissatisfaction among farmers with the pressure that was being placed upon them. They were having to think and manage their operations more like businessmen but, it appeared, the people who ultimately controlled their destiny—the merchants and industrialists of the East—would stop at nothing to take advantage of any success they enjoyed.

Kelley's destiny is to lead farmers

One man who felt this frustration as deeply as anyone was Oliver Hudson Kelley. Born the son of a Boston tailor in 1826, at the age of 21 Kelley answered the call of newspaper editor Horace Greeley who preached, "Go West, young man, go forth into the country." After six months' service as a reporter for the *Chicago Tribune* he moved briefly to Peoria and, later, to Bloomington (now Muscatine), Iowa, where he supported himself as a telegrapher. In Bloomington, Kelley was married to Lucy Earle in the spring of 1849 and the couple "honeymooned" two months later by heading off to the austere Minnesota Territory.

The Kelleys set up their home in the newly incorporated village of St. Paul and when the first territorial Legislature met there a month after his arrival, Kelley was elected messenger by the Minnesota House of Representatives. Other duties included sergeant at arms pro tem and serving as a clerk for the judiciary committee.

Talk about moving the territorial capital from St. Paul 35 miles up the Mississippi to Itasca prompted Kelley to do a little land speculation of his own. He staked a claim near the townsite but when the push to move the capital filed on a split vote, Kelley's dream of riches from real estate faded.

Nevertheless, the Kelleys moved to their land and subsisted that winter on wild rice and cranberries. Oliver traded with the Winnebago Indians who were wintering nearby. The following spring Lucy died during childbirth. Despite the efforts of Oliver's mother who came out from Boston to help care for the child, the baby also died six months later. The next year Oliver married Temperance Lane, a teacher living nearby, who also was a Bostonian. Together they had four daughters.

Kelley, like many others who responded to Greeley's call, had no practical farming experience. Instead, he shared the belief of others that agriculture was a noble career and that without the farmers, America's economy and moral fiber would collapse. Kelley also had a good education and a burning desire to learn the latest and best methods of crop and livestock production.

When Kelley first settled in Minnesota there were only 157 farms in the entire territory. During the 1850s the region grew

William Saunders (1822-1900)

Caroline A. Hall
(1838-1918)

John R. Thompson
(1834-1894)

rapidly, however, and by 1858 farmers in Minnesota were finally able to meet the demands of a growing local market for foodstuffs. General store merchants were the principal buyers of agricultural products, usually trading merchandise for the commodities brought by local farmers. By the early 1860s, this barter system started to collapse because it was incapable of supplying the farmers with enough income to modernize their operations. The promise of greater profit by exporting commodities to other regions of the country attracted Kelley and his fellow farmers. In spirit, at least, they were among the earliest commercial farmers on the frontier.

Early in the 1850s Kelley acted on his conviction that the way to success for frontier farmers was through the utilization of the latest technology and scientific information. The Benton County Agricultural Society (BCAS), organized by Kelley in 1852, started out as a mutual improvement effort where neighboring farmers shared information about agricultural production. There was a library of agricultural books and reports which were under Kelley's care as the society's corresponding secretary. In 1855 he began editing an agricultural section in the *Sauk Rapids Frontierman,* a Democratic newspaper, and for some time he supplied statistical data to the Patent Office, the government agency which assumed some responsibility for agriculture prior to establishment of the Department of Agriculture.

Kelley's county agriculture group gradually expanded its mission from education to include promotion of new farming implements. A livestock and agricultural depot was initiated where livestock, machinery, fruit trees and seeds were sold. The effort was short-lived but the experiment into agricultural activism convinced Kelley he was on the right track. Kelley biographer Thomas A. Woods suggests the society was the original proving ground for the organization which would result from Kelley's labors 15 years later—the National Grange. The BCAS "was the nursery where his hostility and organizational reaction to speculative merchants and monopoly capitalists were born and nurtured," Woods writes.

Perhaps more than anything else, Kelley could be called a promoter. Concurrent with his early farming and agricultural society endeavors, he found the time to develop the townsite of Northwood near his home on the Mississippi. There was a brickyard, headquarters for O.H. Kelley and Company which manufactured Excelsior Metal Polish, a post office, hotel and general store. Although he still kept his farm, Kelley referred to himself as a "notary public, justice of the peace, real estate dealer, and general land agent." The Panic of 1857 brought hardship to all the people

William M. Ireland
(? -1891)

John Trimble
(1831-1902)

of Minnesota and Kelley, who had borrowed heavily to start Northwood, was left with heavy losses. The incident seemed to reinforce his view that the farmer was at the mercy of distant people who controlled the wealth of the nation.

Kelley returned to full-time commercial farming and was again faced with the difficulties of making sufficient profit from his labor. In 1862 his letter printed in the *Country Gentleman* reflected a growing pessimism:

> To one who never opened a farm it may appear very interesting and pleasant; it will do for the boys to talk about, and for men of wealth to recommend, but when you begin without a dollar in ready money, and no team of your own, and work up hill four or five years, the romance fizzles out.... There is no greater curse to farmers than debts and poor fences.... Don't suppose by this I am giving advice without experience. I have had both, and have a little now, but there is a fair prospect of getting out of the snarl before long. Since I made the resolution to keep from contracting new debts, and refuse credit, I have made good progress.

Minnesota agriculture shifted to heavy dependence upon wheat for export and the cost of transporting the commodity to market became a major burden for farmers. The demand for wheat during the Civil War in the early 1860s caused the price to escalate and the expansion of railroads in the state eventually replaced depend-

Francis M. McDowell
(1831-1894)

Aaron B. Grosh
(? -1884)

ence upon river transportation. Freight rates varied radically and as competing lines merged, farmers were at the mercy of railroad monopolies. Woods notes that in 1866 "it cost 35 percent more to ship wheat from Winona to Chicago than from Chicago to New York, a distance almost four times greater." The farmers became even more enraged when they considered the vast subsidization of the railroads through public grants of land. In Minnesota alone, one quarter of the state's land had been given to the rail companies.

Establishment of the Department of Agriculture in 1862 boosted Kelley's idealism and, through the influence of his old friend Minnesota Senator Alexander Ramsey, he received a Washington, D.C., clerkship in the young agency. Leaving his family at the Itasca farm, he worked in Washington through the winter and returned home in the spring of 1865 to plant crops. While in Washington he moonlighted as a correspondent for the *St. Paul Daily Press* and wrote articles for eastern papers such as the *Boston Post* and the *National Republican.* Although his pieces were basically gossip, they reflect a growing disenchantment with the Department of Agriculture.

General Lee surrendered to General Grant at Appomattox on April 9, 1865, and the nation's four-year blood-bath was over. The gigantic task confronting government leaders was reconstruction of the South along with managing the social transformation caused by the end of slavery and break-up of many large plantations. Over one-third of the nation had no effective civilian government and was ruled by the U.S. Army under martial law. One out of every eight Americans at the beginning of the war was now either dead, injured, or homeless. After the assassination of the country's most talented political figure, Abraham Lincoln, there was bitter competition to control the nation's power base. The agricultural climate of the former Confederate States was in confusion; stability needed to be restored in order to renew people's lives and increase production of essential crops.

In October 1865, Kelley received word from Isaac Newton, commissioner of the Department of Agriculture, requesting his return to Washington as soon as possible for "special business." Shortly after reading the letter, Kelley made the trip and learned that Newton anticipated sending him on a tour through the South collecting statistics and information relative to the condition of farming there. Kelley found Newton hesitant to make a final commitment, though, probably because he feared repercussions from sending a

New England Yankee into the South so soon after the war. But the impatient Kelley took the matter into his own hands and scheduled an appointment with President Andrew Johnson. Kelley's bold determination worked and, with the blessing of the president, Newton appointed Kelley for the task on January 1, 1866:

> To O.H. Kelley, Esq.:
> The relations of the Southern states with the Government for several years past having prevented this Department from obtaining the usual statistical and other information from those states, and a prevailing desire for reliable information being manifested on the part of the people, I have determined, with the advice and authority of His Excellency, the President of the United States, to appoint you an agent of this Department, to proceed immediately through the states, lately in hostility against the Government, to procure such information, and report the same to this Department for publication.
> Having reference to the enclosed instructions, you will immediately enter upon the discharge of your duties as such agent.
> ISAAC NEWTON, Commissioner

The instructions charged Kelley with keeping a daily log of observations, gathering statistics and reporting on the "character, quality and price of land,...kind of crops generally produced, and quantity per acre, with the time of planting and gathering, and the facilities afforded in their production, as well as such statistics in reference thereto attainable; also the disposition of the Freedmen to labor, and the feelings of their former owners, and the citizens generally towards them."

A farmers' fraternity takes shape

Kelley already had formed many of his thoughts about the need for organizing farmers. Although some people ascribe the birth of the Grange to the trip through the South, it is more accurate to assume Kelley had recognized the need many years earlier for a national farm organization. The ultimate pattern for the Grange did come to Kelley on the trip, however, and from the South he wrote to his wife's niece Caroline Hall that he felt farmers would respond to a "Secret Society of Agriculturists." He wrote that such a group would help "restore kindly feelings among the people." Her response was enthusiastic, but she also "expressed sympathy for the women of the South." This was the germ which led to the organization becoming a family one.

Kelley was a longtime member of the Masonic fraternity, possessing the distinction of being the first person initiated into the order in Minnesota. In the South, where personal hostilities naturally ran deep only months after the cessation of fighting, the Northern Yankee Kelley could be expected to encounter no little resistance to accomplishing his Department of Agriculture duties. As a Mason, however, he found a bond with Southern members of the fraternity which quickly bridged sectional differences. This experience undoubtedly influenced Kelley's decision to use the fraternal model in forming his new farm organization.

Fraternal orders, particularly the Masonic fraternity, had been influential in American public life since the days of the Revolution. George Washington was master of his Masonic lodge while he served as president. Dating from the same era as the Grange, fraternal orders such as the Knights of Pythias, Eastern Star, Royal Arcanum, Woodmen, Red Men, Shrine and, in a perverse way, the Ku Klux Klan, all attracted unbelievable participation. Americans who had endured years of war and separation longed for fraternity, love and brotherhood.

Kelley's tour of the South was completed in April and, after filing his report with the department, he returned to Itasca via Boston. Visiting Miss Hall allowed her the opportunity to reinforce the concept that women be accorded "full membership" in the new organization; it was an idea which stuck.

Crops were poor that season and family income suffered, so when an offer of a job as a clerk in the Post Office Department was received, Kelley jumped at the chance. With this new position, commencing early in January 1867, Kelley used his spare time discussing his idea for a national farm fraternity with other government employees. Although there were others with whom Kelley conferred, six men plus Kelley are affectionately referred to as the "Seven Founders of the Order" by Grange members. The list of founders, ratified as a National Grange constitutional amendment at its 1874 session, has been termed arbitrary and unclear by some, including Thomas Clark Atkeson, the Grange's first legislative representative and author of the *Semi-Centennial History of the Patrons of Husbandry*. An eighth person, Caroline A. Hall, was granted the distinction in 1892 of being named an "equal to a founder" of the fraternity and in 1915 the Assembly of Demeter recognized her as being entitled to the same position in Grange history as held by the seven founders. Despite the arbitrariness of the list, these eight individuals remain in most members' minds as those responsible for the birth of the Grange. There were, in fact, several others who made equally significant contributions.

John R. Thompson was probably the first to hear of Kelley's plan. An official in the Treasury Department following the war, Thompson was raised and educated in New Hampshire and Vermont. He was a veteran of the conflict and fought in the battle of Gettysburg. Also a Mason, Thompson is credited with contributing his talent to the writing of the sixth and seventh degrees. The sixth degree was first conferred in full form at the 1883 session of the National Grange meeting in Washington, D.C., with the seventh degree making its debut the following year. Thompson was chosen as the first lecturer for the National Grange at the organizational meeting December 7, 1867, and in 1872 he was elected treasurer to fill the unexpired term of William M. Ireland, who had resigned. Thompson also was high priest for almost nine years. Thompson, who was born in 1834, died in 1894 and is buried in Washington, D.C.'s, Rock Creek Cemetery.

William Saunders' name is the one most often mentioned with Kelley's as a principal player in organizing the Patrons of Husbandry. The two had first met during the winter of 1864-65 at the Department of Agriculture. Saunders, an immigrant from Scotland in 1848, had achieved considerable recognition as a landscape gardener. Early accomplishments included designing an estate belonging to Johns Hopkins, Clifton Park near Baltimore, Maryland. Hopkins' bequest of $7 million resulted in the university and school of medicine bearing his name. Saunders is also credited with development of the idea of fixed glass roofs for greenhouses and for introduction of the navel orange into North America. Perhaps his most noted accomplishment, however, was planning the layout of the National Cemetery at Gettysburg at the request of President Lincoln. He was on the platform November 19, 1863, to hear the president deliver his immortal Gettysburg Address and a display at the visitors' center at the cemetery contains a likeness of Saunders and information about his contribution to the national monument. For his services there he received no extra payment and, in fact, was required to pay his own travel expenses for the various trips he had to make to Pennsylvania.

Saunders had secured the Gettysburg assignment because of his position of Superintendent of the Propagating Gardens within the Department of Agriculture. He was appointed at the time of the department's formation in 1862 and remained there until his death in 1900 at the age of 78. Besides the assessment of thousands of plants from around the world for their suitability in North America, Saunders was responsible for landscaping the Lincoln tomb and monument at Springfield, Illinois, and much of the capitol grounds in Washington, D.C.

Saunders was a cautious, individualistic, conservative person, much unlike the impulsive, aggressive and nonconformist Kelley. Indeed, some have attempted to prove that Saunders was the originator of the Grange idea, and it was this speculation which apparently prompted Kelley to write his 1875 book, *Origin and Progress of the Order of the Patrons of Husbandry in the United States; a History from 1866 to 1873.* In his first paragraph, Kelley states, "It is generally acknowledged that the idea of the Order of the Patrons of Husbandry originated with the writer. From its inception he has given it his whole attention...." Kelley's paramount evidence, revealed to undermine Saunders supporters, is a passage from a letter written by Saunders to Kelley in 1869 stating, "You are still driving on and will make your order go. I call it your order, as you not only conceived the idea but are making it go 'unaided and alone.'" Debate about the primacy of founders continued, however, and Atkeson felt compelled to rehash the matter in his 1916 book. He made the pronouncement that the "idea of founding a secret fraternal order of farmers originated with Oliver Hudson Kelley..." That conclusion was repeated by Charles Gardner in his 1949 history, *The Grange—Friend of the Farmer,* and again in 1967 by Grange historian Dr. William D. Barns in an article appearing in the journal *Agricultural History.*

Nonetheless, Saunders did make a massive contribution to the fledgling order. Aside from attempts to keep Kelley's impulsiveness under control—an activity resulting in recurrent friction between the two men,—Saunders contributed most of the Preamble to the National Grange Constitution, a document which Gardner describes as "an illuminating interpretation of the symbolic teachings of the Grange, based upon the importance of agriculture." Saunders, along with Kelley and Francis M. McDowell, was in a select circle of founders of the farmers' group with any remote connection to agriculture; the rest were government officials.

Elected the first national master in 1867, Saunders served at that post during the shaky formative years. He stepped down in 1873 to be an executive committee member for the next three years.

The office of William Saunders in Washington, D.C., has been designated the site of the official organization meeting for the National Grange, December 4, 1867.

One of his five children, Belle Saunders, was a lifelong employee in the Department of Agriculture. One of the first women to secure a clerical post within government, she remained an active member of the fraternity's first subordinate, Potomac Grange, for many years.

Another founder, William M. Ireland, was chief clerk in one of the offices of the Post Office Department and an early confidant of Kelley. Also a Mason, Ireland's suggestions were many when the ritualistic aspects of the new organization were being molded. His zeal for Masonic work eventually secured him a position in 1885 with the famous General Albert Pike, the leader of Scottish Rite Freemasonry in the United States and author of *Morals And Dogma,* a text still used by Masonic students. Ireland was named the National Grange's first treasurer after having turned down the nomination for master due to his inexperience in agricultural matters. He did, however, assume the top post in Potomac Grange in Washington, D.C., and he also functioned as the second secretary of the National Grange following the resignation of Kelley in 1878, serving in that capacity until he joined forces with General Pike.

After that time he failed to show much interest in the order he had helped organize. He died in 1891.

The Rev. Dr. John Trimble, another early friend of Kelley's, served as a clerk responsible for settlement of war claims in the Treasury Department. Prior to the war, he served in the ministry of the Protestant Episcopal Church and, due to health problems, later settled in Kentucky for several years as head of a large school there. With the outbreak of hostilities, the Trimbles moved to Washington, D.C. During the formation of the Patrons of Husbandry, Trimble was fond of playing the "devil's advocate" role by pointing out flaws and errors in the plans. For this reason he was referred to as the "wet blanket" of the organization but his advice undoubtedly resulted in numerous improvements. Trimble refused an office in the new organization for some time, but upon the resignation of Secretary William Ireland in 1885, he accepted appointment as his replacement. At the following convention he was given support by delegates and elected to the post, holding that responsibility until his death in 1902 at the age of 71.

The Rev. Aaron B. Grosh, a Universalist minister who also went into government service as a clerk in the Department of Agriculture, is credited with writing much of the first four degrees. Originally from Pennsylvania, little is known of Grosh except that he was a personal friend of Saunders. His 1876 book *Mentor in the Granges and Homes of Patrons of Husbandry,* long out of print and seldom referred to anymore, served an important function in the organization's early years by clarifying duties of all officers and amplifying the lessons in the ritualistic work. Another writing effort for Grosh resulted in the *Odd Fellows Improved Manual,* a guidebook for that fraternal organization.

Francis M. McDowell of Wayne, New York, was another personal friend of Saunders who became involved with formation of the Grange. McDowell had been a partner in the banking and brokerage firm of Hallett & Company in New York City but in the early 1860s a serious illness necessitated an early retirement. He returned to his boyhood home in mid-state New York where he established a prosperous vineyard. Saunders and McDowell met at a fruit fair in Hammondsport, New York, and, when told of the plans to form a national farm fraternity, he immediately became enthusiastic. Journeying to Washington the following winter, he become acquainted with the others who were working on organizational plans. McDowell corresponded often with Kelley and was selected the first high priest in the assembly of Demeter. In 1873 he was elected treasurer of the National Grange, an office he fulfilled until health required his resignation in 1893, just a year prior to his death. His wife Eva, however, was elected in his place and she performed the duties until 1919.

It is well known that John R. Thompson consulted extensively with McDowell during the writing of the seventh degree but until publication of two books by former high priest of Demeter C. Jerome Davis, few suspected the full measure of McDowell's contribution to this highest expression of Grange ritualism. Davis, a lifelong student of Grange history, combed through original correspondence archived at National Grange headquarters and at Cornell University. The story he puts together is a fascinating account of the origin of the Grange and its ritual.

When McDowell was in the banking and brokerage business, he made numerous trips to Europe to negotiate financing for American railroads. While abroad, he apparently became acquainted with the Duc d'Ascoli of Italy who claimed to be the high priest of Demeter by "apostolic succession" in the ancient Eleusinian Mysteries. In 1858 the duke conferred the same title on McDowell and gave him authority to extend the Order of Demeter to North America. Early correspondence and notes made during formation of the Grange indicate that the founders were fully aware of this connection between McDowell and the 3,000-year-old rituals associated with ancient Greek religious worship of the agricultural goddess Demeter. The seventh degree, the degree of Demeter, was prepared under McDowell's close supervision so it would convey the symbolism of the original as closely as possible.

An interesting confirmation of McDowell's mystery school connection comes from the pen of Kelley. When visiting in the McDowell home in 1868, Kelley was shown portraits of the duke and the vestments and regalia given by him to McDowell. His elaborate description of these items, reprinted in the Davis books, tends to lend credibility to the story.

The last of the "official" founders is Caroline A. Hall. Temperance Kelley's niece was born in Boston in 1838 but later moved with her family to join the Kelleys in Minnesota. She became a teacher and, after her uncle became preoccupied with organization work for the Patrons of Husbandry, she assisted him full-time. Hall was appointed the first Ceres of the National Grange and, as such, was the first female officer of the organization. For awhile she resided in Florida in the town of Rio Carrabelle being developed by Oliver and named in her honor, later returning to Minnesota. She died in 1918 from injuries sustained in an automobile accident. Ironically, a newspaper announcement of her death omitted mention of her important role in organizing the National Grange, concentrating instead on her $100,000 contribution to local charities.

With the cast assembled, the remaining task was the actual initiation of the fraternity. Even with considerable talent committed to the work, the undertaking was not an easy one.

3

Kelley Spreads the Grange Gospel

ALTHOUGH SAUNDERS had spoken of the usefulness of farmer organizations in the past, it was Kelley's enthusiasm and constant stream of ideas which eventually culminated in the Patrons of Husbandry. The other founders contributed input and, at least in the case of McDowell, some cash as well.

Three other individuals added their suggestions early in the formative stages of the Grange. Anson Bartlett, a fruit grower from North Madison, Ohio, is credited with prevailing for the admission of women and young people to the fraternity. William Muir, St. Louis, Missouri, gave aid in ritual development, and A.S. Moss, Fredonia, New York, would ensure the early success of the fraternity by being the driving force behind the first chartered Grange outside Washington, D.C.

With founders and others scattered so widely, early meetings obviously had less than full attendance. Those present on November 15, 1867, made the decision to call their organization the Patrons of Husbandry, adopting the term "Grange" to designate local units. At that occasion William Saunders was requested to write the preamble to the Constitution.

A meeting December 4, 1867, in the office of William Saunders in Washington is recognized as the birthday of the Patrons of Husbandry. The ritual, even though it would undergo radical changes, was roughly outlined and the Constitution was partially agreed upon. The election that day saw William Saunders selected the first national master; Anson Bartlett as overseer; John R. Thompson, lecturer; William Muir, steward; A.S. Moss, assistant steward; William M. Ireland, treasurer; and O.H. Kelley, secretary.

Elected later were the Rev. Aaron B. Grosh, chaplain, and Edward P. Farris of Illinois, gatekeeper. Several of these individuals were elected in absentia.

The next meeting, January 7, 1868, has come to be known as the first session of the National Grange. Potomac Grange No. 1 in Washington, D.C., was formally organized the following day as a proving ground for the emerging ritual work.

The commitment Kelley had to the Grange cause and his almost unreasoning zeal were displayed shortly after these initial organizational hurdles were jumped. He announced to his associates that he was resigning his clerkship in the Post Office Department in order to promote the new organization nationally. Eighty years later, writer Stewart H. Holbrook would capture in words the intriguing character of the man responsible for the continued existence of the Grange in its infancy:

> What was needed at this time was one of those most typical of all American products of the nineteenth century, a genuine fanatic with a purpose. A budding fanatic was ready at hand. He was Oliver Hudson Kelley, born in Boston in 1826... who, in 1867, along with William Saunders and five others organized the National Grange of the Patrons of Husbandry, and became its secretary. A bit later he set out to convert the most individualistic group in America to his idea of an association. It was far from easy. The purpose of the Grange appeared to be somewhat vague. Most farmers thought they had no time for social doings of any sort. Many were actually hostile. But Kelley, though a downright fanatic on the subject in hand, was practical and shrewd. He was filled with boundless enthusiasm, never dismayed, and he had the almost unknown quality—in a fanatic—of a sense of humor. The combination was unbeatable.

Combined efforts of the other founders bought Kelley a train ticket as far as Harrisburg, Pennsylvania, with $2 and half of the Grange funds left over. He was given a letter of credit containing no guarantees, and the power to establish Granges and collect fees. The officers unanimously voted him a salary of $2,000 per year plus traveling expenses, all of which was to be collected by Kelley out of receipts from subordinate Granges he organized.

The adventure began April 3, 1868, but he met with failure at the first stop in Pennsylvania. Although Kelley did collect $15 from a group in Harrisburg, they did not follow through to organize a subordinate. In Fredonia, New York, however, he was successful in organizing Fredonia Grange April 15 through the help of A.S. Moss. That Grange was the first subordinate other than Potomac, the "practice Grange" in Washington. Fredonia Grange is still an

America's first subordinate Grange outside Washington, D.C., was Fredonia No. 1 in Fredonia, New York. The Grange, still active, has been meeting in this building since its completion in 1915.

active group and one national master, Sherman J. Lowell, emerged from its ranks.

Other stops at Pen Yan (New York), Cleveland, Columbus, Chicago and Madison bore little fruit for Kelley and he headed toward his Minnesota home. During the trip, though, he visited personally with McDowell and Bartlett and made plans to chart a somewhat different course of action, grounded in part on his activist experience with the Benton County Agricultural Society. Thomas A. Woods notes, "The real organizational work of the Grange, the lasting work among the farmers themselves, did not really begin until Kelley reached Minnesota. There he began to mold the organization, shaping it to become a powerful voice for farmers. There he was largely free from the objections of the Washington group, and he quickly steered the organization in the direction he wanted it to go." Kelley valued the collective decision-making process and his vision, dating back to the Benton County Agricultural Society, was for a group of farmers who would unite to solve their mutual problems. Saunders and most of the Washington, D.C., group, placed more faith in individual action and self-improvement.

Arriving in Itasca May 1, Kelley set to work on the farm. Several years earlier he had begun concentrating on irrigated market garden crops but as he busied himself with the vegetables, he also continued promotion of the Grange. That summer he began collaborating again with his newspaper publishing friend George Benedict. As associate editor of Benedict's *Sauk Rapids Sentinel,* Kelley acquired a golden opportunity to reach many with his new gospel of farmer organization. He wrote McDowell that "the Editor of the *Sauk Rapids Sentinel* is an old chum of mine. His paper is the organ of the Order, and he wants to make it the head paper of the Order for the State." The Grange's first circular enticing participation of nearby farmers appeared in the *Sentinel* June 19. The first recorded open Grange food social also was advertised in that issue; neighbors were invited to enjoy a "Strawberry Pic-Nic" at the Kelley farm on June 25. The railroad promised to bring participants for half-price where they were invited to pick all the strawberries they could eat at the event. Kelley provided the strawberries, cream and sugar. Banners greeted the merrymakers and the event allowed Kelley to publicize his plans for the Grange in a social atmosphere with many influential people. That pattern is one which remains within the organization.

In the July 3 issue of the *Sentinel* Kelley reports on his picnic and, in another article, tells of the formation of Granite Grange in Sauk Rapids. The Patrons of Husbandry is described as an organization for the "...laboring classes,...combining benevolent and protective features which have been needed in rural districts." Kelley was being a visionary salesman, of course, because the Grange at this point had little to offer. Granite Grange and one which followed shortly thereafter, Cascade Grange in Minneapolis, were both weak and would fold before the end of the year.

Kelley's ability to manipulate the media was exploited as much as possible. He reprinted articles in the *Sentinel* from other sources which created a heightened sense of discontent among farmers, then he countered with articles pointing out the solution for irritated farmers was to join forces with the growing Grange movement. He sent articles to other papers, clipped these and sent them with clippings from the *Sentinel* on to other publications so, eventually, there was so much being printed about the Grange that interest did begin to build.

Even though most of the Grange "movement" was still in Kelley's mind, the strategy began to work. A temporary state Grange was organized in 1868, but it never amounted to anything more than a paper organization. It was reorganized the following year in a permanent fashion. The *Farmers' Union* and the *St. Paul Pioneer* began supporting Kelley's efforts and it was in these publications that some of the more radical of his plans first became known. The Grange would assist farmers in buying and selling cooperatively, helping to eliminate the middleman, and members would be protected from swindlers. An influential circular prepared by Kelley and D.A. Robertson boldly announced the Grange would "protect its members against the numerous combinations by which their interests are injuriously affected." It would also unite farmers in "intimate social relations" that would allow them to work in "combined co-operative association for individual improvement and common benefit." Furthermore, the circular promised the

Oliver and Temperance Kelley lived in this home near Itasca, Minnesota, prior to and during the organizational phase of the Grange. The larger home, which still remains on the property, was begun in 1876 but the Kelleys never spent much time at the farm following its completion.

Grange would supply information about "crops, demand and supply, prices, markets, and transportation throughout the country," and provide for the "establishment of depots for the sale of special or general products in the cities..." This was far beyond what the Washington, D.C., group had envisioned and they were largely unaware of what was happening. Moss and McDowell, when they were appraised of Kelley's vision, were supportive nonetheless.

Kelley later admitted that the start of the Grange as a growing organization began with organization of North Star Grange in St. Paul on September 2, 1868. Woods states this was "the first really permanent Grange in Minnesota, the Grange on which he would build a national organization." Printed articles to the contrary, the Grange at the end of 1868 existed only in Minnesota—most units being within 100 miles of Kelley's farm—with the exception of Potomac Grange, Fredonia, Garden City Grange (a paper Grange organized by Kelley in Chicago), and Newton Grange which was organized by A. Failor in Iowa on May 2.

D.A. Robertson began publishing the *Minnesota Monthly* in January 1869 and his good friend O.H. Kelley used it to help spread the Grange gospel even further. Charles Gardner calls this magazine the first official Grange publication. With this vigorous voice, the reorganization of the state Grange and the help of the strong North Star group, the scene was set for further expansion. Robertson and Kelley engineered acceptance by the state Grange of a plan to appoint an agent to serve as a source of marketing information to members, helping them to increase profits by elimination of middlemen merchants. Although Kelley knew the future of the Grange could rise or fall depending upon the success of this venture, he was nevertheless supportive of it. He went East to consult with other officers about this course of action and the resulting compromise altered the character of the Grange forever.

Woods assesses the compromise as one which met the needs of both the Minnesota Grange members and the Washington leaders:

> Had he [Kelley] remained true to his radical principles, the Grange could have become a powerful rallying point for agrarian dissatisfaction that might well have rivaled the later Populist movement. But the Grange might also have disintegrated if the Washington members had repudiated the Order as they later threatened to do. He decided to compromise, fulfilling some of his own desires and those of the Minnesota Grangers for an activist organizational tactic, yet not offending the more conservative officers in Washington. Members of the Minnesota State Grange claimed that the agency was a local experiment that didn't necessarily involve the Order,

and Kelley agreed that something must be done to "protect our members against impositions now prevalent here, as well as to secure machinery at reduced rates." He was sure that "if they go ahead as they propose, it will have a tendency to break up the combinations between manufacturers and dealers, and bring the retail trade down upon us. This will wake up the farmers, and as soon as a lively fight commences, our membership will increase rapidly."

A business agent was soon named to circulate weekly bulletins to subordinate Granges and to accept quantity orders for merchandise. Kelley's prediction about the membership increasing rapidly would prove true and, thanks to the Chicago-based publication *Prairie Farmer*, that expansion would spread to states other than Minnesota.

4

The Roller-Coaster Years

1870-1877

MINNESOTA GRANGE MEMBERS were becoming even more vocal about economic conditions they felt were disadvantageous to farmers. In March 1870 Kelley wrote to Saunders about farmers' desires for a plan to oppose the "infernal monopolies," echoing concerns he was hearing on a daily basis. Two months later, Kelley received a letter from *Prairie Farmer* associate editor W.W. Corbett pressing for the new Grange organization to fight the railroads, warehouse, insurance and telegraph companies and others that "are crushing the life out of the producing classes." The fledgling Minnesota State Grange was all too willing to do its part and a resolution was passed calling for state Granges to set up cooperative unions to purchase farm supplies in bulk and establish monthly market days so farmers would have direct market outlets for their commodities. By this time state Granges had been set up in Illinois and Missouri and, in early 1871, state units were launched in Iowa and Wisconsin.

With market days underway in Minnesota, Kelley set his sights on regional Grange purchasing agencies in Chicago and St. Louis to act as go-betweens for farmers and manufacturers. He first went to Chicago to enlist the help of friends at the *Prairie Farmer*, then to Missouri and Iowa. The public relations war raged on, and article volume continued at a high rate due to Kelley's stamina. The trip garnered additional support, some of it monetary, and helped plant the Grange firmly in the upper Midwest.

The agent system of cooperative purchasing grew rapidly. Larger subordinates were able to secure sufficient orders from their members in order to enjoy quantity discounts but, in most areas, the as-yet unauthorized county Grange councils pooled orders from all their subordinates. One Grange agent, young Aaron Montgomery Ward, started a catalog business exclusively for Grange members out of a small room in Chicago. His catalogs for many years proudly stated the firm was "The Original Grange Supply House."

The split between the membership out West and the National Grange leadership (composed, still, of the government employee founders) became even more apparent at the January 1871 annual session in Washington. Kelley brought a resolution from Lincoln Grange of Gillford, Minnesota, requesting a constitutional amendment allowing for county Granges. These units would consist of masters and past masters of subordinates and act as intermediaries between the subordinates and the state Grange. A few of these units had already been unofficially formed in Minnesota and Kelley saw them as a tool "to create a local corporation to buy machinery or goods, and [to ship] produce." Arguments fell on deaf ears in Washington and no action was taken on the resolution.

Frustrated, Kelley proposed auxiliary, unaffiliated units to preform these tasks, units which would not officially be part of the Grange but would be controlled by Grange people. Such units would be collectively called the Knights of the Plow. Apparently nothing that formal emerged, but between 1871 and 1873 there were a number of unsanctioned county councils which resembled the structure Kelley envisioned for the Knights. For a time the national officers simply tolerated the councils then in 1874 the Constitution was amended to create Pomona (county and regional) Granges.

With the expansion of the Grange, there also was an increased need to guide the local units in areas other than activist ones. The Grange as a social and educational force was foreseen by the founders, and these elements have always held a prominent place in then functions of the order. One of the first attempts to add some national structure to these organizational elements appeared in 1870 with the appearance of *Songs for the Grange* compiled by Caroline Hall with the assistance of the Rev. Aaron B. Grosh. This book was in common use for Grange meetings until the appearance of the popular *Grange Melodies* in 1891.

The movement was becoming more national in scope and the Kelleys moved to Washington, D.C., ostensibly to place the secretary's office in a place of more prestige. Another, more personal factor helped make this decision: In June 1870 Kelley defaulted on his farm mortgage and a foreclosure sale was held that November, shortly before the move. Although that sale was voided, another was set for the following year. Financial difficulties starting in 1857 with the Northwood development finally reached their logical conclusion. The farm was sold but reacquired in 1873 by Kelley from his nephew, Albert R. Hall, who had purchased it from the mortgage holders. Construction of a presumptuous new house began in 1876 but Kelley would never live there permanently again. The farm remained in the family until 1901.

The national character of the Grange was evident in the numbers Kelley reported to the *Farmers' Union* publication. Thirty-one states had organized Granges within their borders by mid-1873, with the majority of those being in the Midwest. By April that year Iowa boasted 1,000 Granges, more than the nationwide total 12 months earlier. By year's end there were approximately 9,000 Granges with membership totaling an estimated 700,000. State Granges were organized in Alabama, Arkansas, California, Dakota Territory, Florida, Georgia, Kentucky, Louisiana, Massachusetts, Michigan, Missouri, New Hampshire, New Jersey, New York, North Carolina, Ohio, Oregon, Pennsylvania, Tennessee, Texas, Virginia, and West Virginia.

Power shifts to the farmers

The sixth annual session of the National Grange, held in January 1873 in Georgetown (Washington), D.C., was a major turning point for the young but suddenly swelling fraternity. Until that time the national body had been under the control of the founders. At Georgetown the Constitution, as written and rewritten by the founders, was adopted on January 9, and the following day a certificate of incorporation for the National Grange of the Patrons of Husbandry was granted. But perhaps more consequential was the transfer of at least some of the power and control from the founders—those government employees with a vision to help America's farmers—to the farmers themselves. Elected master to succeed William Saunders was 42-year-old Dudley W. Adams, the state master from Iowa who three months before had presented one of history's most biting manifestos calling for farmer organization:

> What we want is a new Declaration of Independence.... We have heard enough, ten times enough, about the hardened hand of honest toil, the supreme glory of the sweating brow, and how magnificent is the suit of coarse homespun which covers a form bent with overwork.... I tell you, my brother tillers of the soil, there is something in this world worth living for besides hard work. We have heard enough of this professional blarney about the honest farmer, the backbone of the nation... We have been too much alone. We must exchange views. Above all, we must think.

Adams, who in 1872 was the first non-founder farmer present at a national session, received the recognition of the founders by being elected to the post of lecturer, filling the vacancy created by John R. Thompson's move to treasurer. A native New Englander from Massachusetts, Adams taught school briefly then moved to the Waukon, Iowa, area to farm. He became prominent in agricultural circles and was an officer in the State Horticultural Society. The Grange greatly interested him when the new group appeared in Iowa and his early involvement earned him election as the first state master in 1871. When he replaced Saunders as national master, his wife replaced Caroline Hall as national Ceres. Follow-

Dudley W. Adams (1831-1899)

ing his two years of service as national master, Adams and his wife moved to Florida where they specialized in growing oranges and other fruit. He died in 1899.

Another "outsider" appeared in 1872 who would go on to high positions of leadership within the Grange. Colonel David Wyatt Aiken, a veteran of the Confederate Army who suffered serious wounds in the battle of Antietam, became enthusiastic about the struggling farm organization when he met with founders in early 1872. Shortly thereafter, Aiken was invited by the fourth Commissioner of Agriculture, Frederick Watts (Isaac Newton had died during Kelley's trip through the South), to be a delegate from South Carolina to an "agricultural convention" in Washington, D.C. After listening for some time without hearing any constructive direction being offered to help America's farmers, Aiken jumped up and began speaking out of turn:

> Mr. Chairman: This is ostensibly an agricultural convention, but I have not heard the word agriculture spoken since it convened. We seem to be gathered here in the interests of commerce and education—the wants of the farmer appear to be ignored entirely. This will not be the case always, however, for there is now springing up among the farmers of our country an organization that will teach them their rights, and, knowing them, they will dare to maintain them. I mean the organization known as the Order of the Patrons of Husbandry.

Later that same year Aiken was elected first master of the South Carolina State Grange and, in January 1873, was elected to the first executive committee of the National Grange, a post he held for 13 years. Between 1881 and 1885 he served as high priest of Demeter. Like many Grange leaders, Aiken attracted the confidence of voters and was elected as a member of Congress in 1877. Voters kept him there until his death 10 years later.

Steering clear of partisanship

The trend which was drawing the Grange toward an activist stance intensified, especially in Minnesota. One of the most interesting expressions of this inclination centers around the appearance of Ignatius Donnelly in Grange circles. Donnelly is now remembered for his books *Atlantis and the Antediluvian World,* a tome arguing for the existence of an ancient civilized continent in the Atlantic, and *Caesar's Column,* an attempt to advance his political ideas by prophetically looking at the future of America. At the time Kelley knew him, Donnelly was a Minnesota politician attempting to rally laboring farmers into a battle against monopolistic capitalists aligned against them. Formerly a mainline Republican congressman, Donnelly later became a spokesman for third party efforts such as the Greenback Party, Farmers' Alliance and the People's (Populist) Party. Near the end of his career he was a vice presidential candidate on the Populist ticket.

In 1873 Donnelly organized Cereal Grange in Hastings, Minnesota, and was promptly elected lecturer. He sought and received permission from Kelley to be a national organizer. Immediately he set out to speak at Granges, convincingly arguing for activist positions. His polished Grange presentations culminated in a political convention in Owatonna, Minnesota, where the Anti-Monopoly Party was formed. Grange members in addition to Donnelly played an important role in the proceedings, something which angered one faction within the Minnesota State Grange. Ever since the birth of the Grange in 1867 there had been an intense disapproval by some members of bringing the Grange into partisan political struggles. Nonetheless, the Anti-Monopolists, with strong Grange support, went on to win many election battles in Minnesota and formed a powerful bloc during the 1874 state legislative session. Actions of that alliance, linked with similar legislative events elsewhere, would eventually associate the Grange name with a significant turning point in American history, popularly termed the Granger Movement. Anti-Monopoly Party activities were also prominent in other Grange states, notably in Wisconsin, Iowa, Illinois, Missouri and Indiana.

Involvement of the Grange in legislative disputes greatly angered Minnesota State Grange Master George I. Parsons, who insisted subordinate Grange involvement in partisan politics violated the National Grange Constitution. Samuel E. Adams, an old friend, neighbor and partner of Kelley's, was on the opposite side of the battle by arguing that the Grange did have a place in the legislative arena. His position prevailed as he unseated Parsons as state master and, in 1877, he rose through the ranks to be elected national master. The outcome of that early debate helped resolve forever the Grange's position regarding its lobbying role. This group of farmers was committed to taking stands on legislative issues consistent with its vision to help the rural class, though only on a non-partisan basis.

A unifying statement adopted

Out in California the Grange was catching on as well, and the first master of the California State Grange, Major James W.A. Wright, was destined to fulfill an important role that helped focus the young organization and guide it through some difficult times just ahead. Born in Mississippi, Wright had been valedictorian of his graduating class at Princeton University. His rank of major was earned in the Confederate Army. Wounded at the battle of Missionary Ridge, he was taken prisoner by Union forces. While being transferred, Wright escaped, making his way home through Canada and the Bermuda Islands to resume fighting for the South. Originally a teacher, he was successful in farming, insurance and writing after moving to California. Following some financial reverses, he returned east to Alabama to resume a career in school administration. He died in 1894.

Wright is best remembered for his leadership in drafting a document which continues to be the blueprint for Grange activity, the *Declaration of Purposes* of the National Grange. The 1874 session was the first to be held outside the Washington, D.C., area and it represents both the shift of power to the members and the geographic concentration of Grange influence at that time in the Midwest. With so many new members, each with a personal agenda, it was visibly apparent that some guide was essential. Wright labored most of two days and nights on the document, completing it at three o'clock in the morning. He received input from D. Wyatt Aiken; John T. Jones, first master of the Arkansas State Grange and afterwards master of the National Grange; N.W. Garretson of Iowa, who had organized the state Granges of California and Oregon; and Ezra S. Carr, a professor of agriculture at the University of Wisconsin and the University of California and prominent historian of the early Grange movement in the West. Carr's wife Jeanne attained eminence in her struggles for equal rights for women.

The *Declaration of Purposes* begins by issuing the call to unite to "labor for the good of our Order, our country, and mankind." Specific objects are headed by the desire "To develop a better and higher manhood and womanhood among ourselves; to enhance the comforts and attractions of our homes, and strengthen our attachments to our pursuits..." An analysis of the *Declaration of Purposes* appears in Chapter 15.

The timeliness of the *Declaration* was exceptional. With this proclamation the farmers, who had secured much of the control of their organization the previous year, were empowered to work together for a specific slate of mutually beneficial endeavors. To the satisfaction of the more militant, there were allowances made for "meeting together, talking together, working together, buying together, selling together, and, in general, acting together for our mutual protection and advancement.... For our business interests we desire to bring producers and consumers, farmers and manufacturers, into the most direct and friendly relations possible. Hence, we must dispense with a surplus of middlemen, not that we are unfriendly to them, but we do not need them. Their surplus and their exactions diminish our profits." The *Declaration,* while voicing the concerns of the farmers in the 1870s by sanctioning the Grange's involvement in economic and legislative areas, set the tone for the organization and transformed it officially into the only fraternity which makes public action a major portion of its activities.

But the *Declaration of Purposes,* critics countered, were too weak and came too late to stop the dissatisfaction which was building with the militant wing. In February, the same month the *Declaration* was adopted, the Grange organized the most subordinates ever chartered in one month—2,239. The total organized that year was 11,941. But the *Declaration's* statements on non-partisanship left many of those new members feeling they had no tools left with which to battle the oppressive forces they saw around them. The pronouncements from the National Grange seemed to counter the enticements made by local organizers, who promised an end to their worries if they joined. As early as 1871 Dudley W. Adams had voiced contempt for the more cautious patrons. "Nothing is more dangerous to the life and purity of a republic than for the best, purest, and most intelligent rural population to abstain from all active *militant* participation in the affairs of government and allow the machinery to be run by lawyers and professional politicians.... Agriculturists *must* take a part in politics and in Government...."

Activists rebelled even more the following year when delegates passed a resolution stating "that the moral, social and intellectual features, being the great and leading features of the Order, should be most sacredly cherished; and that it is the duty of the several State Granges to adopt such measures as will most tend to the cultivation and promotion of these features. Resolved, that all other features *are subordinate to these* and should be kept forever so by this Order." The patient members eventually proved the sensibility of the *Declaration's* position, however; the Grange continued its work successfully while the movements started by the disenchanted flourished for awhile and then vaporized.

Early cooperative experiments attempted

Many in the order speculated that the farmers were so oppressed by middlemen that the only way to attain economic independence was to bypass middlemen altogether with democratic, nonprofit cooperatives. Major Wright moved on from the notoriety gained by drafting the *Declaration of Purposes* to fulfill an important function in this aspect of the organization's development as well. Cooperatives are business ventures in which the customers own the company as members. Each member buys into the cooperative and shares in the surplus according to the amount of business the member has with the co-op. The concept was relatively new to American farmers of the 1870s although it had been tried on a limited basis throughout America for some years.

The granddaddy of all co-ops was one started by workers at Rochdale in England. Since it was felt more information and direct marketing assistance was needed in order to help guide the thousands of cooperatives being established by Granges, Major Wright was sent to Europe in 1876. He was labeled a special envoy to Germany and the United Kingdom, primarily to facilitate an international trading agreement.

The trip was necessary because of a complex proposal to link cooperatives on both sides of the Atlantic. In 1873 Dr. Thomas Worrall had set up the Mississippi Valley Trading Company (MVTC) as a vehicle to expedite trade between the many Grange cooperatives appearing in the Midwest and those of England. During the summer of 1875 the National Grange executive committee became involved. Granges of Georgia had already formed the Direct Trade Union in an effort to forge direct trade linkages between southern cotton growers and mills in Great Britain; agents were located in Liverpool, England, as well as several cities in the American South. Worrall's plans were similar, but Wright's appointment shuttled Worrall to the sidelines.

After visiting Germany, partly to investigate rumors that Germans were interested in organizing Granges, Wright traveled to England, where he met with co-op leaders. He found them torn between their desire to do business with him and their previous ties with Worrall. Wright explained that the Grange people approved of the MVTC concept but were disturbed by Worrall's tendency to deal with members without involving their leaders. Wright was successful in gaining desired changes in the MVTC and its name was changed to the Anglo-American Cooperative Trading Company. Most of the address delivered to delegates by Master John T. Jones at the 1876 session in Chicago was a detailed endorsement of the concept. A majority of the delegates voted to approve the plan, making international cooperation appear inevitable. However, the onset of English economic difficulties caused the enterprise there to evaporate and a lack of economic investment in America by the Grange members scuttled hopes here. The opposition voices heard at Chicago prevailed; Grangers had to confine their cooperative trading to markets closer to home.

And trade they did. Although the grand project for international cooperative trade failed, enterprising Grange members in California decided to try their luck with the concept. "Grain King" Isaac Friedlander had controlled wheat trade in the San Francisco Bay area since the Civil War. Angry Grange growers felt they could boost their profit by unseating Friedlander from his throne and they set about doing that in 1876 by chartering three ships to haul their crops to Liverpool. The voyages returned $1,172,439.26 to the Grange farmers but $27,653.30 had to be paid out in commissions. Their method might have prospered had it not been for the fact that Friedlander was in a position to buy on consignment and extend credit, terms the farmers needed. The king remained on his throne in San Francisco.

Cooperatives, often with dubious underpinnings, were set up by Granges everywhere to enter into virtually any enterprise deemed remotely beneficial to members. Altogether, Grange cooperative enterprises conducted an estimated business volume in the spring of 1876 of $18 million. Domestic cooperative marketing operations were often successful for members such as a wool growers association for growers in Ohio and West Virginia. The Iowa State Grange maintained a resident agent at the Union Stock Yards in Chicago in the early 1870s and, 18 years later, the Maryland State Grange surpassed Iowa's success with even greater sales receipts. Grange historian D. Sven Nordin noted that members "tried marketing their own grains, fibers, and animals largely because they felt warehouse, elevator, and stockyard proprietors conspired against farmers to depress prices paid producers."

Other cooperatives organized during this era prospered for a time. The Texas Cooperative Association stands out as a nineteenth century cooperative Grange achievement; the association survived and flourished for almost two decades.

In Iowa, which had over 100,000 members who could support larger enterprises, the Grange owned patents on a harvester, a hay rake, seeder, and a combined self-rake reaper and mower. Assembly plants were built and sales looked good until rumors spread that the machines were defective. The result was a disastrous depletion

"We Guarantee..."

In the mid-19th century, deficient in laws protecting consumers, frauds and swindlers were common. A goal of early Grange members was to pool their strength and their orders in order to search out bargains and the best merchants. Sometimes even the pools linked up with a less-than-honest agent.

Then came young Aaron Montgomery Ward of Chicago. He had been a traveling salesman throughout rural areas of the Midwest since moving there in 1865 and his idea for a catalog firm marketing directly to rural people evolved while he was bouncing between sales calls in his buggy. Locating the firm in a big city allowed easy access with manufacturers, and large wholesale orders permitted the lowest retail prices possible. Customers would order by mail with goods being shipped COD to the nearest rail station.

Ward saved some money but was unsuccessful in convincing skeptical friends to invest. In 1871, on his own, he purchased a small amount of goods in preparation for his new business but the great Chicago fire, originating in Catherine O'Leary's barn, destroyed Ward's holdings. By August 1872 Ward had saved more money and, this time, was joined by two friends who supplied needed capital.

The first price list was a single sheet listing 163 items, most of them priced at $1 each. The list, circulated only to Grange members, announced "Grangers Supplied by the Cheapest Cash House in America" and boasted that "We find our business is increasing to such an extent that our present quarters are entirely too small." Actually, the business was only beginning and the Panic of 1873

of state Grange assets. Missouri members in 1874 were told they had built or had in the works 18 grain elevators and warehouses, eight gristmills, three meatpacking plants and 26 manufacturing plants making everything from cheese to plows. Three Grange banks were chartered in Virginia in 1875.

A pamphlet published in 1875 by Kelley outlined the basics of successful Rochdale cooperatives and the doctrines were adopted the following year by the Grange. However, the advice came too late; the order and its cooperatives had already entered a rapid decline. In spite of the large number of cooperatives which failed in this period, the Grange remained unified in its support of cooperation and a resurgence of interest in forming cooperatives

---

nearly crushed it. Ward's partners became nervous and he bought them out.

Ward began going to Grange meetings and in a speech near Bloomington, Illinois, he offered to entertain order-takers from McLean County to three days and two nights in Chicago—all expenses paid—if they pooled an order of $300 or more. The Grange master appointed a committee to round up customers and the goal was achieved.

A major blow came with a November 1873 *Chicago Tribune* editorial which warned in its headline, "Grangers beware. Don't

One of the earliest catalog illustrations was this woodcut of a "Regulation Grange Hat," sold exclusively by Montgomery Ward & Company.

in the 1920s through the 1940s would result in ventures with greater permanence.

Nordin postulates two prevailing attitudes toward business which were apparent in the Grange of the early 1870s. One faction staunchly opposed capitalism as it was practiced in the last half of the nineteenth century. This faction, led by Master (1885-1892) Milton Trusler of Indiana, especially disliked "trusts, monopolies, and shylocks." Trusler and his companions felt that governmental action to redistribute wealth was necessary in order to avoid an inevitable class conflict. Nordin quotes Trusler urging Grange members to do some "serious soul searching" since "there must be something radically wrong" when a system allowed some to earn

---

Patronize Montgomery Ward & Co.—They are Dead-Beats!" Ward acted quickly, found the article was written with scanty, fallacious information, and convinced the paper to investigate thoroughly. On Christmas Eve the *Tribune* took it all back, touting Ward's policy allowing customers to refuse payment if they were not satisfied with the goods. "It is difficult to see how any person can be swindled or imposed upon by business thus transacted," the *Tribune* said.

Business with Grange members continued to grow, his assortment of goods increased and bulk orders from Grange secretaries began flooding in. One of the first illustrations used in an early catalog showed a gentleman wearing a "Regulation P. of H. Hat—All Wool." The Grange hat, "manufactured expressly" for Montgomery Ward & Co., sold for $1.25. The 72-page 1875 catalog expanded the guarantee by pledging to refund purchase and shipping costs if any goods were not satisfactory.

In that same catalog Ward bragged, "From a small beginning, we are now the largest exclusively wholesale house in America devoted to supplying the consumer direct. When we introduced our system in 1872, we were looked upon with scorn by the monopolies and suspicion by the Patrons themselves. In the short period of three years, we have saved the consumers directly over one million dollars and, indirectly, millions by breaking up monopolies and forcing dealers to sell their goods at fair prices. This Herculean task has been accomplished through the power of the Granger organization."

GRANGERS

SUPPLIED BY THE

Cheapest Cash House IN AMERICA.

At the Earnest Solicitation of many Grangers, we have consented to open a House devoted to furnishing

FARMERS & MECHANICS

Throughout the Northwest with all kinds of

Merchandise at Wholesale Prices.

You can readily see at a glance the difference between our Prices and what you have to pay your Retailer for the same quality of goods.

No.	Article	Price
1.—12	yards best quality Prints	$1.00
2.— 8	" good quality Bed Tick	1.00
3.—10	" Lancaster Gingham	1.00
4.—10	Fine Brown Cotton Muslin	1.00
5.—10	" Heavy Sheeting—Indian Head—yard wide	1.00
6.—10	" Bleached Cotton, yard wide	1.00
7.— 3	" Heavy Cassimere, for Pants or Coats	1.00
8.— 1	Corsets, Beauty style, imported	1.25
9.—15	yards Delaine	1.50
10.—10	" Empress Cloth	2.00
11.—10	" All Linen Russia Crash Toweling	1.00
12.— 1	Call Bell, best Silver Plate, side strike, and 1 Butter Knife	1.00
13.—10	yards Japanese Striped Silk Poplin	1.25
14.— 1	Silver Plated Castor, solid band frame, with five bottles	1.25
15.— 7	yards good quality Cotton Flannel	1.00
16.— 1	Extra Heavy Plated Butter Dish	1.50
17.— 1	Lotta Hoop Skirts	1.00
18.— 1	Silver Cake Basket, extra heavy plate	1.75
19.—10	yards Linen Diaper	1.50
20.— 6	Heavy, extra plated, Silver Napkin Rings	1.50
21.—10	yards extra fine Dice Diaper	1.25
22.— 1	Extra Plated Silver Drinking Cup, lined with Gold Plate	1.00
23.—10	yards Fancy Poplin Dress Goods	1.50
24.— 1	Extra Silver Goblet, lined with Gold Plate	1.25
25.— 7	yards Blue Denim	1.00
26.— 1	Silk Lined Case, containing one Extra Plated Knife, Spoon, Napkin Ring and Gold Tooth Pick	1.00
27.— 2	yards Fancy Cloth, for Pants	1.00
28.— 1	Gentleman's Toilet Set, containing 2 Wade & Butchers Razors, Tooth Brush, Nail Brush, Comb, Hair Brush, Lather Brush, Razor Strop, Shaving box and Soap, for	1.00
29.—12	White Handle Knives and Forks	1.00
30.— 7	Grain Bags, and 1 Pair Buck Gloves	3.00
31.— 2	Orange Colored Undershirts	1.25
32.— 2	" " Drawers	1.25
33.— 3	Yards Blk. Silk finished Velveteen	2.00
34.— 1	Backgammon Board with Checkers, Dice and Cup	1.00
35.— 4	Yards Black Silk Fringe, 3 inches wide	1.00
36.— 3	Boxes Paper Collars, 3 Neck Ties, and 1 Collar Button	1.00
37.— 6	pair Ladies' Colored Wool Hose	1.00
38.— 6	" Men's British Cotton Socks	1.00
39.— 3	Ladies' Scarfs, 2 Lace Collars, and 1 pair Sleeve Buttons	1.00
40.— 1	Winter Wool Cap, and 1 pair Boys' Buck Gloves	1.00
41.— 8	pair Child's Balmoral Stockings	1.00
42.— 5	yards Valenciennes Lace	1.00
43.— 2	New York Mills White Shirts	2.50
44.— 4	yards best Stripe Hemp Carpet	1.00
45.— 5	" all wool Ingrain Carpet	2.50
46.—	White Rose Blankets, each	1.50
47.—	Gray Colored " "	1.25
48.— 2	pair Men's Cassimere Pants	3.00
49.— 1	" " " "	1.65
50.—12	" " Cotton Socks	1.00
51.—10	yards Colored Alpaca	2.25
52.— 1	pair Buck Gloves, and 1 pair Suspenders	1.25
53.— 1	Fur Hat, 2 pair wool Socks, 1 Gold Vest Chain, Octagon link, double plate	2.50
54.— 3	yards Plain Cassimere	1.00
55.—12	Bleached Linen Napkins	1.00
56.— 1	Embossed Wool Table Cover	1.00
57.— 1	Hoop Skirt, 1 Bustle, and 1 Hair Braid	1.00
58.— 1	Ivory handle Silk Fan, and Sleeve Buttons	1.00
59.— 1	pair Alexander Kid Gloves, all shades	1.00
60.— 2	" Josephine " " "	1.00
61.— 3	1-2 yards good Red Flannel	1.00
62.— 3	" " White "	1.00
63.— 1	Silk Fan, and Handkerchief Ring with Chain	1.00
64.— 8	Linen Towels, with red borders	1.00
65.— 2	Oil Cloth Table Covers	1.00
66.—10	boxes Paper Collars, cloth-lined button-holes	1.00
67.— 6	Fine Combs, 6 Coarse Combs, 1 Hair Brush and 5 papers English Pins	1.00
68.—12	yards one-inch wide Jaconet Ruffling	1.00
69.—12	new style Ruches, for the neck	1.00
70.— 8	pairs Ladies' White Cotton Hose	1.00
71.— 6	pairs Army Wool Socks	1.00
72.—10	yards inch-wide Ribbon, all shades	1.00
73.—24	spools Thread, 200 yards each, all colors and numbers	1.00
74.— 1	pound Woolen Yarn	1.00
75.— 5	yards Victoria Lawn, best quality	1.00
76.— 2	Wool Shawls, for children, or shoulder Shawls	1.00
77.— 1	Silk Parasol, walking-stick handle	2.00
78.— 1	" new style, short handle	1.00
79.— 1	Silk Fan and pair Kid Gloves	1.00
80.— 2	Undershirts	1.00
81.— 2	pairs Drawers	1.00
82.— 6	yards best quality Jaconet	1.00
83.— 4	yards Spanish Dress Linen	1.00
84.— 1	New style Balmoral Skirt	1.00
85.— 1	Printed Felt Skirt	1.25
86.— 5	yards Swiss Mull	1.00
87.— 5	Linen Shirt Fronts	$1.00
88.— 3	Neck Ties or Scarfs for Ladies	1.00
89.— 3	boxes Paper Collars and 1 pair Brace Suspenders	1.00
90.— 2	Boy's Winter Caps, new style	1.00
91.— 6	yards extra fine Hamburg Edging	1.00
92.— 2	Lunch Table Cloths	1.00
93.— 1	pair 2 1/2 yd Nottingham Lace Curtains	1.00
94.— 2	extra fine damask Table Cloths	1.25
95.— 1	Ostrich Plume and 3 bunches fine French Flowers	1.00
96.—10	yards imported Beaver Brand Black Alpaca, send for sample	3.25
97.— 1	fine Marseilles 10-4 Quilt	1.40
98.— 1	white honey-comb Quilt	1.00
99.— 1	Lady's Night Dress and 3 hem-stitched Handkerchiefs	1.00
100.— 1	Chemise and 2 hem-stitched Handkerchiefs	1.00
101.— 2	Lady's white six-tuck Skirts	1.00
	(The above underwear are all made of Hill's Cotton.)	
102.— 2	pair Buck Gloves	1.00
103.— 1	pair Gauntlet Buck Hand Gloves	1.00
104.— 5	yards Kentucky Jeans	1.00
105.—10	pounds best quality Cotton Batting	2.00
106.—10	" medium " " "	1.60
107.—10	yards very fine Alpaca, assorted colors, in remnants of from 1 to 3 yard pieces, for children's wear	2.25
108.—16	yards genuine Irish Poplin, all shades, green, light brown, rose, slate and drab	15.00
109.—15	spools Belding Bros. 50-yard Sewing Silk, assorted colors and letters	1.00
110.—10	yards Garnet 4 mole-fold imported Alpaca	3.25
111.— 3	yards bleached Table Damask	[illegible]
112.— 2	[illegible]	[illegible]
113.— 1	1-4 yard fine West of England Black Broadcloth, double width	4.00
114.— 1	plain Japanese Silk pattern in all shades, genuine goods	6.00
115.—12	Gent's Linen Handkerchiefs	1.00
116.—12	Lady's " hem-stitched Handkerchiefs	1.00
117.— 1	Oreide hunting-case Watch, lever, 13 holes jeweled	6.00
118.— 1	" " Lady's Watch, diamonds	8.00
119.— 1	silver plated hunting-case Watch	6.00
120.— 1	Josephine Stripe Shawl	2.00
121.— 1	extra heavy double Plaid Shawl	3.50
122.— 1	Secretary Writing Desk, spring top, fancy design, very stylish, with paper, envelopes, pen and pen-holder, all complete	1.00
123.—	The Correspondence Desk, after the style of General Grant's, Imitation of rosewood, lock and key furnished, with paper and envelopes	1.00
124.— 1	Portfolio, plain, with 3 pockets, lock and key furnished, with paper and envelopes	1.00
125.— 1	extra fine Portfolio, 6 pockets in gilt	1.00
126.— 1	plain Gold Ring, 14 k. all sizes	2.00
127.— 1	enameled " " "	3.00
128.— 1	Lady's Seal Ring (20 patterns) 14 k	3.00
129.— 1	" " garnet and pearl settings	3.00
130.—	Gentlemen's and Ladies' Cluster, Alaska Diamonds, Rubies, Moss Agate, Onyx, Bloodstone. All of the above are genuine and warranted	3.00
131.—	Gold Masonic Pins Square and Compass, assorted styles	1.00
132.—	Chased Shields, Pins, enameled emblem in center	1.00
133.—	Odd Fellow's Pins, 3 links, assorted sizes	1.00
134.— 1	Extra fine Opera Glass, screw extension	1.00
135.— 1	Ice Pitcher, extra plated	8.00
136.— 2	Extra fine double rolled plated Bracelets, with two tassels, equal to solid gold	1.50
137.—	Jet Bracelets, with chased gold center	1.00
138.—	Plain Jet Bracelets	.50
139.— 1	Guard Watch Chain, fancy patterns, double plated	1.00
140.— 1	Solid Silver Guard Chain	1.00
141.— 1	Lady's Set, Pin and Ear Rings, Etruscan gold	4.50
142.— 1	" " " " Medallion and Coral	5.00
143.— 1	" " " " Garnet, imported	4.50
144.— 1	" " " " Fine Onyx, set in gold	3.00
145.— 1	" Gold Locket, plain	1.50
146.— 1	" " " chased	2.00
147.— 1	" " " enameled	2.00
148.— 1	Gold plated Opera Guard Chain, with 1 and 2 tassels	5.00
149.— 1	Lady's solid gold Ear Drops	3.00
150.— 1	" " " Pin	3.00
	[All of the above which are marked as gold you will find as represented. The others are equal to solid gold and will wear for years.]	
151.— 1	Album, fine Turkey morocco, bevel edges, with hooks, contains 100 pictures	$1.00
152.— 3	yards fancy plaid all-wool Flannel, 1 yard wide	1.00
153.— 2	1-2 yards Opera Flannel	1.00
154.— 1	Gent's Cassimere Coat (send size)	3.50
155.—12	Cakes fine Honey Soap, 10 papers Sharp's Needles and 12 papers assorted Pins	1.00
156.— 1	All-wool Henrietta or Fifth Avenue Ottoman Striped Shawl	2.50
157.— 3	yards all-wool Cassimere	1.50
158.— 2	yards best quality Waterproof, double width, gold or black mixed	2.00
159.— 5	yards wool Linsey	1.00
160.— 1	Bronze Medallion Work Box, partitioned and finished complete	1.00
161.— 1	Fancy plated Shell Card Case, very fine	1.00
162.— 1	" " Wire Casket and 2 bottles Cologne	1.00
163.— 1	Stereoscope and 6 views, with walnut frame, good glass	1.00

It is with great pleasure that we present you with our Catalogue. We find our business is increasing to such an extent that our present quarters are entirely too small. Our new store on Clark street will be one of the largest and best arranged in the country for shipping goods promptly. We are also prepared to make purchases of all kinds of Merchandise which we do not keep, for our customers, charging them only five per cent. on the net cost. We do this simply as an accommodation.

All goods will be sent by express (Collect on delivery), subject to examination. In this way you can see just what you pay for. Any one sending us orders will please send the number opposite to the articles they wish sent. When convenient, as many as possible should club together, making one order. In this way the goods can be shipped at much less expense. Samples of piece goods sent on application by enclosing ten cents to pay postage, etc.

Address MONTGOMERY, WARD & CO.,

Box 517, Chicago, Ill.

millions while others wallowed in poverty.

A conservative element countered Trusler's group by disavowing radical changes while admiring "Horatio-Alger-type plutocrats." This group, whose ideals were summarized by Maine State Grange Master (1894-1898) Edward Wiggins, discouraged "any antagonism between capital and labor" while pointing out that the "interests of each are identical."

"Nevertheless," Nordin continues, "the wide assortment of Grange cooperative enterprises reflected general antibusiness attitudes. Most Grangers distrusted entrepreneurs, and their suspicions engendered programs aimed at breaking up trusts and monopolies and punishing thieves and swindlers. In effect, the order tried to become a watchdog against fraud, deceit, and theft."

The cooperatives, mostly of them seriously undercapitalized and poorly managed, faced a serious challenge with an economic depression called the Panic of 1873. Grain prices fell and farmers found it increasingly difficult to pay cash for needed goods at the Grange "cash-only" cooperative stores. Farmers were dedicated to the anti-monopoly posture of their Grange and they saw the cooperatives as the answer to their economic problems. Unfortunately, when the co-ops began to fail, the farmers lost confidence in their fraternity as well.

Membership decline moves power eastward

The growth of the Grange in the early 1870s was phenomenal. At the close of 1875 the secretary's report showed 858,050 members in states across the nation, in "Indian Territory" and Canada. Since the growth was occurring spontaneously and at such a vigorous pace, it is believable that total people claiming Grange membership at this point in its history could well have exceeded one million. The largest concentration of Grange power, interestingly, was in the Ohio River Valley and in Missouri, with about one-third of the members living in Ohio, Indiana, Kentucky and Missouri. Other large Grange states included Iowa, Texas, Tennessee and Pennsylvania. So prominent was this geographic distribution that the executive committee in 1875 pushed to have the national headquarters removed to Louisville because that was a mid-point for membership.

The earlier days of organizational poverty were over for now be-

John T. Jones (1813-1907)

cause the influx of members brought a boost of income. With the coffers full and debts paid, delegates to the 1873 session let their aversion to asset accumulation becloud their judgement somewhat and they voted some disbursements which could be considered the beginning of the Grange's persistent commitment to community service. The panic had economically devastated many farmers but additional ruin followed a destructive Louisiana flood and extreme ravages of grasshoppers in Nebraska and adjacent states. Delegates decided to disperse the accumulated wealth of the National Grange by dribbling it to a number of states which had experienced difficulties. A total of more than $18,000 was dispensed. Charles Gardner notes these funds were a minor help to those whose lives had been ruined, but the depletion of the treasury almost crippled the National Grange in the years ahead.

A more immoderate move to reduce the surplus built up by the National Grange was a reduction of annual dues to the national body from 10 cents per person to five cents and a one-time refund to subordinates amounting to $54,825—a mere $2.50 per subordinate Grange. D. Wyatt Aiken later characterized the disbursements as "an extravagant squandering of the funds of the National Grange" and programs of the national body would be severely limited in a few years because of the lack of reserves.

Arriving at the height of Grange popularity, John T. Jones, master of the Arkansas State Grange, was elected national master at the November 1875 Louisville session. He and his wife were delegates to the 1874 session and at the February 1875 session he was elected to the national executive committee. (There were two sessions that year because of a change of months for the events from February to November. Sessions have been held in November since 1875.) Serving as national master for two years, Jones was a staunch supporter of cooperatives. His background included graduation from the University of Virginia and many years as owner of large cotton plantations. He was twice elected district judge early in life and passed away in 1907 at the age of 94.

The downward spiral of members was almost as dramatic as the onrush of early interest. From the official high of 858,050 in 1875, the order dwindled to 124,420 members just five years later. During the '80s there were fluctuations, but the all-time low point for dues-paying members was 106,782 in 1889.

Analysis of the membership decline in the mid-1870s has flourished since Solon Justice Buck's classic study *The Granger Movement* appeared in 1913. Although later scholars have disputed some of Buck's conclusions regarding the causes of the decline, there are some areas of general agreement. Problems encountered by the cooperatives were definitely promoters of dissatisfaction even though those problems were not entirely the fault of the Granges.

Disorganization resulting from extremely rapid growth was probably a major factor in the slippage in membership. The Grange simply grew too quickly for it to stabilize and provide continuity of services for the new units. Another aggravating ingredient was the fact that the growth occurred before the organization had even established its identity.

The composition of the membership was a point of stress as well. Most members were farmers and those farmers were traditionally independent types who found working together a difficult transition to effect. There was a continual eruption of suspicions, particularly of the leaders and anyone connected with the organizational funds. Grange members addressed themselves as "brother" and "sister" and like siblings, open quarrels surfaced.

There were some instances of graft as well as unfounded accusations; resulting trials in the Grange judicial system tended to polarize members rather than unite them.

One nationally noticed abuse involved a Grange chartered in downtown Boston, Massachusetts, composed of wealthy grain dealers, commission men, and individuals prominent in newspaper circles. Since it became apparent the subordinate was actually subverting the work of the organization, the National Grange had to finally pull the subordinate's charter and censure the Massachusetts State Grange for not taking appropriate action as requested earlier. Another big city Grange, this one in New York's Manhattan, had been chartered by O.H. Kelley himself. The master of that Grange, Robert Farley, was Kelley's brother-in-law and he had secured business contracts with Granges with Kelley's help. Farley proved to be dishonest in business dealings, however, and he also used his position in the Grange to proselytize for a particular political candidate. In 1875 that subordinate's charter also was revoked. The scandal intensified and despite Kelley's written disavowal of Farley's company, the Grange founder had to endure attacks on his character by New Hampshire State Master Dudley T. Chase at the next National Grange session. Even though he retained his secretary's post that session, Kelley's reputation was

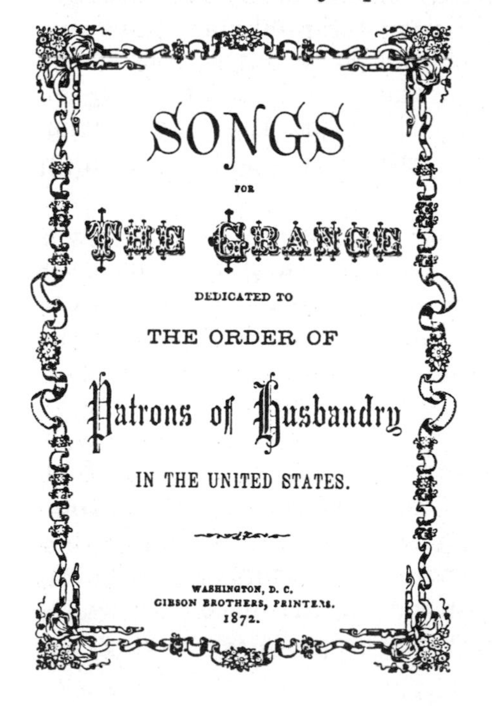

The song book by Caroline Hall and Rev. Aaron Grosh helped solidify musical elements in the subordinate Grange meeting.

smeared and his enthusiasm for the movement he started began to wane. These public squabbles, and others like them, did their part to weaken the order.

In desperation, Kelley renewed his old plan to have a separate movement within the Grange itself. In 1870 he had proposed the Degree of Demeter to McDowell, but it apparently never went anywhere. Set up during the 1875 Louisville session, Kelley called the new body the Degree of the Golden Sheaf and following the convention he tried through letters to entice others to participate. Kelley's chief interest was to provide a medium of expression for the Grange's radical leaders since they were being thwarted by conservative elements within the organization. The move apparently made little headway, but the effort did result in passage of a resolution in 1877 barring secret societies within the Grange.

William Saunders, unhappy with the 1875 move of the national headquarters to Louisville, severed his ties with the Grange in November of that year. He joined forces in 1879 with his friend and former Grange member Elizabeth Thompson, a reformer and philanthropist, to form the American Workers' Alliance. Kelley did relocate to Kentucky with the headquarters but resigned three years later in order to devote time, he said, to land speculation in Florida. The squabbles within the national leadership circles undoubtedly influenced his decision to leave. Saunders returned to the Grange in 1880 and Kelley also attended an occasional national session, but neither held office again. As Nordin says, "If prominent men like Kelley and Saunders left the order out of protest, certainly countless others must have" left for similar reasons.

Still others pulled out of the Grange in protest against the perceived reluctance of the organization to adopt a militant posture while even others left because they thought the Grange had already fulfilled its purpose. Many of the radicals shifted their allegiance to the Farmers' Alliance and those who felt the job was done cited new willingness expressed by lawmakers to attend to farmer problems.

Religious and racial attitudes also contributed to the drop-off of Grange membership in the mid-1870s. Studies have shown that the Grange was most popular with those who were from a better educated part of society, people with family roots in New England who espoused moderate Protestant theology. Despite intense efforts, the fraternity never made much progress organizing the masses of immigrants flooding the Midwest from Germany and Scandinavian countries, largely because of the influence of wary clergy. The immigrants mistook the Grange's "secret" characteristics and its ritual as being in competition with their church and accused the order of teaching a false brand of Christianity. A scarcity of foreign names on early member rolls indicates that the clergy was successful. The apex of this criticism was printed in the *Augustana* publication in 1873:

> The Grange is the devil's last trump card; it is, without doubt, the most dangerous movement that has been instituted up to this time. It was started by the Free Masons; it will also accompany Free Masonry to destruction and will be interred in the same wicked grave toward which all honest souls have an aversion. Among all the people on earth, those least likely of forming a secret, selfish league with idolatry for divine service and insanity for its creed are the solid farmers.

Other church publications picked up the tone of these prejudices, creating doubt in the minds of some devout patrons.

Regionalism also played a role in the Grange's successes and failures, even though early leaders did everything possible to avoid it. Grange success in the deep South has been mixed over the years. Some southern states had impressive early activity but those gains were quickly lost when the hard times of the mid-1870s arrived. Racial attitudes of early members may have been a contributing factor. Although some Granges in the Reconstruction South willingly admitted members regardless of race, they were probably the exception. Nordin points out that in Mississippi "the Grange was often a front for the Ku Klux Klan. The farmers' organization with its features of secrecy and brotherhood and its legitimate objectives was subverted to serve as a cloak for the devious work of recalcitrant opponents of Reconstruction." It is ironic that the farm group conceived as a vehicle to aid the poor farmers of the South—and none were poorer than the former slave tenant farmers—would fail to attract the enduring active involvement of those who could have used it the most.

In defense of the tendency to avoid these southern problems, it could be stated that the national body made every effort possible to avoid being entangled in regional issues which would lead to factionalism. The more conservative outlook, while it alienated many of the early organizers, did equip the organization to weather its roughest trial. In retrospect, this period resulted in the most well-known achievement of farmer-activism, the Granger Laws.

5

First Triumph

FARM PROFITS in the 1870s depended as much upon cheap farm to market transportation as they do now. The railroads, because of some of their high-handed, expensive practices, were singled out by the emerging Grange movement as the source of all economic evils for the nation's farmers.

Even before the completion of the first transcontinental railroad in 1869, tracks were linking isolated communities throughout the nation. With the railroad came the promise of prosperity but, in many locales, the prosperity failed to materialize as expected.

Massive land give-aways to the railroad companies by the government were resented by early settlers who had to buy their property at inflated prices. Then, to make matters worse, railroads were taxed for their property at a fraction of the rate charged to farmers. Iowa State Master A.B. Smedley pointed out in 1873, for example, that his state's farmers paid 20 to 50 mills per dollar value of their land while the railroads were assessed only four mills per dollar value of their developed property.

Grange arguments stressed the semi-public nature of American railroads because their very existence depended upon the public contributions of lands. A Wisconsin court case had upheld that notion by stating the railroads were "public highways, like bridges, town roads, etc., and as such were subject to the same rules." The argument went on to assert that in the land grant acts there were phrases granting states the power to regulate freight and passenger tariffs—something the Grange members collectively wanted desperately. There was ample precedent for regulation of railroads since the Rhode Island Legislature had passed the first such law back in 1839.

In an effort to boost their own profits, railroads granted the most favorable rates to long hauls. Highest rates, generally, were charged for shorter hauls to points served by competing businesses such as river towns with barge and ship terminals.

At the onset, efforts to enlist support of legislators in discussing any form of railroad regulation were stymied because of a longstanding railroad practice of giving free passes and additional favors to the lawmakers, judges and others in authority. There were even instances of free passes being given to Grange leaders on their way to convention, a cunning attempt to sway their allegiance toward the railroads.

As early as 1870 Grange interests in Minnesota prevailed and Republican Governor Horace Austin was obliged to promise in his inaugural speech a thorough investigation of railroad business practices. Resulting legislation failed to clear the Legislature. During the 1871 legislative session, Minnesota lawmakers passed a law creating a railroad commissioner who could investigate and make recommendations. Also that session, the Jones Railroad Bill was successful due to Grange agitation with maximum rates for freight and passengers being set for all Minnesota railroads. Ironically, the railroads simply ignored the law.

In response to the railroad arrogance, the recently successful Minnesota Anti-Monopolists, headed by Ignatius Donnelly, achieved a victory in 1874 by passing a bill modeled after a one-year-old Illinois law creating a railroad commission. The commission would have authority to regulate rates and, if the railroads continued to stay in non-compliance, the commission would place the companies in receivership. Thomas Woods notes that "Much to the chagrin of state control advocates, railroad rates actually increased under the commission system."

Impetus for the Minnesota actions came from Illinois. Because of pressure from many sectors, including rural residents, an act was approved March 10, 1869, mandating regulation of common carriers within Illinois. Further refinements were passed in 1871 and 1873. The impact of the Granges in the initial act is disputable since the organization was still in its infancy in the state. D. Sven Nordin searched the Illinois State Archives and could find no petitions from Granges supporting the proposal. Nevertheless, Grange members joined with other farmers and merchants to fight for the latter laws, as evidenced by petitions from Granges reaching the Legislature in 1873 and 1874. *The Prairie Farmer,* long a supporter of the Grange, helped rally rural backing for railroad reform.

Grange input also was vocal in the states of Iowa and Wisconsin where similar legislation was passed and, collectively, the laws became known as the "Granger Laws."

This spate of regulatory legislation did not humor railroad executives and their response was a series of eight court cases which were dubbed as the "Granger Cases." These cases culminated in decisions from the U.S. Supreme Court in 1877 which firmly established the right of government to regulate business interests by ruling that "where property has been clothed with a public interest, the legislature may fix a limit to that which shall in law be reasonable for its use."

The first case to reach the Supreme Court was *Munn vs. Illinois.* The 1871 Illinois law regulated maximum rates for grain warehouses and elevators and required these businesses to apply for a license. Since the Munn warehouse would not comply, the court levied a $100 fine. Their appeal to the Illinois Supreme Court

*Foundation for Social Improvement**

Central to the concept behind the "Granger laws" was the idea that business "affected with a public interest" could and should be required to meet certain reasonable public expectations. Once this idea and its implications gained a foot-hold, it was applied to a wide variety of situations.

For example, in 1897 the Attorney General of Minnesota advised the Governor that a proposed commission to establish minimum wages for women and children would be constitutional. The Attorney General drew an analogy between the proposed minimum wages commission and the railroad regulation boards which were first established under the Granger laws.

The concept of public welfare as a basis for legislation was extended into a multitude of areas where reformers found social injustices. In the famous Oregon cases of *Miller vs. Oregon* and *Bunting vs. Oregon*, the concept was upheld by the Supreme Court as a valid basis for maximum hour and minimum wage regulation.

Some of this legislation was addressed directly to the physical and moral benefit of individuals who were simply unable to cope with the host of inequities and misfortunes which dogged them in an industrialized community. Other law making concerned bank reform, more effectual corporate regulation, tax reform, and conservation of natural resources. All of these measures had been adin 1873 resulted in a decision which upheld the law and the lower court decision, and the U.S. Supreme Court concurred. On the same day the high court ruled on *Munn vs. Illinois,* the justices applied this decision regarding the constitutionality of states to regulate business on the collection of railroad cases.

With this defeat the railroads had two courses of action: They could simply accept the controls and adjust their business accordingly, or they could oppose the laws and fight for their repeal. Whenever the latter action was chosen, Granges rose up in outspoken support of business regulation for the common good.

The Supreme Court decision far from settled Grange concerns about monopolies in general and railroads in particular, nor were all the problems with railroads contained in the upper Mississippi Valley, as the Granger Laws would seem to indicate. Grange members kept insisting the freight rates were excessive and, at the 1879 Canandaigua, New York, National Grange session, stated

---

vocated by the Grangers or their successors through the years when *laissez-faire* reigned.

As a whole, this legislation may fairly be described as evidence of the process of a maturing society and adjusting to the necessities of human dignity in an industrial age. The process had not been smooth or painless. The fact remains, however, that social legislation in the United States sought remedies for what they conceived of as inequities in the social structure within the existing constitutional framework of politics and government. It has left intact the concept of free enterprise and individual freedom of choice. Government regulation has been conceived of as working to preserve, rather than supersede, these freedoms.

For these reasons, the Granger movement left a commendable legacy. Those who can claim it as part of their heritage have good reason to be proud....

It is clear that the "Granger Cases" had great impact upon the constitutional development of social legislation in the United States. First, they sank the first roots of Supreme Court acceptance of social legislation in a free-enterprise, industrial society. They introduced into a *laissez-faire* mentality the idea that private rights must be subject to limitation by the government in the interests of social justice. Second, the language of the *Munn* case is such that

that "The railroad companies and other corporations engaged in transportation have assumed the right to charge 'just such rates for transporting freight as the commodities entering into commerce will bear.'" The solution, delegates felt, was for Congress to create a National Board of Control, "invested with full power to fix and regulate the freight rates which may be charged by railroad companies and other corporations engaged in interstate commerce."

As early as 1874, National Master Dudley W. Adams had seen the need to carry railroad control all the way to Congress. In his master's address he said, "I see no solution of this question but for Congress to avail itself of its constitutional right to regulate commerce between the states, and for the states themselves to regulate the tariffs within their own boundaries.... To rely on competition for relief will bring only renewed disappointment. Our past history shows that the rapid increase of railroads has only

---

it could be used to sustain the growth of the idea of social legislation. For many years a Supreme Court majority was unwilling to concede broad power to the legislature for the purpose of regulating private interests. But they were willing to admit that some regulation of some interests was necessary. They could take comfort in the idea of affection with a public interest. At the same time, a more liberal court could find in *Munn* the concept that the legislatures had a broad power to do what seemed necessary to ensure social justice. Third, the concepts first developed in the Granger Cases provided a viable alternative for the American society to two repugnant courses of political development. One would be the prepetuation of a *laissez-faire* system, which could simply not work in a heavily industrialized, complex community. The other would be state ownership of the means of production. The fears of the 1930s have not materialized.

The Granger Movement [of the 1870s] was short-lived. Most of the laws passed in its name did not work well. But it was the beginning of the movement in this country for viable social legislation. The roots it sank have gone deep.

***Excerpted from a winning essay (" The Impact of the Granger Movement Upon Social Legislation") in the National Grange Centennial contest for law students, written by John C. Miles Jr. and published in *Legal and Economic Influence of the Grange*, © 1967 by the National Grange.**

resulted in more gigantic combinations."

All this disquiet ultimately led to passage of the Interstate Commerce Act of 1887. State regulations were modest attempts to grant the relief sought by the Grange; the ultimate accomplishment came with the Interstate Commerce Commission and its authority to regulate railroads nationally.

Attitudes on the Supreme Court between 1876 and 1934 were very pro-business, the Granger Cases notwithstanding. The court consistently limited the *Munn vs. Illinois* ruling to regulation of public utilities until the 1934 case of *Nebbia vs. New York,* which permitted regulation of wholesale and retail price of milk. Following that decision, state legislatures had the authority to exercise "reasonable" control over business practices.

In 1966, in honor of the centennial of the Grange's founding, an essay contest for law students was held by the National Grange. Entries were to be on the "Impact of the Grange on Social Legislation" and judging was done by a panel chaired by Judge Thurman Arnold, U.S. Court of Appeals and head of the Antitrust Division of the U.S. Department of Justice from 1938 to 1943. The four winning essays and Judge Arnold's presentation address, given at an awards ceremony during the 1966 session in Minneapolis, were printed the following year in a 100-page book, *Legal and Economic Influence of the Grange 1867-1967.* Each winning essay traces the development of government sovereignty and authority to regulate business for the common good back to *Munn vs. Illinois.* Examples are cited of many areas which also have their source in this legal doctrine but go beyond the regulation of public utilities. Because of *Munn vs. Illinois,* our legislatures have been free to respond to multiple public needs in the areas of civil rights, hours and wages of employees, sale of alcohol, child labor and other realms of social concern.

Other battles with monopolies were yet to be fought by the Grange, culminating a few years later with passage of the Sherman Antitrust Act. But for the youthful Patrons of Husbandry, their earlier struggles with railroad regulation would be seen as a mighty accomplishment. Many years afterward, Judge Arnold called them " The Grange's greatest victory."

6

Finding A Niche

1878-1897

THE ACTIVIST AGENDA for the Grange, as conceived and carried out by O.H. Kelley and his closest associates, was at the same time responsible for both the rapid spread of the order during the early 1870s and its eventual deterioration during the latter 1870s and 1880s. As popularity of the movement spread, many farm families were attracted initially because of the promises made by overly optimistic organizers. The Grange, they felt, could solve the problems of the farming class, ushering in a utopia of good prices, improved living conditions, enhanced respect from other segments of society and a heightened sense of self-worth. When the desired changes were slow to materialize, discouragement set in and the less patient turned their attention in other directions.

Despite portraits of the Grange painted by some scholars, the Patrons of Husbandry did not die during this period. Even though a few of the founders and many early members took their leave, those remaining were determined not to see their grand experiment fail. The struggle with the railroads and other monopolies was not over. Government at all levels was in need of Grange attention. Living conditions on the frontier were far from perfect and the work of the farmer and his family was unusually burdensome and in need of technological improvement. Perhaps the more conservative founders were right: Education, social interaction and a less confrontive approach to lawmakers might work after all.

Kelley's old friend Samuel Emory Adams entered the national master's chair at the worst possible time. From a high point of popularity in 1875 when 858,050 dues-paying members were enrolled, membership had steadily declined. The drop of nearly 130,000 in 1876 was minor compared to the almost 400,000 additional members who would walk away by the end of 1878.

Adams, who was elected at the 1877 session in Cincinnati, was a Minnesota neighbor of Kelley's. The two had been involved in some real estate endeavors together during the 1850s and it was Adams who led the Minnesota State Grange into a strong activist posture by unseating the conservative state master in 1874. He kept the state post while serving as national master 1877-1879. He was state master of Minnesota a total of eight years in two different terms and his interest in Grange service is evidenced by his 20 years as master of Minneapolis Grange, until his death in 1912. His other fraternal ties were with the Masons, and at the time of his death he was lieutenant grand commander of the Ancient and Accepted Scottish Rite. During the Civil War he attained the rank of lieutenant colonel and in later life he held positions in Minneapolis city government and was twice elected to the Minnesota State Senate. His wife, Augusta, was secretary of the Minnesota State Grange for 18 years and national Flora and Ceres, serving two years in each post.

Adams achieved his national Grange position, after 26 ballots,

Samuel E. Adams
(1828-1912)

at a time when his friend Kelley was undergoing the ordeals which ultimately resulted in his departure from the order the following year. Kelley felt the national officers were too reserved and their reluctance to allow the Grange to battle for the farmers in the way he envisioned was promoting its demise. The disbursement of needed reserves in 1874 was also causing hardships but, in a desperate attempt to attract new initiates and hold present members, total dues were reduced at the 1877 session from $5 to $3 annually for men and from $3 to $1 for women.

It is revealing to note that the membership base shifted radically during this period of the organization's history and this move introduced individuals into the order who eventually exerted a strong influence with the Grange's policies. Only 13 percent of the members, D. Sven Nordin notes, lived in the six New England states, Ohio, New York and Pennsylvania in 1875. Just 10 years later, though, three-fifths of the members resided in that region and by 1900 those nine states held 83 percent of the fraternity's dues payers. Nordin calls this membership shift the "second Granger movement."

There was a flourishing interest in the Grange in eastern provinces of Canada during the fraternity's early years, reaching its zenith in 1879 with over 30,000 members. Although membership decline paralleled that in the U.S., subordinate Granges continued activity in Canada for many years.

Education, social enrichment become goals

Saunders and many of the other founders identified more strongly with the portion of Kelley's portrayal of the Grange as a social movement for farmers, feeling uncomfortable with entanglements in business ventures and Kelley's insistence on collective political or legislative activity. Conservative forces won a partial victory with the adoption of the *Declaration of Purposes,* containing restrictive clauses against partisan political involvement.

With the departure of Kelley and many early Western patrons, the order collectively began to redefine its methods of operation. Although there was general agreement that the role of the Grange included legislative involvement—the Granger Laws had proven the effectiveness of organized action by farmers—the direction of that involvement on a national level was becoming more structured and controllable. At the 1878 session in Richmond, Virginia, the first recognizable national legislative committee was set up with the appointment of D. Wyatt Aiken of South Carolina and A.P. Forsyth of Illinois (both members of Congress) as a committee "to take charge of such petitions and memorials to Congress adopted or ordered prepared by the executive committee, and to bring the subjects contained in them to the attention of Congress in such manner as they shall deem most expedient."

Education began to emerge as one of the Grange's most exigent issues. The preamble of the Constitution, penned by Saunders and adopted in 1873, stated "The ultimate object of this organization is for mutual instruction and protection; to lighten labor by diffusing a knowledge of its aims and purposes; to expand the mind by tracing the beautiful laws the Great Creator has established in the Universe; and to enlarge our view of creative wisdom and power." The *Declaration of Purposes,* accepted the following year, said, "We shall advance the cause of education among ourselves, and for our children, by all just means within our power. We especially advocate for our agricultural and industrial colleges, that practical agriculture, domestic science and all the arts which adorn the home, be taught in their courses of study." This was bold stuff for the 1870s and was undoubtedly included because of the persistence of women members.

In Richmond, delegates approved a resolution, advanced by Tennessee State Master T.B. Harwell, based upon the recommendations made the previous year by Kelley. The resolution recommended states "have the study of the elementary principles of agriculture introduced into the public schools by legislative enactment." Apparently this is the first recorded action by any group urging an agriculture curriculum in elementary and secondary schools. Kelley, of course, had touted education as at least one of the chief saviors of the farmers. New methods of crop and livestock production were being discovered and innovative implements and hybrid varieties were coming on the market so fast that farmers were finding it difficult to keep up. Many, of course, did not, but Kelley represented those who valued the latest information and he took pride in possessing intellectual skills necessary to gain from it. Having agriculture classes in the public schools would help involve and train young people from farm homes so they would be able to profitably engage in the industry when their time came. Texas State Master A.J. Rose told his members in 1882 "that education is the leading feature of the order" and "nothing increases debt, vice, superstition, and crime so much as ignorance." His injunction is reminiscent of phrases sprinkled throughout the degree work and it prompted Nordin to comment that the Grange members really wanted schools to "inculcate pupils with a mythical grandeur of agrarian life."

Schools in late nineteenth century rural America were anything but ideal. Public education originally had its start in Kelley's home state of Massachusetts, with that state also passing the first compulsory school attendance law in 1852. As city school systems began to implement advanced public educational opportunities through high schools, those in rural districts were feeling some disenchantment with the quaint one-room school. The Grange came to many of these areas at a time when farm parents were starting to recognize the value of education, especially "practical" lessons which would help the children develop vocational skills, stay on the farm and avoid the multiple temptations to move into the cities. Departing from commonly accepted teaching techniques, the Grange leaders postulated that their children would learn far more through hands-on experience coupled with instruction than they were by the rote memorization method common in schools of the time.

Grange members, however, realized that for their children to experience the education they needed, parents would have to take matters into their own hands. Rural residents have always been fiercely loyal to local control of their schools and in some instances the Grange people went one step farther by forming their own schools. In Alabama, where the state Grange education committee in 1875 urged subordinates to start independent schools, at least four Grange institutions appeared. Similar schools appeared in North Carolina, Mississippi, Louisiana, California and Michigan.

Calls for vocational agriculture education

These early attempts to tailor-make a curriculum for rural children did not enjoy longtime success, though, and a desire to reform the existing public system took their place. Kelley's 1877 plea "to relieve distress and avoid future troubles by encouraging the establishment of industrial schools and making agriculture one of the principal studies" placed the Grange in the forefront of contemporary educational innovators. Novel, too, was Kelley's insistence that young women be given equal opportunity. "By all means let the girls have the same opportunities as the boys. They will excel as florists and horticulturists. How many there are who could be in easy circumstances with happy homes, and others competent even to manage farms, had they the requisite knowledge." This topic of vocational agriculture education in public schools—for both boys and girls—appeared on the National Grange session agenda every year between 1877 and 1900. These Grange hopes were largely fulfilled in 1917 with the passage of the Smith-Hughes Act which provided for vocational and agriculture education nationwide.

Common Grange statements over the years, beginning in the early days of the order, concern efforts to upgrade qualifications for teachers, elevate courses of instruction for those taking teacher training in college, and, beginning in 1896, included calling for increases in salaries so as to attract the most capable men and women for the teaching profession. These progressive views were generally held throughout the Grange, but a few isolated examples of a less broad-minded approach have survived. One which illustrates the long struggle with mistrust between North and South comes from a subordinate Grange near Bowling Green, Mississippi, which felt their community would be better off if all teachers with a northern background were expelled. They argued "the harmony, peace and prosperity of our country demand that our public schools should be conducted by competent teachers of our own people and not by foreigners."

Public school finance has been a proverbial topic of Grange concern. Rural and small town schools were almost universally funded at a much lower rate per pupil than schools in cities and Grange members could easily see that the imbalance resulted in inferior education for their children. Proposals in the early years of the Grange were less sophisticated and even included suggestions from Alabama members to tax dogs or implement a poll tax to support schools. Most schemes, however, called for some state or federal aid to rural districts. Concern has always been expressed that control of the schools should remain local, but in 1896 the National Grange went on record favoring "one grand national system" of schools. In later years that position was abandoned in favor of federal aid to rural districts "only when adequate safeguards to assure local control are provided."

Inequality of educational opportunity became glaringly obvious with the rapid expansion of high schools in cities. Toward the end of the century, Grange resolutions concerning consolidation of country schools with larger districts in order to access high school opportunities for farm children created bitter disputes. Secondary education was favored, but by 1896 only Massachusetts had a law requiring high school for every child. Advanced education beyond the one-room school was usually unavailable or inaccessible for farm children. Eventually, because of pressure from farmers, local and statewide plans were devised and implemented to expand educational opportunities for rural children.

Agriculture goes to college

By adopting the specific language in the *Declaration of Purposes* pertaining to agricultural colleges, the Grange delegates were voicing a strong protest about the shortcomings of the land grant college system. Congress had, with the passage of the Morrill Act in 1862, set up the land grant college structure. The federal government, as it did with the railroads, gave blocks of land to the states which would, in turn, produce income to support the establishment and maintenance of colleges. Each institution was required to teach agriculture, military science and engineering. While approving of the intent of this act, Grange members were faced with the realization that some states failed to fulfill their promise to provide agriculture training and funds were being used to sustain liberal arts programs.

The Grange favored separate colleges of agriculture and in 1884 Representative D. Wyatt Aiken successfully engineered legislation requiring a congressional investigation of the money diversion practices. The House Committee on Education conducted an inquiry but when Congress failed to act further, the Grange resumed its pressure. At the 1892 National Grange session delegates were told that in 13 states with Morrill Act universities, only 770 students were engaged in agriculture studies and only 304 had earned degrees in agriculture. Conversely, in 13 other states with agriculture and mechanical arts colleges separate from universities, a total of 4,386 students were enrolled in agriculture programs and 2,616 had graduated.

National Grange pressure had been important in securing passage of the Hatch Act of 1887 which established agricultural experiment stations in conjunction with land-grant colleges. The experiment stations were charged with the mission of conducting scientific investigation and experimentation as well as disseminating practical information on agriculture to farmers. With colleges and universities jumping to capture funds for this new function, Grange observers were becoming even more vigilant in their oversight role.

The agriculture school and experiment station complications in West Virginia were not only typical of what occurred elsewhere, but the conflicts also produced a Grange leader who would go on to national prominence. West Virginia University had been founded in 1867 as the land-grant college for the state. Originally called the Agricultural College of West Virginia, the institution quickly became a liberal arts university with little practical instruction in agriculture being offered. The West Virginia State Grange began to act, and with the Hatch Act and establishment of an experiment station in Morgantown, agriculture research began in earnest in their state. Grange members still felt agricultural

Thomas Clark Atkeson (1852-1935)

The connection between the Grange and the Chautauqua Institution was strong from the early days of both movements. This Grange building on the Chautauqua grounds, completed in 1903, still stands. (Chautauqua Institution photo)

education was virtually nonexistent in West Virginia and found their state overseer Thomas Clark Atkeson to be an effective spokesman. Atkeson was a practical farmer, well educated, and articulate. The National Grange and other groups had pushed the Morrill Act of 1890 through Congress to provide for some additional funds for agriculture, mechanical arts, natural and economic sciences and similar subjects at the land grant colleges. The legislation convinced the West Virginia State Grange and the State Board of Agriculture, with Atkeson as a member, to began pressuring West Virginia State University to expand its agriculture education program.

In response, the regents created a chair of agriculture and offered the position to Atkeson in 1891. It was the first time the university had ever had a professor of agriculture and Atkeson implemented a broad-based course of study leading to a Bachelor of Agriculture degree. Further conflicts erupted, he was dismissed in 1893, and the agriculture classes were assigned to the director of the Agricultural Experiment Station. This intensified Grange dreams for a separate institution but Atkeson's ambition was for reappointment to his former position. A reorganization of the board of regents was effected in 1897 and Atkeson's cousin, Governor George W. Atkeson, appointed him as a member representing the state's farmers. By this time, T.C. Atkeson was master of the state Grange and in this dual role he also was able to secure appointment as the dean of a reorganized College of Agriculture. Success resulted, and enrollment grew from 10 in 1897, when Atkeson assumed control, to about 40 in 1902. Atkeson remained dean until 1910, gaining national recognition for his work. His greatest accomplishment during this stage of his life was, perhaps, his ability to keep the university from becoming dismembered, in spite of national Grange policy to the contrary, while agriculture education was being firmly implanted. Atkeson, who served as state master until 1921, would go on to fill an important National Grange role as the organization's first staff lobbyist in Washington, D.C. During his tenure as dean he had the distinction of organizing one of the nation's first student Granges in order to equip agriculture students with the leadership skills their communities desperately needed.

Adult education championed by early Grangers

Leadership ability and practical training was essential back home by those who couldn't go to college and the Grange's response to this need is perhaps the most far-reaching accomplishment of the organization's history. Provision had been made in the Grange meeting structure for a regular educational or entertaining feature. The "lecturer's hour" generally did not last that long, but the time set aside for the program was used, and is still used, to present information to enlighten, educate, amuse and help make life more productive and happy. In early days, programs were often about new techniques in farming. Women-oriented programs focused on methods to lighten and improve domestic chores. Usually, these programs were "home spun," but the study and practice necessary to put on a good presentation molded many members for public service. Special speakers, such as Ignatius Donnelly or other political figures, sometimes pushed the Grange meeting beyond the boundaries of non-partisanship but, nonetheless, members could never say they didn't receive some fresh, challenging idea.

The appearance of a new Grange in a community which had relied solely upon the local church and school for its social, educational and cultural advancement made a tremendous difference. With the fast growth of the Grange in the 1870s, there were, almost instantly, tens of thousands of presentations being made each month where, before, there had been none. Being part of a national organization with instant name recognition also allowed the local Grange to attract the attention of politicians, visionaries and roving lecturers with each appearance spreading innovative ideas.

These efforts within the Grange dovetailed nicely with another movement of the time which, in hundreds of districts, joined forces with the Grange. Chautauqua County, New York, the birthplace of the first subordinate Grange, also was the birthplace of another movement dedicated to popular education. Dubbed the Chautauqua movement, it traces its beginnings to the efforts of Dr. John Heyl Vincent, a Methodist clergyman, and the wealthy Akron, Ohio, farm implement manufacturer Lewis Miller. Their novel idea was to have a summer school for Sunday school teachers in the relaxing atmosphere of a camp on the shores of Chautauqua Lake. The first assembly opened August 4, 1874, and the summer series has continued to attract capacity crowds ever since. Over the years the Chautauqua Institution has grown and the beautiful grounds comprise hotels, administration buildings, a library, numerous private homes, a massive outdoor covered amphitheater seating in excess of 6,000, restaurants, a post office and other sites of interest. In 1888 the first "Grange Day" at the Institution was held, beginning a long tradition which continued until the late 1950s. A Grange hall was built there in 1903 by the Chautauqua County Pomona Grange with the financial help of Cyrus E. Jones, a Grange member and manufacturer from Jamestown, New York. The building, which still stands and is used as a personal residence, was valued at $35,000 when built and contained a hall for meetings and bedrooms where prominent Grange members spent the night.

At the 1890 kickoff of Grange Day at Chautauqua, the institution's daily newspaper, *The Assembly Herald,* welcomed the members of the Grange in its August 1 edition as "men allied for objects of mutual improvement and of general good." The following year the *Herald* reported over 7,000 Grange people flooded the Chautauqua grounds for Grange Day festivities and in 1892 former President Rutherford B. Hayes was chair of the Grange Day program with National Master Joseph Brigham featured as the keynote speaker. "These men and women here present will pass away," Brigham prophesied, "but...the [Grange] will exist while the great industry of agriculture shall exist. Agriculture must be the last industry to survive when the end of all things in this world shall come. I believe that so long as this industry shall exist, there will be difficulties that will render organization necessary." Brigham's address was followed by one delivered by Dr. Trimble, one of the Grange founders. Picnic dinners were served each year in a tent near the Grange building.

The concept of a summer school was a new one when it was proposed by Dr. Vincent. Home study through correspondence also was a fresh idea which had its start at Chautauqua. So, too, was the liberal, tolerant approach to new ideas and the willingness to be exposed to opposing points of view, an attitude which characterized both the Grange and Chautauqua.

But one idea, although not entirely original, spread the influence of the Chautauqua Institution across the nation and it involved

This 1904 poster advertises August Chautauqua events. The annual Grange Day program was a popular, regular feature for decades. (Chautauqua Institution)

thousands of Granges and their members. People distant from Chautauqua were hearing about the summer sessions there and they longed for the experience. Distance and lack of funds for travel prompted citizens to organize copycat Chautauqua meetings and contract for a series of speakers, musicians and entertainers to visit their local five-day to one-month cultural event. Contact with the "outside world" through the traveling speakers linked settlers, particularly in the West and Midwest, with the heritage they felt they had lost.

One of the best known individuals traveling the Chautauqua circuit was William Jennings Bryan, the presidential candidate on both the Democrat and Populist tickets and a popular hero for nineteenth century Grange members. Bryan, who shared Chautauqua tents with Mark Twain, Josh Billings, Wendell Phillips, Julia Ward Howe, Senator Robert La Follette, Eugene Debs and others, had a fiercely loyal following and was memorialized by one supporter who said "only one greater ever walked this earth and He never trod American soil."

Chautauqua events at local parks and in traveling tents continued to draw crowds until 1932. Although little known now, Chautauqua programs reached an estimated one out of 11 people—men, women and children—in the entire United States each year. In 1924, for example, the *New Republic* stated that "last year, more than 10,000,000 people bought in excess of 35,000,000 tickets to individual Chautauqua performances." In those hot tents, rural and small town people heard nationally-known speakers introduce them to concepts which had been topics of lecturer's hour for decades: pure food laws, school lunch programs, graduated income tax, slum clearance, free textbooks, temperance, juvenile courts, physical fitness, movements called Camp Fire Girls and Boy Scouts. Some of these were first discussed at Chautauqua Lake, refined and then introduced cross-country by the lecturers. Those not original with the Grange were championed by the organization and, in many instances, made reality because of its efforts.

Making education fun at the fair

Agricultural fairs became another medium for rural education. Although fairs date back to Medieval times, the contemporary county and state fairs trace their American origin to Elkanah Watson who, in 1811, organized the Berkshire County Fair at Pittsfield, Massachusetts, as the first rural event of its kind. As today, the fairs of the 19th century gave farmers and homemakers the opportunity to display the fruit of their labor, swap ideas, listen to presentations on new farming techniques and witness demonstrations—all in a festive atmosphere. In counties without existing fairs, Grange members often took the lead to establish a local annual fair. State fairs also resulted from Grange efforts and today they remain as the foremost way to display the best products of our farms. At many fairs there is a separate building or an aisle within the agriculture building dedicated to displays constructed by local Granges.

Grange picnics and encampments emerged as a hybrid, containing elements of both the Chautauquas and county fairs. One of the first and largest was the Williams Grove Picnic and Encampment which began near Harrisburg, Pennsylvania, in 1874. Grange families camped on the grounds for a week, taking in the commercial, industrial and agricultural exhibits. Although there were educational features, it is certain most of those attending were there for the fun and fellowship. Up to 100,000 would participate, with 50,000 or more being present on the big days. Chautauqua-like lectures were a staple at the encampment with big-name speakers including saloon-busting Carrie Nation and Dr. Anna Howard Shaw, minister and physician, the first woman licensed to preach by the Methodist Church in the United States. Another notable guest was Oliver Hudson Kelley who, in 1894, reminisced about the early days of the Grange from the Williams Grove podium. At that same location Governor Woodrow Wilson opened his formal campaign for the presidency in 1912. Grange picnics, especially centered around the fourth of July, emerged everywhere and, in some localities, they are still important functions. The Trask Bridge Picnic in northern Illinois, although originating later, earned the reputation of being one of the largest and most enjoyable with a large agenda of speakers each year.

The picnics and encampments are indicative of the fraternal and social aspects of the Grange that began to be more firmly planted following the near collapse of the mid-1870s. Members camping at Williams Grove, Trask Bridge or one of the hundreds of other similar conclaves would agree with an earlier Grange spokesman who, in 1873, wrote in the Charleston *Rural Carolinian* that even though he could save money with early Grange cooperatives and these business involvements were "by no means unimportant objects ...[of the order], we shall make a great and in the end a fatal mistake, if we take these to be the sole or even principal ends of the organization.... The Grange is primarily a social institution—a bond of union and a guarantee of good fellowship and kindly fraternal feeling. It brings together in its meetings the fathers, mothers, sons, and daughters of the neighborhood."

Farmer institutes, special educational meetings often conducted by staff and students of the state experiment station or the agriculture college, were organized or sustained by Granges and often held in Grange halls. The concept began in Mississippi due to pressure from the state Grange and its state master, subsequent national master Israel Putnam Darden. The model was successfully followed elsewhere with participants eagerly supporting the Grange agenda, and eventually led to establishment of the Cooperative Extension program.

Legislative battles include RFD, opposing trusts

The pattern for successful legislative involvement had been set early in the Grange's experience. With the great prestige gained through enactment of the Granger Laws, members continued to press for the causes which meant so much to them. Major thrusts of legislative activity during this period concerned the growing menace of business monopolies, efforts to secure mail delivery in rural areas, technicalities of the election process, the shortage of credit for farmers, and the need for improved roads.

Monopolies, cartels and trusts had always been a concern of Grange leaders because they blocked competition and allowed one interest to control the supply, trade and price of a commodity. Invariably, farm producers suffered the most because they had to battle monopolies of shippers, grain and livestock buyers and producers of agricultural implements and supplies. Later they were faced with unregulated monopoly control of electric utilities and oil companies, a confrontation which resulted in a resurgence of Grange cooperatives in the 1920s through the 1940s.

The Granger Laws were examples of how a monopoly could be regulated to protect the public and many Americans, including those in the Grange, began pressing for more control of the massive business organizations that mushroomed in the last decades

Jonathan J. Woodman (1825-1907)

of the nineteenth century. The result was the Sherman Antitrust Act enacted in 1890 with strong support from the Grange. It declared illegal "every contract, combination in the form of trust or otherwise, or conspiracy, in restraint of trade or commerce among the several States, or with foreign nations." Further clarification was offered with the passage of the Clayton Antitrust Act of 1914, a law which also encouraged the formation of farmer cooperatives by removing some serious barriers.

Aside from the Granger Laws, Rural Free Delivery (RFD) is probably the Grange accomplishment most often mentioned by members. Although the Grange cannot take full credit for rural mail delivery, the organization certainly played an important role in its development. Massachusetts pioneered in 1639 by offering the first postal service in America. Congress authorized a postal service in 1789, but the system was cumbersome until the expansion of railroads and the development of the adhesive stamps in 1847. Despite initiation of free delivery in cities in 1863, by 1890 nearly three-fourths of the people still had to pick up their letters at the post office.

The Grange first started the clamor for rural delivery in the organization's infancy, but members were universally greeted with derision for this innovative idea. Common perceptions were that farm people either didn't read or seldom received any mail so, therefore, they did not need delivery. The popularity of shopping through the mail, introduced by Montgomery Ward, convinced the Grange people that country residents would sufficiently take advantage of the mail to make it practical. Developments in education were raising the standards of rural literacy; even in the 1850s, Kelley and his neighbors had subscribed to agricultural journals. The Chautauqua Literary and Scientific Circle was the forerunner of the modern book clubs and, for the first time, all citizens had ready access to educational materials through the mail.

In 1891 controversial Postmaster General John Wanamaker—called the "father of the modern postal system"—proposed mail delivery to everyone, much to the elation of Grange people nationwide. On March 3, 1893, Congress appropriated $10,000 for an experimental rural delivery system but Wanamaker felt this was insufficient. Three years later Congress again appropriated $10,000 and the combined amount allowed an adequate test in West Virginia. By the end of that year, routes were in operation in 30 states and Carroll County, Maryland, was the first to have complete rural mail service in 1899. The Post Office annual report in June 1897 cited a number of beneficial effects of rural delivery including increased postal receipts, enhanced value of farmlands, road improvements, and better prices for farm commodities due to accessibility of market information by farmers. The report also noted, "To these material advantages may be added the educational benefits conferred by relieving the monotony of farm life through ready access to wholesome literature and the keeping of all rural residents, the young people a well as their elders, fully informed as to the stirring events of the day. The moral value of these civilizing influences cannot be too highly rated."

Charles Gardner cites a woman for originating the idea of RFD during a discussion in her Grange meeting. A resolution was drafted which went to the Pomona Grange and on to the state and National Granges, making the Grange the first organized group in the nation to seek mail delivery for country residents. Furthermore, in 1887 the Grange went on record favoring establishment of a parcel post system for small packages, such as those sent out by Montgomery Ward & Co. Package delivery at that time was controlled by a group of five express companies and rates were high. This proposal took longer to usher in but victory was final with the enactment of the present parcel post system on August 24, 1912.

Good roads become important to farmers

Grange legislative efforts originated with transportation issues and they continued to occupy much of the organization's attention. Besides concerns about railroads, the young Grange attempted to keep alternate modes of shipping available in order to enhance competition—and, hopefully, lower prices—between carriers. Hence, there were Grange voices pushing for domestic canal construction, channel deepening and widening in rivers to allow for increased navigation, improvements in ports, harbors and wharves. Additionally, western Grange people in particular fought for a canal across Nicaragua in order to speed delivery of goods to and from the West Coast. The Nicaragua route was eventually abandoned in favor of one in Panama.

Israel Putnam Darden (1836-1888)

When the bicycle craze of the 1880s and 1890s focused the nation's attention on the quality of its roads, farmers were there to voice their needs as well. Although the federal government had built roads during the Civil War, the practice was abandoned after the conflict, with the exception of occasional military roads. Some Granges felt roads were the responsibility of county governments, but the predominant opinion was that states should be accountable for highways and there should be some national aid. Everyone, especially the farmers and bicyclists, agreed that the roads were in miserable shape.

In 1893 Congress appropriated $10,000 to the Department of Agriculture to establish the Office of Road Inquiry, an action supported by the Grange. From that modest beginning, federal involvement grew and the office evolved into the Bureau of Public Roads with its responsibility of coordinating federal-state road building partnerships. By the end of the century the subject of roads, highways, canals and railroads was far from settled in the eyes of the Grange and transportation would continue to be a hot topic at many Grange conventions to come.

Grange presses for election reform

Another rallying point for Grange conventions at this time had to do with the election process. Ballots for various elections commonly were printed by candidates and political organizations and distributed to voters by them, a practice which led to confusion and fraud. Massachusetts in 1888 was the first state to adopt the so-called Australian ballot in state elections, a process that provided for printing and distribution of ballots by government agencies, the blanket ballot listing names and party affiliations of all candidates for all offices, and secret voting under the supervision of government. That same year the National Grange endorsed the system and urged its adoption in all the states. Beginning in 1885 the Grange started its longstanding support of primary election measures.

Populist ideas such as direct election of U.S. senators found fertile ground in the Grange and both movements espoused democratic, popular government. The U.S. Constitution provided that state legislatures elect senators from that state but the Grange was vocal in support of popular election by the growing group of qualified voters. One of the earliest appeals for the right of voters to select their own senators came from delegates at the 1885 Oregon State Grange convention. "By past experience," they warned, "we know the corrupting influence of money in the election of U.S. Senators; therefore, it is the opinion of the State Grange of Oregon that the constitution of the United States should be so amended that all officers be elected by the direct vote of the people, irrespective of sex, and that our representative to the National Grange bring the matter before that body." The struggle for direct elections was a long one and finally resulted in the seventeenth amendment to the U.S. Constitution in 1913, which instituted the practice.

Populist causes entice Grangers

The Populist movement owed much of its strength to a group known as the Farmers' Alliance. Many of the more militant early members of the Grange moved their allegiance to the Alliance following the decline in the mid-1870s. The Alliance, unlike the Grange, did not shy away from partisanship and political maneuvering, although both groups were essentially working for the same general uplifting of conditions for rural Americans. In the Alliance, business activities similar to earlier Grange exploits were set up. Alliance-sponsored candidates were elected to state legislatures, and in the 1890 elections several governorships and 30 U.S. Congressional seats were won by Alliance supporters. This achievement led to the formation of the People's or Populist Party the following year. The new party had widespread support not only from the Alliance but also from members of the Grange, former members of the Greenback Party, and labor groups such as the Knights of Labor. The party platform paralleled many policies of the National Grange by calling for abolition of the national banking system, institution of a graduated income tax, direct popular election of senators and the adoption of referendum. Other party planks supported the free coinage of silver as a method to improve economic conditions for laboring people. The party's 1892 platform was written by O.H. Kelley's early Grange organizer, Ignatius Donnelly of Minnesota.

Prior to the 1896 presidential election, a large number of Populists sympathizers took control of the Democratic Party convention and succeeded in nominating their staunch supporter William Jennings Bryan as that party's candidate for president. Even though Bryan received 176 electoral votes, he lost the election to Republican William McKinley by a slim margin of 609,687 popular votes. Following the election, the Populist Party split and eventually disappeared after the elections of 1908. With the demise of the Populist Party, the Farmers' Alliance also declined and with them departed the hope of changing negative conditions for America's farmers and laboring classes through a separate political party. For at least the second time in its history—and Donnelly was present both times—the Grange narrowly escaped entanglement with partisan politics and the formation of an independent party. During the first decade of the next century, however, the Grange would again be enmeshed in partisan politics, this time because of its national master and legislative committee.

Some of the Populist positions became less significant because of rapid changes in the American way of life in the late 1890s and early years of the twentieth century. Discovery of new gold fields dampened the Populist cause for free silver and the improvement in economic conditions made a third-party-approach less appealing. The most popular policies of the Populists, and the Grange took these on as its own, were being assimilated by a movement which would later be called Progressivism. William D. Barns, in his outstanding history of the West Virginia State Grange, notes "the importance of agrarian rebels of the Granger and Farmers' Alliance persuasion is that they dared to face directly the dilemma of a rural way of life confronted with a closing frontier and a rapidly developing industrial and financial capitalism.... But the most tragic failure of the mass of farmers was their continued propensity to organize rapidly and desperately only when their backs were against the wall, coupled with their unwillingness or inability to remain organized for extended periods of time."

The Grange was to benefit, however, from better times and from the collapse of the Alliance and the People's Party. As Lowell K. Dyson states in his book *Farmers' Organizations,* the Grange had "established a solidly progressive but not radical reputation." Beginning in 1900, the Grange would begin another rapid climb in membership that would continue with only minor fluctuations for the next 50 years.

National Grange attracts strong leaders

Organizational developments within the Grange also contributed to its improved prestige following the near disastrous failure of the 1870s. Following Samuel Adams' one-term leadership of the National Grange, delegates elected Michigan State Master Jonathan J. Woodman as master at their session held at Canandaigua, New York, in 1879. After some moderate success in the California gold rush, he had returned to Michigan to farm. For 12 years he was a member of the Michigan Legislature, serving as speaker in 1869 and 1871. President Hayes appointed Woodman as one of the U.S. commissioners to the International Exposition at Paris. His first wife, Harty, was national Pomona and Ceres, and following her death Woodman remarried Olivia J. Carpenter, pastor of the Universalist Church at Farmington, Michigan, and a prominent spokesperson for the temperance movement.

Even though the National Grange had no available funds due to the give-aways of the mid-1870s, Woodman worked tirelessly to help avert the decline. During his administration of six years (he

James Draper (1842-1907)

was the first national master to be reelected to a second or third term) the fight continued for an effective Department of Agriculture with a seat in the president's cabinet—a change that transpired in 1889. A widespread "cattle plague" alarmed national delegates in 1880 and at that session they passed a memorial to Congress asking for immediate action to "arrest the spread" of the disease. The resolution resulted in the Bureau of Animal Industry within the Department of Agriculture in 1884. That event, according to *Century of Service: The First 100 Years of the United States Department of Agriculture*, "marked the establishment of the first bureau in the new Department" and "its regulatory powers initiated a new departure in Government control."

A well-educated man who had been both a teacher and principal of a school, Woodman enthusiastically encouraged the Grange's increasing emphasis upon education. In his address at the 1882 session in Indianapolis he said,

> There is no subject so intimately connected with the welfare of our Order as that of education. No class of our people are better prepared to enjoy, or would be more benefitted by, a well-educated mind and heart than the cultivators of the soil; and no occupation in life is so well calculated to develop a man morally, mentally and physically as that of agriculture, or which requires closer study, deeper thought or a greater need of the application of science to obtain practical results.

Two years later, Woodman was able to report that "we have no cause for discouragement in the general condition and work of our Order" because the roughest of times had passed. He was acutely aware of the temptations to dabble in politics and asserted that "no instance has come to my knowledge where the Order has departed from its wise and well-defined non-partisan policy, and lent its influence to aid the special interest of partisanship. There have been encouraging indications of an increasing interest among Patrons in the general politics of the country; but the Order has held its course steadily onward, battling for the right, and for men and principles rather than party."

A southerner, Israel Putnam "Put" Darden of Mississippi, captured the post of national master in 1885 and he was reelected in 1887. Darden's service to the Grange ended abruptly with his death on July 17, 1888. He had been a captain in the Confederate Army and was subsequently a member of the Mississippi Legislature. From one of the wealthiest families of his county, he was able to graduate from the State University at Oxford. This fostered his in-

Joseph H. Brigham
(1838-1904)

tense interest in higher education and he was a leader in the founding of the Agricultural College at Starkville, later named Mississippi State College, and the Girls' Industrial College at Columbus. A monument to Darden was later erected to his memory at Mississippi State University. Darden was a charter member of Phoenix Grange at Fayette and he served as state master from 1877 until his death. His first wife, Mary Lou, was national Pomona for five years until her death in 1884 and his second wife, Kate, served as national Ceres four years.

Legislative action interested Put Darden greatly, probably because of his experience in advancing education in his home state. Political pressures were great on the Grange due to the agrarian unrest evidenced in the rise of the Farmers' Alliance and Populist movements. Darden, in his first master's address, stressed that the Grange at all levels was not a "political or party organization." But, he exhorted, "A national farmers' organization without the power to discuss the political rights of its members would be a farce beneath the dignity of intelligent men. The farmers want an organization that will use its influence upon the legislatures, state and national, to protect their interests, just as other class organizations protect the rights of their members; and no organization can long maintain standing with them if it does not render such assistance. We have been trying resolutions and petitions long enough and to little effect. Let us try the remedy that has been suggested at nearly every session of the National Grange; let us, with our ballots, send men to the legislatures, state and national, who will equalize and reduce taxation; restrain corporations from oppressing the people; have the finances managed in the interest of the people; keep our public domain for actual settlers; prevent gamblers from pricing our productions, and extend the same protection to the farmer and to the manufacturer. For this great work the Grange was organized, and it is not born to die, nor will it fail in the accomplishment of its purposes."

James Draper, Massachusetts state master, was thrust into the master's position due to his position as national overseer at the time of Punam Darden's death. A market gardener from Worcester, he later transformed his farm into a nursery. In 1874 he also began manufacturing cement drain and sewer tile. A Mason, his interest in ritual resulted in contributions to enhance the impressiveness of the sixth and seventh degrees and he served as high priest of Demeter from 1887 through 1889.

After serving in the post for four months, Draper was a candidate for election as national master for the remainder of Darden's term of office but was defeated by Col. Joseph Henry Brigham of Ohio at the 1888 Topeka, Kansas, session. Brigham had been Ohio state master and for six years served on the national executive committee. His popularity resulted in a total of nine years as national master, a longevity record which was not to be broken until the election of another Ohio man, Louis J. Taber, in 1923.

Brigham came to his national post well prepared since he had served two years in the Ohio Senate, was sheriff of his county four years, a trustee of the Ohio State University for six years, president of the Wool Growers' and Sheep Breeders' Association three years, and a member of the board of control of the Ohio Agricultural Experiment Station seven years. Following his national leadership role with the Grange in 1897, he was appointed assistant secretary of the U.S. Department of Agriculture by his good friend, President William McKinley.

An imposing figure, Master Brigham led the National Grange through its slow recovery, with his manner and reputation of strong leadership earning new respect for the organization in the halls of Congress.

Pivotal advancements

A significant development during this time was provision of insurance coverage for Grange members. Casualty insurance was, in most areas, unavailable for farm families, but it was becoming more of a necessity. Typical of early efforts to cooperatively provide for themselves what business was unwilling to do, Grange members in Washington state banded together in 1893 to form the Washington Fire Relief Association, following the example of the Lower Columbia Fire Relief Association formed by the Oregon State Grange in 1884. Both businesses operated by means of the loss assessment method. Participants paid a nominal premium to

Papillion Grange members in Blair, Nebraska, turned out in force for their float in the 1891 Labor Day parade. (Nebraska State Grange photo)

cover forms and incidental costs and then additional assessments were levied when any loss occurred. The Washington group changed its name to Grange Fire Insurance Association in 1936 and, with the inauguration of auto coverage in 1943, the name was shortened to Grange Insurance Association. The mutual company continues to serve Grange members in numerous Western states from its headquarters in Seattle. Other insurance endeavors would spring up elsewhere in the country.

During Brigham's administration were two pivotal advancements which would forever change the character and structure of the Grange—development of the juvenile Grange and the emergence of initial agitation for a separate committee to work with women's interests.

O.H. Kelley had first recommended activities for children of Grange families and, in 1886, members in the state of Texas began forming units of youngsters. Since these groups proved feasible, delegates to the 1888 session of the Texas State Grange adopted a juvenile Grange ritual. Three months later the delegates at the National Grange session instructed the executive committee to monitor the Texas experiment and report their findings. At the 1890 national session a favorable report was delivered and a revised juvenile Grange ritual was adopted for national use. Few units were organized, however, until after 1900 when enthusiasm for the idea caught on, especially in the state of Ohio. Further refinements of the concept would be made and the name eventually changed to junior Grange, but the original Kelley idea would remain: "to entertain and instruct the children in the rural districts and get their minds interested in the study of the beauties of Nature, as well as to afford them some rational recreation."

Grange mothers were, of course, the power behind the juvenile Grange. After nearly 30 years in the Grange, women of the 1890s were waking up and starting to assert themselves. Their presence, viewed skeptically by some early Grange organizers, was having a dramatic effect upon the organization and, in just a few years, the impact would be felt by everyone in America.

7

"The World's Greatest Equality Club"

WHEN GRANGE MEN AND WOMEN assembled in Rochester, New York, for the 37th session of the National Grange in 1903, they were given a compliment which, by that time in the organization's history, was received enthusiastically. Speaking before the delegates in her last public appearance, the woman suffragist Susan B. Anthony admitted she had always been able to recognize a "Granger woman as far off as I could see her, because of her air of feeling herself as good as a man." Even though the leadership provided by the Grange in recognizing the rights of woman has always been acknowledged, earning that distinction was a struggle which took several years to win.

Kelley, of course, had from the start insisted on including women in the Grange, giving credit for the idea to his wife's niece, Caroline Hall. In his September 4, 1867, letter to Anson Bartlett of North Madison, Ohio, he outlined his plans: "As our wives and daughters are generally attractive features in rural life, I have planned the work to have them active laborers with us, in full communion, and propose to make male and female form for each degree. Among civilized people in the country, this will make the meetings of the Lodges sociable reunions." Bartlett replied that "Your idea of female membership is all right, and will give general satisfaction.... I would like to see, not only women admitted to membership, but boys and girls as well,—boys at fourteen to sixteen years of age, and girls of twelve to fourteen. There is a time in the life of every farmer's boy when he becomes disgusted with farm life. At or before that time I would admit him in the Order (not to full or complete membership), and try to educate him to a love of the occupation."

It was Bartlett who suggested calling local units of the new organization something other than "lodges" and by the time he became the first national overseer of the organization the term "Grange" had been adopted to signify the subordinate chapters.

Bartlett said nothing about electing women to positions of responsibility even though the founders, in the second National Grange Constitution, devised four new offices which could be held only by women—Ceres, Pomona, Flora and stewardess (called lady assistant steward since 1873). There is some evidence that the founders initially created these ceremonial offices in order to ensure possession of the more responsible posts by men. One of the founders, The Rev. Aaron Grosh, implied this in his 1876 book *Mentor in the Grange and Homes of Patrons of Husbandry* by stating that women were candidates for all offices "except, perhaps, the few offices whose titles and duties would probably render them undesirable to the sex...." Reflecting male attitudes of the time, Kelley and the others apparently thought women would enjoy the essentially ceremonial positions which Mrs. J.B. Olcott, Pomona of the Connecticut State Grange characterized in 1887 as "three Lady graces [who] sit in distressing dignity, like so many wax-figures...." Kelley told Francis McDowell in 1868 his impression that women were generally pleased with their roles and regalia. The Grange was like "a fancy dress party," and women "like that, you know." Reacting to this relegation to a ritualistic post, Cordelia Atkeson, wife of Thomas Clark Atkeson, complained at the 1901 national session that there was no "real reason" for her to report as Ceres because the office had given her nothing to do. The frustration felt by Mrs. Atkeson and Mrs. Olcott was shared by many other early Grange women and they improvised in their offices by working to promote causes of interest to female members. It is important to note, however, the requirement that each Grange fill the female offices did ensure at lest minimal participation from women.

Grosh did not question the inclusion of women in the order and conceded that everyone would benefit from the close association of men and women. "Woman needs our Order far more than does the sterner, hardier sex; and the Order needs her for man's improvement. Her gentle influence, her innate tact in all matters of good taste and propriety, her instinctive perceptions of righteousness and purity—all these are needed in the Grange and also in society at large, from which she has been so much excluded, but into which our Order is rapidly introducing her."

The record shows that male patrons were much in need of the "gentle influence" exerted by the female members. Donald Marti, in his exhaustive study of women in the Grange, tells about eastern Indiana's Olive Grange. Women were in the background in that subordinate and "brothers had to be reminded to bring 'their women' to an installation of officers" in 1889. The group had bought six spittoons for the hall from dues money, thinking that would be enough for the regular crowd at meetings. Two years later, however, "they voted to fine brothers who continued to spit on the floor. Penalties escalated from five cents for the first offense to expulsion for the fourth. The Olive Grangers aspired to gentility, but the Order's uplifting influence was working slowly in their part of Indiana."

Disagreement about the role of women in the fraternity would emerge quickly. Early voting records unearth some common attitudes which made the presence and activity of the women in the fraternity even more crucial. At the Wisconsin State Grange's 1875 session a total of 253 votes were cast for state master and 35 for Pomona, numbers which manifest the level of importance attached to the women's offices. That same year 87 Iowa State Grange delegates voted for master, 61 for Flora, 58 for lady assistant steward, 57 for Ceres and 46 for Pomona.

More than likely, imbalance in voting for women offices represents the male tendency to leave the women alone to run their own portions of the Grange structure. Men were largely disinterested in the offices which were criticized by the women themselves as being less important than those held by male members. Especially in regions of the South, men actually apologized for the Grange's inclusion of women and disavowed that their farm group had any interest in improving the standing for American women. D. Wyatt Aiken, the Congressman who actively organized Granges in South Carolina, confessed that the presence of women had probably made the Grange unpopular in his state. Another South Carolina organizer, William Simmons, said that the "woman membership feature...appeared to be a very objectionable one."

Moving into leadership roles

Women would gradually assume a more prominent leadership

role in the Grange, however. In order to clarify mixed signals coming from National Grange sessions, the California state master ruled in 1873 that any member was free to run for any office, but it would be three years before a woman would attempt election to a state Grange post.

One of the first subordinates to elect a woman as master was in Howard County, Indiana, in 1877, and a year later Flora Kimball, a well-known campaigner for equal suffrage, was named master of her Grange in San Diego County, California. High-ranking spots in state Grange leadership also began to be filled by women, but in a minor way. The first was Julia Garretson who became state lecturer for Iowa in 1874. Her husband's success as the Grange organizer who planted the organization on the West Coast probably helped her win the breakthrough election. Sallie J. Back served as lecturer for the Indiana State Grange from 1881 through 1886. However, as historian Donald Marti discovered, "Never before 1895 was any woman Master of a state Grange, nor did more than seven women hold" the state Grange offices of master, treasurer, secretary or lecturer "in any one year." In 1895 Sarah G. Baird began a 17-year stint as master of the Minnesota State Grange and the statistics of women in leadership would continue to improve throughout the twentieth century.

An early novel feature was the design of the first degree so men and women had separate ceremonies, a practice which continued until 1889 when the two were combined. One phrase in the original woman's degree set the tone for later activism on the part of female members by instructing that woman "was intended by her Creator to be neither the slave, the tyrant, nor the toy of man, but to be his helpmeet, his companion, *his equal.*" This provocative statement was written by Anson Bartlett.

Social isolation of farm women was an original motivating factor for including women in the Grange. Caroline Hall, after moving to Minnesota, was fully aware of the problem faced by the farm wives and mothers who could never see their chores completed. A Wisconsin Grange woman shared a long inventory of her typical daily duties with readers of their state Grange *Bulletin* in 1880. Her husband's insensitivity made the day in question even worse when he brought in an unexpected dinner guest and then asked his wife to mend his coat so he could go into town with the friend after supper. The wife was left home, of course, and she wrote at the end of the day that "My head aches, my back aches, and my heart aches."

The exceptionally hard work of farm women, extreme isolation and lack of opportunity to visit other people were problems which Grange organizers hoped to fix. Statements in degree work and Grange publications, subordinate lecturer programs, and the evolving level of participation and leadership by women all combined to instruct husbands about women's needs. Husbands were urged to help lighten the load for their wives and put forth some effort to make the home more comfortable and attractive. Wives were told to improve themselves, study, elevate the beauty of their homes and make use of new tools and methods which lightened the work burden. Just as the Grange was elevating the standing of the farmer himself by promoting new production practices and the use of modern machinery, the organization was consciously trying to raise the standard of living for the rural homemaker as well.

In many areas of the country women flocked to the Grange because of opportunities they found there. The church often was the only other possibility for social contact and the role for women in most congregations was much more restricted than in the Grange. Even though women were still expected, in most subordinates, to take charge of the food and children, they had a level of participation and responsibility which was expanding.

Studies have shown, however, that the majority of the women in the early Grange were the rural counterparts of their middle class sisters in town. They came from the more successful farm families, they had the better farms and homes. The women were literate and interested in the world around them, as can be seen by their frequent writings in Grange publications. The Chautauqua Literary and Scientific Circle home reading program was enthusiastically embraced by rural Grange women and their efforts were instrumental in organizing summer Chautauquas as well as educational programs at county fairs. By 1901 they occupied the majority of the lecturer positions in subordinates, according to an estimate made by Kenyon Butterfield, former editor of Michigan's Grange paper before he assumed the presidency of Michigan and Massachusetts agricultural colleges. In this capacity, women were able to help mold the policy and activity of the Grange. These were exceedingly capable women.

Michigan women gain responsibility early

Michigan produced an outstanding lineup of woman leaders in the Grange with one of the most widely known being Jennie Buell, state lecturer for many years and also state secretary. A recognized leader, Buell authored a column for lecturers in the *National Grange Monthly* and later put her guidance for officers together in a book, *The Grange Master and the Grange Lecturer.* She noted that in the first years of the Grange, lecturers actually did lecture, but "duties have since changed from those of a 'lecturer' to those of a teacher." Assuming that the lecturer was a woman, Buell wrote she "must know people as well as facts; she must know how to arouse the indifferent members; she must tactfully draw out the stored-up funds in the non-communicative members; and she must incite to competition and rivalry those who are not moved by finer mo-

---

A new Generation Grange Woman

Michigan's reputation for producing exceptional female Grange leaders was assured with the careers of Mary Mayo, Jennie Buell and Olivia Woodman. But one more, Dora H. Stockman, was waiting in the wings.

Born in a log cabin in 1876 to Grange parents, Dora followed the route taken by many rural women in her day by passing a teaching examination at age 14. Her teaching career began at age 16 and she married the next year. The couple had an unsuccessful adventure with farming before opening a store in Arcadia. "A saloon and two blind pigs, together with a German beer garden decided us to move to Benzonia, in 1895," she wrote in her biography.

Dora took correspondence courses and eventually earned bachelor's and master's degrees. By then her husband was successfully farming and she settled into a career as a housewife, mother of two children, and teacher. A prolific writer, her work appeared in Grange publications, and her two children's books were published. Grange service included 16 years as state lecturer, the post previously held by the famous Jennie Buell.

Grange service was the school which prepared many women for public service, and Stockman endures as one of the best examples of this pattern. In 1919 she started 24 years on the Board of Agricul-

tives." Marti observes that Buell's description shows "the Lecturer had become less an authority and more a manager of human relations." These transformed lecturers accomplished their responsibility by expressing what a modern researcher calls "the female view that one strengthens oneself by strengthening others." The early male lecturers who authoritatively lectured were being replaced by tactful teachers and in the process the office was being feminized.

The lecturer's hour, now firmly under the guidance of women in a majority of the subordinates and under their watchful eye in all the rest, was evolving from a time in the meeting when husbands learned about latest achievements at the state experiment station to an opportunity for everyone to broaden their intellectual horizons. Buell credited the lecturer for shaping members' "ideals concerning their home and farm surroundings, rural schools, and

---

ture, the governing body for Michigan Agricultural College. She was the first woman in Michigan to hold an elective office.

Stockman began work in 1930 toward a doctorate in sociology

(continued next page)

Dora Stockman (1872-1948)

local community conditions" and she was "somewhat responsible for the attitude which the members hold toward issues...such as taxation, the land question, conservation of natural resources, transportation, rural school improvement, control of packers, collective bargaining," and other issues. This broadening of the programs at the Grange meeting was similar to what was happening concurrently with the traveling Chautauqua circuits. Rural people were assuming a proactive stance by supplying the necessities for their own adult education.

When it came to farm children, the Grange women were dedicated to securing formal educational opportunities for their daughters and the Grange became their vehicle to achieve that goal. Their view was that education for both the boys and girls should be vocational in nature and, especially for the young women, home economics or domestic science training was seen, ac-

---

at Michigan State College, but never completed her dissertation. However, she had the distinction of being the first woman to receive an honorary Doctor of Laws degree from Michigan State.

In 1938 she successfully ran for the Michigan House of Representatives, holding that seat until 1946. Her notable accomplishments in the Legislature were support for state aid to local schools, school lunch programs, and a plan for added years of high school which foreshadowed modern community colleges. Grange women of previous generations would have been proud of her adamant stand for heavy taxes on alcohol and tobacco products. She died in 1948.

Early in her Grange career, Stockman felt the need for organized activities for children. Since juvenile Granges were still unknown in her area, she brought Grange children together in units called Four Leaf Clover Clubs. The four leaf clover was adopted as an emblem, and out of these early efforts grew the 4-H club movement.

Grange women had always been fighters, dedicated to their causes and quick to accept leadership when the opportunity presented itself. The sacrificial labors of several generations of female Grange activists created the environment where Dora Stockman and other rural women would be able to claim the public role that they filled so well.

cording to Marti, as "the discipline which they expected to free women from mindless drudgery just as agricultural science was supposed to lift farmers out of traditional ruts." Beginning in the 1870s, because of the influence of vocal women members, domestic science coursework in the agricultural colleges was an official Grange dream. Iowa State College (now University) and the State Agricultural College of Kansas (now Kansas State University) were two early institutions which began offering courses on domestic science for women in the 1870s. Most women enrolled in colleges prior to the turn of the century studied pedagogy, but in the early 1900s, when Grange demands helped expand popularity of high school home economics classes, more women majored in that field in preparation for careers as home economics teachers.

One Grange leader who fought hard for vocational education for women was Mary Mayo of Michigan. A farm wife and perhaps the best known Grange woman in the country between the early 1880s and her death in 1903, Mayo told her friend Jennie Buell of a snub she had received from a former high school classmate while shopping in Battle Creek. The acquaintance criticized Mayo for marrying a farmer because, she said, farm women could only "work hard and make lots of good butter." Mayo later recalled, "I knew that I did work hard and that I made good butter, but it made me indignant to think that this was the measure of my life, and that of every farmer's wife." She and her husband used the affront as a springboard to improve themselves by reading old school books together and being actively involved in both the Grange and the Chautauqua Literary and Scientific Circle. She later became a speaker for Farmers' Institutes (lecture series sponsored by the agriculture colleges), Grange meetings and Chautauqua events. Her 1877 address called "A Higher Standard of Culture for Housekeepers" set the stage for Mayo's later work for home economics education for women, a battle which she headed during her 14 years as chair of the Michigan State Grange committee on women's work. While in that capacity she also organized "Fresh Air Work," a program which provided summer outings for urban women and children to Grange farms. Michigan State University memorialized Mayo's contribution to its home economics department by dedicating Mary Mayo Hall as a dormitory for women in 1931.

Temperance becomes a crusade

One of Mayo's other passions, a preoccupation shared by most of her Grange contemporaries, was the temperance movement. She was probably behind the 1883 Michigan State Grange statement that called temperance "one of the essential principles upon which our Order is founded." At the 1878 national session, delegates had officially positioned the Grange in opposition to the use of alcohol by passing a resolution stating "that the members of our Order should carefully consider" the corrupting influence of intemperance "before casting their ballots for anyone for office—town, county, state or national—who is in sympathy with the liquor traffic, or who is addicted to the habitual, or even moderate, use of intoxicating drinks." The vote was not unanimous but out of the 11 dissenting votes, seven were from southern delegates. Most of the Grange members of the time, especially the women, were painfully aware of the consequences of excessive use of alcohol and they were dedicated to working for a public ban on its sale. Their efforts would culminate in a 1905 Grange resolution which threatened members with expulsion from the order if they sold liquor. A year earlier the Grange had gone on record favoring a law "prohibiting the manufacture and sale of cigarets *[sic]* or cigaret *[sic]* papers within the United States of America."

The predominant organization fighting for prohibition, the National Women's Christian Temperance Union (WCTU), captured the participation of many Grange members and its history shares the Grange's connection with the Chautauqua Institution. According to Chautauqua historian Theodore Morrison, the Union "resulted from discussions by a number of women during the first session of the [Chautauqua] assembly" in 1874, making the WCTU "virtually an offshoot of Chautauqua." Women around the country who were involved with Grange or Chautauqua groups rallied behind the new association. The growing activism of women in the Grange could in part be due to the influence of the WCTU and its chief spokesperson, Francis Willard. Her concept of "home protection" called women to become a driving force for reform in order to keep the evils of the world from overwhelming their homes.

From the many examples available of early Grange women activists, several stand out because of their dedication and involvement. One of the earliest was Jeanne Carr, wife of Dr. Ezra Carr, a university professor and author of an early history of the Grange on the West Coast. She was involved in formation of the California State Grange in 1873 and immediately was placed on various committees. In 1876 she ran for state lecturer but lost on the third ballot. The following year she was elected state chaplain and finally attained the lecturer post in 1879. Her stand for women's rights was clear, and in 1876 she told state Grange women, meeting apart from their husbands, that their organization might be the "'entering wedge' to shatter the false system of laws that has so oppressed women for all time." She was sent by the State Grange as its representative to the state constitutional convention to speak on behalf of equal suffrage.

Eliza C. Gifford was another product of the remarkable Chautauqua County, New York. A farm wife, she was active on behalf of the Grange and woman suffrage causes through the WCTU. Her husband, Walter, served two terms in the state legislature, organized Granges and cooperative fire insurance companies, and served as master of the state Grange between 1890 and 1894. Gifford, who in 1894 named the Grange as the "greatest equality club the world has ever known," was successful in having her 1881 resolution endorsing equal suffrage passed by the New York State Grange by the deciding vote of the presiding officer.

Two other Chautauqua County women, Carrie E.S. Twing and Elizabeth Lord (Mrs. Bela B. Lord), also attained prominence for their speeches at Grange gatherings favoring woman suffrage. Lord, who served as lecturer for the New York State Grange, spoke widely for the Grange and WCTU.

Succeeding Mary Mayo as chaplain of the Michigan State Grange was Olivia Woodman, serving until her death in 1929. An ordained Universalist minister, she was active in the state Grange before marrying Jonathan J. Woodman, a widower and past state and national master. She spoke widely, represented the state Grange on the board of Michigan's anti-saloon league, and worked as president of her county's equal suffrage association. Other groups claiming Olivia Woodman's devotion were the Order of the Eastern Star, the Ladies of the Maccabees, and both her local and state federations of women's clubs.

Out West, the Rev. Minnie Fenwick was elected the first lecturer of the new Wyoming State Grange in 1913. In addition to serving small congregations in the area, she helped her husband establish a farm and raised four children. The WCTU was her outlet for social activism as well, and she was the Wyoming state president of the group for five years. Nearby in Colorado, Agnes Ludwig Riddle blazed her name into Grange history in a dynamic way. She was born in Silesia (now part of Poland) in 1865 and immigrated to the U.S. as a teenager. Trained as a nurse, she worked in a Colorado hospital after marrying dairyman Joseph Riddle. Later she was elected secretary of the state Grange and was named a member of the advisory board for Colorado's agricultural college. In 1911 she was elected the first woman legislator in Colorado, serving as a Republican state senator for one term. Marti observes, "When she won her senate seat, women in most of the country could not yet vote."

Taking up the suffrage banner

It is interesting to speculate that the zeal for universal temperance actually may have shaped Grange women's attitudes toward equal suffrage. The WCTU early on recognized that it would take more than men's votes to enact legislation prohibiting the manufacture and sale of intoxicants; women had to have the right to vote if the temperance platform was to succeed.

The Grange's various statements in resolutions and degree work represent a lofty attitude toward women, and female members began arguing soon after the organization was formed that these pronouncements constituted an implied pledge to work for equal suffrage. Although not all women wanted the franchise, those in favor of suffrage finally prevailed within the Grange. Beginning with the California State Grange in 1878, other states adopted policies supporting equal suffrage until the National Grange finally adopted the policy in 1885:

> Resolved, that one of the fundamental principles of the Patrons of Husbandry, as set forth in its official *Declaration of Purposes*, regulating membership, recognizes the equality of the two sexes. We are therefore prepared to hail with delight any advancement in the legal status of women, which may give to her the full right of the ballot-box, and an equal condition of citizenship.

Grange women did not enjoy this full endorsement of woman suffrage without setbacks, however. One delegate protested that "It's ridiculous to give women equal voice with men. Any organization that does that cannot live. What right has a woman to come into the Grange and vote on resolutions concerning public questions, when she does not even have a vote for Congress? My wife is a better woman than I am a man, but she has no business voting on civic questions. She does not know enough to do so." Apparently this man was not willing to admit the success of enlightenment efforts being promoted by the Grange lecturer's hour and the Chautauqua Literary and Scientific Circle.

Although the Grange never swayed from its endorsement of woman suffrage, delegates at the 1914 session in Wilmington, Delaware, hotly disagreed on how the goal might best be accomplished. A contingent led by progressive State Master C.B. Kegley of Washington argued for National Grange endorsement of the pending universal suffrage amendment to the Federal Constitution then being debated in Congress. Citing recent accomplishments in state legislatures, another Grange camp fought for a state-by-state approach to gaining voting rights for women. After long debate, the latter side won and the resolution for a federal suffrage amendment was turned down. The policy adopted did, however, firmly state the Grange position by declaring that the organization was "unqualifiedly and emphatically in favor of woman suffrage."

The next year the arguments resumed at the national convention in Oakland, California. Kegley, as chair of the committee examining the suffrage resolutions, presented an extensive report, containing a summary of the Grange's tradition of support for woman suffrage:

> On behalf of the National Grange your committee views with keen satisfaction the present encouraging position of the woman suffrage movement. We are proud of the fact that the Grange was the first great body in this nation to adopt woman suffrage, and to safeguard it by providing for the equality of women with men in the exercise of all rights, privileges and governing powers in its organic laws. Thus the Grange having, both by precept and example, been the pioneer in this "new freedom," it is eminently fitting it should take a foremost stand in the movement to give to all women their right of suffrage.

Maine State Master Clement S. Stetson agreed and announced that "This injustice to women has been tolerated too long." When the debate was finished, delegates reversed the National Grange policy adopted the previous year and favored a woman suffrage amendment to the U.S. Constitution.

Efforts to secure for women the right to vote on a statewide basis were first successful in the West. Wyoming Territory first recognized that right in 1869 and, largely due to agitation by suffrage groups, the states of Colorado (1893), Utah and Idaho (1896) and Washington (1910) followed with legislation. In 1911 California fell in line with Kansas, Oregon, Arizona, Nevada and Montana passing similar legislation during the next three years.

The entry of the United States into World War I probably did more to advance women's rights than all the petitions and protests of the previous 50 years. Grange women joined others in doing work formerly done by the men now in Europe, proving to the nation that differences between the sexes were not as great as had been assumed. Articles in the *National Grange Monthly* during the war touted these accomplishments, quoting a New Jersey woman who reiterated an Englishman's statement that women's war efforts proved they could do "anything with practice." She added that women willing and able to keep the nation going while the rest of the world was at war ended "the delusion of ages, that woman's work must consist only in the performance of household duties." She was skeptical that "any great reform will come at once with the inauguration of woman suffrage" because women's votes would not instantly improve the nation. Allowing women into the voting booth would be only "one step" in the progress of democracy, but it would go far in easing "sex antagonism" by terminating an injustice that had long embittered women.

Shortly after the end of the war, Grange women, after a half century of prodding, applauded passage of the nineteenth amendment to the Constitution which gave them the full right to vote. The amendment was later ratified by 36 state legislatures and became law on August 26, 1920.

Prohibition is a national issue

The other driving cause of Grange women, prohibition, was resolved during that era as well. Temperance movement lobbying resulted in several states going "dry," beginning with Georgia and Alabama in 1907. In 1917 Congress passed a law prohibiting manufacture of all liquors with the exception of beer and wine and, later that year, President Wilson issued a proclamation reducing the alcohol content of beer. The eighteenth amendment to the Constitution, popularly called the Prohibition Amendment, was ratified on January 16, 1919. Its effectiveness was short-lived, of course, since it was repealed with ratification of the twenty-first amendment in 1933.

With equal suffrage and prohibition concerns finally put to rest, some Grange women of the early 1920s were tempted to feel like those members in the mid-1870s who presumed all the work was over (or, to paraphrase the words of the closing ritual for Grange meetings, "the labors of the day [were] completed"). That was far from the case, however, and few women took much time away from the full range of activities they had, by this time, woven into the Grange structure.

Women oversee juvenile Granges

With the implementation of the juvenile Grange in the late 1880s, Grange women had a means within the organization to aid their children in gaining valuable lessons while they developed leadership skills. Although interest in juvenile Granges grew slowly at first, it reached movement proportions first in the state of Ohio. The first reported Ohio group, although not an official juvenile Grange, was formed in Lorain County by Harriet Mason, an Oberlin graduate and a charter member of Wellington Grange. She was typical of many Grange women of her era in that she was a rural school teacher, active in her Grange with service as state Grange lady assistant steward from 1896 to 1900. For the next four decades she was women's editor of *The Ohio Farmer* and she spoke extensively throughout the state on women's and Grange issues.

Ohio juvenile Grange work took off after appointment of Harriett Harris as the state's juvenile Grange organizer in 1900. She organized German Juvenile Grange No. 1 in Darke County the next year with others following shortly thereafter. In 1915 Ohio State Master, and later National Master, Louis J. Taber pressed national delegates to approve a uniform style juvenile charter, constitution and bylaws for use in all states.

Ohio successes stirred interest across the nation and juvenile Granges, most of them under the wing of a Grange woman, sprung up everywhere. These units, later called junior Granges, kept many Grange women occupied in a function with far-reaching, positive results.

Women's work becomes national fixture

The other primary outlet enjoyed by women in the Grange was their home economics committees. The first recorded reference to a specific women's department within the Grange is contained in a resolution passed at the 1888 Topeka, Kansas, session: "Resolved, that there be added to the list of standing committees of the National Grange a committee of three women on 'Woman's Work in the Grange,' and that they report at the next session of the National Grange." This action resulted from prodding by Addie S. Hale of South Glastonbury, Connecticut, and she became the new committee's chairperson. A pamphlet issued by the committee recommended similar committees on state and subordinate levels. Their duties were to "keep house in the Grange" which meant calling on absentees, encouraging them to return, and aiding the "lady officers" in their special duties. The next committee report urged Grange women to become informed on "all legislative questions vital to the purity and intelligence of our homes, press for legal equality of the sexes and help other groups—especially the WCTU, women's clubs, humane and kindergarten societies—in working for social purity."

Michigan, under the tutelage of Mary Mayo, enthusiastically participated in this new woman's work endeavor. Charity work characterized the Michigan woman's agenda, with the Fresh Air project topping their list. Designed to allow urban women and children to have summer farm outings, a total of 51 people in 1894 were guests on Grange farms. By 1897, 707 visitors had participated in the program's first four years and 18 city children had been adopted by farmers.

Although none could match Michigan's success, many other states did form committees. Notable accomplishments included Iowa and Illinois fund drives to help flood victims and New York women who copied the fresh air program and raised money for starving Russian peasants, for which they were thanked by Count Leo Tolstoy. Kansas committee members were not shy about topics they chose for examination and one year they discussed the question of whether mothers were competent teachers of sex hygiene and listed books on sex that might be useful to mothers. But problems evolved in many states because committee goals were nebulous and involvement was spotty. Interestingly, Colorado adamantly refused to participate and Rhode Island's state master confessed that men in his state "did not take kindly" to the idea. His state equivocated, but finally a woman's work committee was formed and it kept active long after most others disappeared.

Grange sisters from Colorado prevailed, nonetheless, and at the 1893 Syracuse, New York, session one of their own, Grace Booth Working, read a resolution claiming "that woman's work in the Grange is not sufficiently distinct from man's work to justify the continuance of the national committee of Woman's Work." With adoption of the resolution, the national committee was dead. Women in state and subordinate levels disagreed, and quietly continued their activities.

With the increasing interest in domestic science and home economics, Grange women began to feel there was a definite place for a national committee to oversee the organization's efforts in these fields. Elizabeth H. Patterson, wife of Maryland State Master and experiment station director Dr. Harry J. Patterson, can be given much of the credit for initiating the permanent committee which remains within the Grange as the women's activities department. In 1910 she introduced a successful resolution authorizing appointment of a standing committee on home economics "whose duty it shall be to promote and develop the interests of this subject in every way possible; and to make a report upon this subject to the National Grange at its annual sessions." Delegates at the 1909 session had heard Elizabeth Patterson read a paper in which she shared her excitement about the burgeoning university discipline of home economics. Women were still managing their homes, she said, as their mothers and grandmothers had done. Science could simplify their work and allow freedom "for the more important and permanent interests of the home and of society."

The new committee, with Patterson as its chair, embarked on a program to enlighten Grange women about scientific housekeeping. Because of U.S. involvement in the war, the committee in 1917 began focusing on efficient food use so more could be sent overseas. The next year the emphasis remained, but Herbert Hoover's Food Administration, which had prompted the committee's endorsement of food conservation in the first place, was criticized for not sufficiently involving rural women. Red Cross work was supported and the government was condemned for encouraging cigarette smoking among soldiers.

The united efforts of women members of the "world's greatest equality club" were significant in achieving woman suffrage and, undoubtedly, their persistent talk about temperance paved the way for not only the ill-fated Prohibition Amendment but also for greater public awareness and understanding of all substance abuse problems. But perhaps even more profound were the tens of thousands of rural women who, because of the example set by female Grange leaders, were able to stand a little taller and feel every bit as good as a man.

8

Golden Jubilee

1897-1923

THE YEARS BETWEEN the Spanish-American War and World War I were good for the nation and its farmers. The Grange saw its membership base expanding during the period and, with the exception of some embarrassing disruptions during the Bachelder and Lowell administrations, the organization continued an upward spiral that began in the early 1890s.

With the disintegration of Populism as an organized force following the 1896 William Jennings Bryan-McKinley presidential election, many Grange members and others interested in reform became part of a broad-based political movement known as Progressivism. The progressives would continue fighting for some of the issues raised by Populists while adding others.

Aaron Jones succeed Col. Joseph H. Brigham as National Grange master, being elected to the high post at the 31st National Grange session held at Harrisburg, Pennsylvania, in 1897. A prosperous farmer from South Bend, Indiana, Jones traced his Grange involvement to 1873 when he became a charter member and first master of Pennsylvania Township Grange near his home. He was Indiana State Grange master for a total of 27 years, over a time span ranging from 1879 to 1913. Before being elected national master, Jones had been national overseer for two years and he was on the national legislative committee a total of 14 years, ending in 1911. Local accomplishments included a role in organizing Indiana's first county-wide farmers' mutual fire insurance company and service for 10 years on the State Board of Agriculture. He died in 1928 at the age of 90.

Brigham had been appointed assistant secretary of agriculture by President McKinley, and his vacant national master's seat was hotly contested. With Jones' victory and Brigham's new position in the Department of Agriculture there was progress made in patching up ill will which had existed for several years between the Grange and the department. In 1899 the Department of Agriculture had gained cabinet status, a long-sought Grange goal, and President Cleveland's first secretary of agriculture, Norman J. Colman of Missouri, was a past master of Potomac Grange and former commissioner of agriculture for the department. Colman didn't last long in his new position of responsibility and, unfortunately, his successors were less enthusiastic about Grange proposals.

Colman's replacement as agriculture secretary was Jeremiah M. Rusk of Wisconsin, a non-farmer whose selection was viewed as a political appointment. After a short seasoning period, however, Rusk earned some confidence from Grange members and, at the 1890 Atlanta, Georgia, session he also secured an official endorsement.

That warmth of feeling quickly dissipated after the appointment of Secretary J. Sterling Morton in 1893. A very conservative man, Morton embarked on his career in the Department of Agriculture

Aaron Jones (1838-1928)

by slashing the budget, laying off employees and cutting salaries of many that remained, including a blanket reduction of women's salaries to a base of $1,200 a year or less. Morton had been an acting governor in Nebraska who repeatedly was embarrassed by being rejected by voters in elections for governor and senator. He also worked as a farmer and an editor, and is best known for his ideas resulting in the establishment of Arbor Day in 1872. Even though he shared his enthusiasm for conservation with the Grange, Morton sullied his reputation with members by attacking the organization from the rostrum at the Congress of Agriculture, part of the World's Columbian Exposition in Chicago, October 16, 1893. The worst enemies of the American farmer were not the pests which attacked his crops, Morton said. Rather, "The most insidious foe of the farmer is the professional farmer, the promoter of Granges and [Farmers'] Alliances, who for political purposes farms the farmer."

Reaction within Grange circles was instantaneous and explosive. The following month, at the national session, resolutions were adopted which strongly condemned Morton's speech as "unbecoming a gentleman, much less a high official, even a member of the President's Cabinet, who condemns and censures all farmers' organizations, specifically mentioning the Grange."

The Grange had to deal with Morton for another four years, until he was replaced in 1897 by a Scottish native and Iowan, James Wilson. The Grange worked closely with Wilson, even after the death of Assistant Secretary Brigham on June 29, 1904. Wilson's illustrious background included service in the Iowa Legislature, the U.S. House of Representatives, teaching at Iowa Agricultural College, directorship of the college's experiment station, and writing for various farm journals. Even though he was popular, serving under three presidents, Wilson angered the Grange in 1911. With talk about temperance flowing like wine, it was understandable that Grange members reacted negatively when Wilson consented to act as an honorary president of the National Brewers' Congress. Wilson, of course, recognized the close tie between the brewing industry and agriculture but ideology got in the way, and the Grange rebuked his link with the alcohol trade. The farm group was especially sensitive because of recent revelations which linked the Grange itself with the notorious Whiskey Trust.

Nahum J. Bachelder (1854-1934)

Flirting with partisan politics

Aaron Jones was replaced as national master in 1905 by Nahum J. Bachelder, a Grange member with an imposing background. Grange service had included six years as national lecturer and 12 years as New Hampshire state master. Educated at Dartmouth and the University of New Hampshire, Bachelder farmed, served on the state board of agriculture and, in 1902, was seated as New Hampshire's governor for a two-year term.

The election of Bachelder as national master was evidence of a subtle shift within the organization. With the exception of Saunders and the brief, four-month administration of James Draper, all previous national masters had come from the Midwest or South. Membership had shifted east, however, and the policies of the organization were becoming much more conservative. The fiery influence of Kelley was dying out with the decline of interest in the Midwest, and the more reserved tone of recently inducted New England members was becoming more prominent.

Bachelder assumed his new post with vigor. A staunch

Republican, Bachelder was a strong supporter of President Theodore Roosevelt. At the 1905 Atlantic City session where Bachelder was elected, the delegates had wholeheartedly endorsed 13 of the president's major goals. Some of these goals were hold-overs from the Populist movement and most had been Grange policy for some time. Among those policies which shared space on both the Grange's and the president's platforms were popular election of U.S. senators, antitrust legislation, a parcel post law and postal savings banks, national aid for highway construction, pure food and drug legislation, strengthening the Interstate Commerce Commission and revisions of salaries for federal office holders. A telegram from the delegates to Roosevelt stated, "the farmers of this country want neither more nor less than a 'square deal,' and we unanimously endorse the manly efforts President Roosevelt is making to secure equal opportunity for the individual, and the common people, against the arrogant power of aggregated wealth, and, irrespective of party, pledge ourselves to support his efforts in that direction in every way possible."

Legislative activity for the Grange was, at that time, controlled by a legislative committee and, under Bachelder's direction, it became the principal avenue of Grange involvement. Under the domination of Bachelder, past Master Jones and West Virginia State Master T.C. Atkeson, the committee did everything possible to cheer the president's Republican agenda.

The need for a national publication to air the Grange's viewpoints was promoted energetically by Bachelder. There had been numerous Grange-oriented newspapers over the years and in 1877 *The Grange Record* was published briefly by the National Grange but discontinued due to lack of funding. During Bachelder's term as national lecturer he had issued the *National Grange Monthly Bulletin* with the sanction of the executive committee. On November 6, 1907, his new weekly publication, the *National Grange Official Organ—Patrons of Husbandry* appeared, with the national master as editor-in-chief. The new paper frequently brought the Grange to the fringes of its non-partisanship by promoting the president. During election years, the cover photographs were of Roosevelt, and on April 22, 1908, there appeared a notice for a composite print made up of 500 different poses of the president. The print, which was offered as a premium for new subscriptions, was billed as "Part of the Most Wonderful Photograph Ever Made." Then, in the September 28, 1910, issue, appeared a photo of the former president being introduced by Bachelder before a crowd of 10,000 at a Utica, New York, Grange-sponsored event. The president's speech was recurrently interrupted, we are told, by glances at Bachelder and the expression, "Isn't that so, Governor?"

Bachelder's "scandal" dated from his first year as national master. In 1905 he "hired" the New York firm of Allen and Graham to plan and execute the legislative committee's campaigns. To the end, Bachelder maintained his belief that Joseph Allen and Whidden Graham were attorneys but, in reality, neither of them practiced law. They were lobbyists. The fascinating arrangement with the National Grange provided that the Grange would receive Allen and Graham's services at no cost. With their efforts, the Grange maintained a middle ground between progressive insurgents in the Republican Party and stubborn conservatives who supported President William Howard Taft, Roosevelt's successor.

The national leadership's methods of action alarmed some of the most progressive Grange people and, by 1910, several state Granges (Washington, Maine, Pennsylvania, Michigan, Kentucky, Oregon, Colorado and Ohio) combined to form an alternative voice in Washington, D.C., called the Conference of Progressive Granges. Their primary concerns were that the National Grange had come under the control of radical forces, dedicated to keeping the organization from advancing. A dominant bone of contention was the voting system employed at National Grange sessions. Each state Grange had two votes, that of the master and spouse, regardless of membership of that state Grange. The progressives felt votes should be more closely aligned to membership. New England Granges, they said, formed alliances with state Granges having insignificant membership in order to control the national body. Financial transactions were kept secret and little legislative work was being done.

The progressive state Granges met each year in conjunction with the National Grange convention, attracting the admiration and participation of Oliver Hudson Kelley during his last years. One conference goal was to maintain a presence in Washington, D.C., for progressive Grange interests, something they felt was not being accomplished by the legislative committee or Allen and Graham. Much of the successful legislative work done on woman suffrage and parcel post has been credited to the Conference of Progressive Granges. The conference led to the formation of the Farmers National Council, which opened an office in the capital to mount an extensive lobbying effort under the direction of Grange activist George P. Hampton. Farm lobbying authority William P. Browne credits the council with the eventual move of National Grange operations back to Washington, D.C. "Had it not been for the council's presence in Washington," Browne wrote, "the Grange itself probably would have stayed away." This was the era, too, which gave birth to the local Farm Bureaus, the American Farm Bureau Federation and the National Farmers Union, the latter being a group which grew from the ashes of the Farmers' Alliance.

The reality of having state Granges forming their own lobbying arm because of perceived weakness, inaction and mishandling on the part of the national leadership prompted retaliation. At the 1910 National Grange session in Atlantic City, the executive committee pressed charges against Hampton and J.W. Helme, editor of *The Michigan Patron.* Hampton and Helme were not present and four out of every five national delegates voted to expel them from membership because of articles they had published about alleged political and financial misconduct at the organization's national level. Bachelder had to concede, nevertheless, that his opponents in the Conference of Progressive Granges—with the able leadership of State Master C.B. Kegley of Washington—had considerable strength, and he was submitted to an intensive grilling by a committee representing all state Granges. As a concession, Bachelder agreed to relinquish his powerful newspaper and in its place appeared the *National Grange Monthly,* a publication which would last until the early 1960s.

A hot issue in 1911, the Canadian-American Free Trade Agreement proposed by President Taft, also contributed to Bachelder's woes. The Grange position was for elimination of trade barriers and for establishment of a non-partisan tariff commission. However, the Taft plan, while eliminating barriers for most goods, allowed entry into the U.S. of certain Canadian agricultural commodities and farmers felt this would unfairly hurt their interests. "Free trade for all if free trade for the farmer!" was the slogan in Grange publications and Allen and Graham put together packets of petitions with a cover letter which went out to all subordinate Granges from Bachelder's office in New Hampshire. Free mailing was courtesy of Bachelder's close friend, Republican Senator Jacob H. Gallinger, and the U.S. taxpayer. Tens of thousands of other pieces of Grange mail concerning the reciprocity issue poured through the senator's office, making use of his franking privilege.

The legislation, after easy passage in the House, was bogged down in the Senate where the national master testified that it violated Republican promises made in 1908. Two days after Bachelder's testimony, Republican Senator William J. Stone of Missouri announced he was going to unearth the truth about the rumored connections between Allen and Graham and the National Grange. Stone suspected Allen and Graham were not the attorneys Bachelder represented them to be, but lobbyists who, while working free for the Grange, were being paid by large business interests which would gain by Grange victories. Allen, Graham and Bachelder were subpoenaed and the May 31 hearing was reported widely throughout the nation. Under oath Allen and Graham admitted they were reimbursed for their work for the Grange by interests such as the American Newspaper Publishers Association, the National Lumber Association, the American Pulp and Paper Association, the American Woolen Company, the American Protective Tariff League and a group of distillers known as the Whiskey Trust. The Whiskey Trust was anxious to see the Grange successful in its efforts on behalf of the Denatured Alcohol Bill and the other groups would suffer along with the farmers if the Taft Canadian reciprocity bill passed.

The Grange, because of the connection with Allen and Graham, was publicly humiliated, its effectiveness shattered and the membership disillusioned. The aftermath was a change in national leadership that fall, and a loss of nearly 100,000 members the following year. The Canadian-American trade agreement finally passed Congress over Grange objections but was eventually rejected by the Canadians.

Although it could be considered a borderline breach of non-partisanship as outlined in the *Declaration of Purposes,* the close link existing between the Republican Party, President Roosevelt and the Grange under Bachelder—aided by the efforts of the Conference of Progressive Granges—did result in accomplishment of some longstanding Grange goals. One of the first, passed shortly after Bachelder's election, was the Pure Food and Drugs Act of 1906. The Grange began calling for legislation in 1881 to regulate the purity of foods and medicines sold to the public. The language of the successful bill and much of the regulatory rules developed later can be credited to Dr. Harvey W. Wiley, head of the Department of Agriculture's division of chemistry. Wiley often paid tribute to the Grange for its efforts in behalf of this legislation, which has been of tremendous benefit to consumers. Popular support for the legislation, which had the blessing of President Roosevelt, came from wide distribution of Socialist Upton Sinclair's novel *The Jungle*. The book angered and mobilized consumers because it revealed unsanitary conditions existing in Chicago's meat packing plants.

Conservation assumes a new priority

Perhaps President Roosevelt's greatest legacy to America was his devotion to its natural resources, an attitude he shared with Grange members and leaders. Like the Grange, Roosevelt felt vast tracts of forest land, potential parks, mineral wealth and sites suitable for development of electric power and irrigation should remain in the public domain for the benefit of all citizens. Wise use of these holdings was stressed and those large business interests which exploited resources were held out as enemies of all Americans.

Gifford Pinchot
(1865 - 1946)

During this era of rapid corporate expansion, efforts by companies to gain title to government land were reminiscent of the earlier land-grabbing railroads. Delegates at the 1903 national session went on record favoring the 160-acre limitation for land grants set up originally in the Homestead Act. The Grange had also supported the same 160-acre limitation in the Reclamation Act of 1902, which ensured benefits from federal irrigation projects would be made available only to families farming smaller tracts. This provision would require Grange input several more times in the decades ahead because new technologies would make small farms increasingly uneconomical, even for family-owned enterprises.

An early prudent move Roosevelt made to ensure success of his conservation policies supporting his good friend and longtime Grange member Gifford Pinchot. Pinchot had been appointed, in 1898, chief of the Forestry Division for the U.S. Department of Agriculture. The Grange supported expansion of the division and, in 1901, it was elevated to the status of a bureau within the department. In 1905 a new unit called the Forest Service was added to the Bureau of Forestry with the duty of administering the forest reserves transferred to its jurisdiction from the Interior Department. Later that year the entire bureau was redesignated the Forest Service and subsequently the forest reserves were renamed national forests. One of the most scenic of the national forests, located in Washington state, is named for Pinchot. Setting aside land was a driving passion for Roosevelt and during his presidency more than 148 million acres became National Forests. Pinchot was appointed by Roosevelt as chair of the National Commission on Conservation in 1908 which released an inventory the next year of the nation's total resource base.

One of Pinchot's most widely known contributions was with the Country Life Commission, President Roosevelt's pet project organized to study rural life and make recommendations to Congress. Dr. Liberty Hyde Bailey, head of the commission and dean of the College of Agriculture at Cornell University, was well-known to Grange members because of his appearance at the 1903 national session. The endeavor Bailey's group undertook in 1908 was one which the Grange had sought since 1879, and the commission's 1909 report pinpointed deplorable living conditions and the high degree of poverty which the Grange had said existing in the nation's rural areas.

The president's message to Congress about the report set the stage for later involvement of farmers in rural electrification. "It is the obvious duty of the Government," Roosevelt said, "to call the attention of farmers to the growing monopolization of water power. The farmers above all should have that power, on reasonable terms, for cheap transportation, for lighting their homes, and for innumerable uses in the daily tasks on the farm." The commission's findings also promoted renewed interest in cooperatives but the president's endorsement of cooperation angered Congress and, because of it, they refused to print the commission's report. No action was taken on the commission's work until establishment of the Rural Organization Service in the Department of Agriculture in 1913.

Pinchot's dogged dedication to conservation got him into some trouble during the Taft administration. He was convinced that Richard Ballinger, secretary of the interior, was abandoning conservation policies instituted during the Roosevelt years and brought suit against him. Ballinger received support from the president and Pinchot was fired for insubordination. Pinchot taught at the Yale University School of Forestry, his alma mater, and in 1922 was elected Republican governor of Pennsylvania (campaigning against another Grange member, Democrat John A. McSparran), serving in that capacity until 1935. He was a popular speaker for many years at Grange events throughout the country.

Congressional waste angers Grange leaders

A persistent thorn in the Grange's side was a longstanding Congressional practice of sending free seeds to rural constituents—all at taxpayer expense. This practice, the Grange said, did nothing to advance agriculture and was viewed as a nuisance calculated to win popularity votes. While Secretary of Agriculture Morton was unpopular with Grange leaders, he did win their praise for his attempts to thwart Congress by refusing to buy the seeds for their give-away. Angered, Congress passed a resolution forcing Morton to comply.

By 1912 the seed program had grown to such proportions that 49,570,370 packets of vegetable seeds, 9,624,565 packets of flower seeds, 3,118 packets of tobacco seeds, 12,000 packets of cotton seeds, 16,133 of grass seeds, 11,040 boxes of bulbs, 24,350 grapevines, 91,320 strawberry plants and 2,021 citrus trees were passed out that year. Often the seeds were sent too late in the season or were, in the words of National Master Oliver Wilson, "old and unreliable." At the 1913 National Grange session Secretary of Agriculture David F. Houston helped Grange members forget some unfortunate statements made in his speech by promising that "next year the distribution of ordinary vegetable and flower seeds may be discontinued." Houston failed to prevail and the seed dissemination continued until 1923.

The Populist movement, the progressives and the Grange all emphasized the need for government to be responsive to the voters. One bold idea, with precedent in Switzerland and New England town meetings, was direct legislation through the initiative process. Although the first Georgia state constitution, adopted in 1777, allowed voters the exclusive right to propose amendments to the state constitution, no state allowed voters to initiate all types

---

Early initiative leads to U.N. agency

International agricultural trade and development had been of interest to Grange members since before the ill-fated Mississippi Valley Trading Company in the early 1870s. However, one California Grange member, David Lubin, did more than think about international conditions; he started a movement which would eventually lead to the current Food and Agriculture Organization of the United Nations.

Lubin wrote extensively about agricultural topics and one of his articles, suggesting an international organization dedicated to advancement of farming around the world, caught the attention of King Victor Emmanuel III of Italy. In 1905 the king proposed such an agency be established with headquarters in Rome. Named the International Institute of Agriculture, the organization eventually attracted membership of over 60 nations.

In 1926 National Master Louis J. Taber was named by President Coolidge as one of the U.S. delegates to the agency's biennial session. Prominent participants in the institute over the years included many Grange people.

Due primarily to the agitation of National Master A.S. Goss, the International Institute of Agriculture was integrated into the new Food and Agriculture Organization of the United Nations in 1945. Headquarters of the FAO were also located in Rome.

---

of legislation until South Dakota granted the right in 1898. Oregon's pioneer initiative process, achieved with the help of the State Grange, followed in 1902 and it served as the model for other states. President Theodore Roosevelt noted the innovation originated in order to counter a corrupt legislative system: "The movement for direct popular government in Oregon...was in part the inevitable consequence of the betrayal of their trust by various representatives of Oregon in the national and state legislatures."

The Oregon process allowed voters to petition for legislation and, if enough petitioners signed on, the question would be put to the voters at large on an upcoming statewide ballot. Citizens also could invoke a referendum on acts of the legislature and petition to initiate amendments to the state constitution. Writing about the Oregon process, historian Joseph D. LaPalombara said, "there exists almost complete unanimity in the conviction that the advent of the initiative and referendum must be regarded as one of the most important landmarks in the history of American political institutions within the twentieth century."

Neighboring Washington State Grange members envied Oregon's success and state masters Jesse Wing and Carey B. Kegley made initiative and referendum their top legislative priority. Washington's first victory was adoption of the direct primary law in 1907, a measure which allowed all interested candidates for a public office to file a declaration of candidacy, pay a filing fee and appear on the primary ballot. Voters would then vote to select the top candidate for each party with leaders facing off in the general election. The Grange, in alliance with other groups, later secured the rights of initiative and referendum for Washington, and soon several other states—mostly in the West—followed suit.

Grange interest in tax issues evolves

In spite of negative overtones created by alliances with unpopular forces, the Bachelder administration did see a stabilization of Grange views on taxation and economic policy which would bear fruit shortly after Bachelder's retirement. The National Grange had favored, since 1880, "the immediate enactment of a graduated income tax, to the end that all wealth may bear its just and equal proportion of the expenses of government...." Part of the

Grange's appeal included leniency for low income citizens with heavier responsibility being placed on those who could afford it. There were some disagreements within the organization, however, about the number and types of taxes the Grange should support. At the 1906 session in Denver, Colorado, a committee on taxation presented arguments which settled the question. The committee, composed of state masters T.C. Atkeson of West Virginia, Obadiah Gardner, Maine (later elected as a U.S. senator from that state), and ex-governor C.J. Bell of Vermont, favored a collateral inheritance tax as well as an income tax. National Master J.H. Brigham had prepared Grange members 12 years previously by stating, "A graduated inheritance tax may be deemed one of the most equitable forms of taxation. It does not interfere with nor discourage enterprise, but allows a man to control and enjoy his accumulations whilst he may; but when his power to enjoy is gone, the law steps in, and, whilst leaving an ample share to those who probably never earned a dollar, returns a portion to those who have earned the wealth which he has concentrated. Such forms of taxation tend to distribute more equally the burdens of government and act as a check against the dangerous concentration of wealth in the hands of a few families or individuals."

Those were the days of John D. Rockefeller and Andrew Carnegie, J.P. Morgan, William Randolph Hearst and Jay Gould. Hard-working farmers in the Grange were improving their financial picture because farm prices nearly doubled (faster than the cost of inputs) during the decade prior to World War I. For generations American farmers would look back at this time and call it the golden era of American agriculture. But in spite of their new-found affluence, the farmers demanded assurances that the escalating costs of government would be spread evenly; the early Grange mistrust of capitalists and their money was far from forgotten. And, in 1913, with the passage of the federal income tax law, one longstanding Grange goal was realized. All able citizens would be required to contribute to the cost of government based upon their income. Sales tax measures, on the other hand, have generally been opposed by the Grange because their support by wealthy interests reveals a lop-sided approach. Sales taxes tend to impact citizens with lower incomes much more than the wealthy and, as delegates said at their 1925 Sacramento session, "Any just system of taxation requires that taxes be levied in proportion to benefits received and the ability to pay."

Oliver Wilson (1849-1924)

In 1909 the Grange began speaking out against practices which, at the end of the century, continue to dominate Grange discussions. Since the days of Alexander Hamilton there had been those who favored centralized and branch banking, but the farmers in the Grange viewed their local banks as community institutions, sympathetic with their credit needs. Large banking interests, they feared, would drain local money to the large cities, making it unavailable to farmers and small town residents who needed the credit. The Federal Reserve Act of 1913 could be viewed as a compromise between central bank and local bank interests in that the Federal Reserve brought uniformity in banking regulation and practices while it allowed the presence of local banks.

At the 1911 National Grange session in Columbus, Ohio, the disgraced Nahum Bachelder refused to be a candidate for national master. Delegates, in a hotly contested race, finally chose their national lecturer, Oliver Wilson of Illinois, as Bachelder's replacement. He had been state lecturer for eight years, starting in 1885, followed by 16 years as state master. Although he had four years' experience teaching in rural schools, he had spent most of his life as a full-time farmer. His interest in education and agriculture combined and he has been given credit for implementing the farmers' institute work in his state. Wilson, a strong conservative, was not counted among those in the Conference of Progressive Granges and his election dashed the hopes many held for reform.

Wilson was immediately confronted with the consequences of the Bachelder scandal. Even though membership plummeted by more than 87,000 in 1912, the next year gains exceeded this loss. Extension and organization work continued, resulting in the Nebraska and Montana state Granges being reorganized in 1911 and 1912 respectively. The Wyoming State Grange was formed in 1913 followed by North Dakota in 1914 and Oklahoma in 1916.

At the 1912 session in Spokane, Washington, delegates again placed the Grange in the forefront of the temperance movement by issuing a plea to prohibit interstate commerce of intoxicating liquors. An additional recommendation was for uniform laws in all states governing the organization and operation of farmer cooperatives. The next year the Grange celebrated the seventeenth amend-

The FFA inspired by Grange

The Grange had fought a long battle for inclusion of vocational agriculture education in the nation's schools. Victory came with passage, in 1916, of the Smith-Hughes Vocational Education Act.

Vocational agriculture teachers found their effectiveness could be stretched if they augmented classroom work with extracurricular activities. Clubs eventually were formed, composed of class members. Virginia seemed to lead the nation in its network of clubs and a statewide coalition of the groups was called Future Farmers of Virginia.

Henry C. Groseclose, a Virginia agricultural education leader and an active seventh-degree Grange member, was asked to develop a ritual and procedures for the new clubs. He utilized some Grange tools and the familiar Grange blue and gold colors. The ritual Groseclose wrote was adopted in 1926 in Virginia and two years later, at the formation of the national Future Farmers of America organization, it was accepted for use by all clubs in the country.

Groseclose served as the first executive secretary of the national FFA (1928-1930) and its first national treasurer (1928-1941).

ment to the Constitution allowing for direct election of senators.

As the National Grange approached its golden jubilee session in 1916, there was a flurry of legislation passed for which the organization had been working for many years. The Smith-Lever Act of 1914 began the Agricultural Extension Service and it was followed in 1917 with passage of the Grange-supported Smith-Hughes Act which provided further for vocational and agricultural education. The Clayton Antitrust Act in 1914—a revision of the Sherman Antitrust Act—encouraged the formation of farmer cooperatives and, in 1916, Grange insistence for better highway and road funding paid off with the passage of the Federal Highway Act which provided for federal cooperation in construction of rural post roads.

The Federal Reserve Act, according to some farm representatives, had created a system beneficial to big industry but contained few rewards for agriculture. Compromise legislation, the Federal Farm Loan Act, signed by the president in 1916, established cooperative national farm loan associations and joint-stock land banks—an innovation which survives in our present Farm Credit System. There would be a system of 12 district federal land banks under the supervision of a Federal Farm Loan Board. This was the precursor to the Farm Credit Administration, formed in 1933.

Even though the Grange had been vocal about tariff matters for decades, the Canadian-American reciprocity treaty further convinced leaders there was need for an impartial fact-finding tariff commission to provide information and guidance for Congress. The Tariff Commission was established in 1916 and it would eventually have two former national masters—Sherman Lowell and Herschel Newsom—as commission members.

Grange members everywhere celebrated their fraternity's fiftieth birthday in conjunction with the annual session in November 1916. The long struggle for organizational recognition was rewarded by the appearance and words of welcome from President Woodrow Wilson at the convention's opening reception. T.C. Atkeson helped his own rise to prominence and that of the Grange itself by publication that year of his *Semi-Centennial History of the Patrons of Husbandry.* Once existing only as a dream of O.H. Kelley, the Grange had finally established itself as a permanent American institution.

Pronouncements for peace escalate as war looms

Anniversary celebrations were muted somewhat by events in Europe; a war was raging and Americans dreaded involvement. Master Wilson, a devout Quaker, spoke often in defense of the Grange's position opposing warfare and was undoubtedly pleased when the 1916 session endorsed the president's League of Nations proposal. The League, delegates said, embodied the Grange's reliance upon arbitration to settle international differences. Even earlier, in 1903, delegates had said, "We deplore the continued prevalence of the military spirit and feel the fallacy of the claim that extensive preparation for war is the best means of preserving peace, for nations thus prepared are like pugilists in the ring, watching for an opportunity to strike an effective blow." Peacetime military training and conscription also had been opposed believing, instead, "that such training should cease and in its stead the principles of virtue and peace be implanted; and that boys should be taught that a nation's greatness and power do not lie in its arsenals and mighty naval fleets, but in the honesty, sobriety, integrity, morality and intelligence of the great mass of her people." Grange activist and former national Lecturer Mortimer Whitehead chaired the Universal Peace Committee, a Grange group dedicated to the cause of peace.

When Congress declared war upon Germany in April 1917, the organization and its members supported their country's decision. Grange men in every state went to the battlefields and those at home opened up their Grange halls for Red Cross work. Subordinate funds, and those of individual members, purchased Liberty Bonds and the agricultural nature of the organization placed it in position for encouraging increased production of foodstuffs. This wartime activity was not viewed as a compromise of the organization's stand for peace and arbitration of international disputes; rather, it was a demonstration of the Grange's endorsement of democratic principles and the need for all citizens to honor decisions made by those in authority.

With the completion of the war and Oliver Wilson's fourth term of office as national master, the top leadership position in the National Grange again shifted eastward with the election of Sherman J. Lowell in 1919. Lowell was a Chautauqua County, New York, fruit and grape grower who belonged to the first farmers' Grange, Fredonia. His Grange service included offices at Fredonia and in the Chautauqua County Pomona Grange, and lecturer, overseer and master of the New York State Grange.

Lowell was a conservative Republican businessman who believed, as Charles M. Gardner points out, "in the principle of more business in government and less government in business." He was staunchly opposed to establishment of a national Department of Education within the federal government and he voiced his disapproval of proposals to locate the executive departments of the National Grange in Washington, D.C.

Dissenting voices are silenced

One of the greatest challenges to the National Grange, only briefly alluded to by Gardner, reinforced post-Bachelder caution within the National Grange. With the death of the progressive State Master C.B. Kegley of Washington in 1917, that state's Grange leadership was assumed by the fiery William Morley Bouck. He strongly believed in the policies Kegley had fought for and was not afraid to speak his mind. Problems emerged at the

Sherman J. Lowell (1858-1942)

state Grange's 1918 session at the Walla Walla High School. Even though the Grange had an agreement to use the school, the school board told the Grange representatives at 10 p.m. the evening of June 5 to vacate the building. The excuse given was the reelection of Bouck who, they claimed, supported the Nonpartisan League (a political party alleged to be disloyal to the war effort). Department of Justice archives reveal, however, that Walla Walla business people had been frightened by a group known as the Employer's Association of Eastern Washington who feared establishment of cooperatives that would diminish their business income.

Contrary to allegations, Bouck made numerous speeches supporting President Wilson's war efforts and he also shared with crowds some other radical ideas such as government ownership of railroads and utilities and new taxes to pay for war expenses rather than government borrowing. On June 12, 1918, in a speech at tiny Bow, Washington, he called the European conflict a "rich man's war." In August he was indicted by a grand jury at Seattle for allegedly violating the just-passed Espionage Act of 1918 because his Bow speech was an attempt, the jury felt, to discourage the sale of Liberty Bonds.

Problems began to emerge between the National Grange and Bouck. Kegley had often pointed out his belief that the national body had become reactionary. Evidence of that, Bouck and Kegley felt, were the policies of Bachelder, Atkeson and, now, Lowell. As Washington Grange historian Gus Norwood notes, "Bouck was bitterly disappointed because the National Grange refused to request a two-year extension of federal railway operation. He was more than disappointed when an overture by the American Federation of Labor was rejected by the National Grange." Lowell visited the 1920 State Grange session and his speech there was reviewed negatively in *The Grange News,* the State Grange newspaper.

That fall Bouck campaigned for Congress on the Farmer-Labor ticket, gaining 40 percent of the vote and coming in a close second to the Republican candidate. At the November national session Bouck was subjected to a Grange trial for charges of "injecting partisan politics into the Grange" and seven other points. The Grange court convicted him on five trumped up charges, he received a reprimand from Lowell, and was forced to sign a loyalty oath. Bouck's 1921 master's address at the state Grange convention showed his bitterness, prompting Lowell to presume Bouck's oath had been broken. Lowell sent a second reprimand and called the

National Grange executive committee together to suspend Bouck until another formal trial could be held in November.

Bouck, who must have felt like Kelley during his struggles with the other founders on the executive committee, finally decided to break that fall with the Grange and form a new organization which would not have to do constant battle with a national body. He was painfully aware a fair hearing would be impossible, given the attitude of national leadership. During the Bouck years the Washington State Grange experienced a 50 percent boost in membership, but Bouck took about one-fourth of all the members with him to the Western Progressive Farmers group he formed. Through his efforts the new organization became national in scope in 1926 but it eventually faded away.

Kegley, Bouck and other progressive Grange leaders repeatedly expressed hesitation about T.C. Atkeson's emerging prominence within the National Grange structure. Outspokenly conservative, Atkeson was named the National Grange's first legislative representative in Washington, D.C., undoubtedly as an effort to counter the effective lobbying being done by George P. Hampton and the progressive Farmers National Council. Other competition was being experienced from the Farmers Union, organized in 1902, and the American Farm Bureau Federation, formed in 1919. Despite Lowell's protests, the move to locate the Grange firmly in Washington, D.C., progressed and, in 1920, a resolution was passed which established a "Washington Building Fund."

It is a credit to Lowell that he was able to keep the National Grange growing and prospering despite the presence of so many counter forces. When he retired from the national master's post, he was appointed by President Coolidge to the U.S. Tariff Commission. He died in 1942.

Insurance programs expand

One notable accomplishment of the Lowell years was establishment in 1923 of the National Grange Mutual Liability Company (now National Grange Mutual Insurance Company) at Keene, New Hampshire. The mutual insurer was formed to provide automobile insurance for Grange members. A network of Grange member agents was recruited and the company grew quickly, expanding to several other states. Casualty insurance was added in

1936 and today the company writes insurance in 14 states along the Eastern Seaboard.

National Grange Mutual was preceded by the Farmers and Traders Life Insurance Company, organized in 1914 at Syracuse, New York. Formed by Grange leaders with the direction of New York State Grange Master E.B. Norris, the company began as a service to Grange members. It was organized as a stock company but was, in 1955, reorganized as a mutual life insurance company. It presently serves 24 states and the District of Columbia.

Juvenile Grange activities, which were becoming more popular each year, were expedited with adoption of uniform national rules at the 1922 Wichita, Kansas, session. Charters for the units, formerly issued by state Granges, would thereafter be granted by the national body and a position of National Grange juvenile superintendent was created. The first holder of the new post was Harriet H. Dickson of Ohio. The national superintendent was responsible for encouraging organization of new juvenile units and ensuring their activities were well structured.

The Grange's use of radio to promote its endeavors began at the 1922 Wichita session when a coast-to-coast hookup featured a talk by Leslie R. Smith, Massachusetts State Grange master and national executive committee secretary. The broadcast proved to be popular and from 1923 through 1942 the National Broadcasting Company aired an hour-long program each year from the National Grange conventions. For many years NBC also allocated an hour per month for a Grange program of discussions and special speakers. Widely circulated national magazines regularly featured actions of the Grange. This favorable publicity helped the organization advance at all levels.

The Grange had passed some important milestones during the first two decades of this century. The activities of the Bachelder administration and subsequent maneuvering which ensured the prominence of cautious, conservative and moderate policies would have a lasting effect upon the character of the organization. Goals and programs once dreamed of by Kelley would become those of other, more adventuresome organizations and the Grange would assume the middle road in most legislative matters. The long tenure of Lowell's successor would place the Grange squarely in the center of the Washington scene and its role would continue to evolve into a place of prominence with the emergence of the Farm Bloc.

9

The Farm Bloc

1923-1941

SENATOR ARTHUR CAPPER of Kansas was a freshman congressman in 1919, the same year Grange lobbyist T.C. Atkeson set up shop in Washington, D.C. Encouraged by his success in making a transition from the Kansas governor's mansion to the halls of Congress, Capper vowed to do all he could for America's farmers. Capper agreed with his fellow Grange members when he stated that our "national prosperity is dependent primarily upon agricultural prosperity" and that without good times on the farm "the Nation cannot have a continued growth and development."

Capper's Grange membership was something he wore proudly and he quickly formed close ties with Sherman Lowell, Atkeson and other Grange leaders. Capper noted that even though Americans, as always, had great confidence "in the man on the land," they also had "developed an apathy toward the real needs of agriculture." The strong political structure from which Capper emerged as spokesman became known as the Farm Bloc and its influence would be strong on Capitol Hill for nearly three decades.

The Farm Bloc was an unofficial alliance composed of key members of Congress representing farm states, the strong Secretary of Agriculture Henry C. Wallace (a member of the family which published the popular *Wallace's Farmer* in Iowa and not to be confused with Henry A. Wallace, President Franklin D. Roosevelt's secretary of agriculture), and the general farm organizations which were only then establishing permanent residence in Washington, D.C. The Grange was still the oldest and largest of the farm groups, followed by the American Farm Bureau Federation formed by representatives of 300,000 members in March 1920, and the National Farmers Union, a group organized in the South in 1902 which had a strong membership base in the birthplace of the Grange, the upper Middle West. The NFU worked in Washington with the National Board of Farm Organizations, formed in 1917.

Capper and others realized that none of the farm groups represented all of agriculture; farmers were fiercely independent and reluctant to organize in any permanent fashion—a hesitancy which was best illustrated in the Grange during the 1870s. Each farm group had a slightly different agenda, appealing to a specific type of member. Before the early 1920s these groups were still not working well together despite the fact that collectively they held enormous power to influence change. C.B. Kegley and the Conference of Progressive Granges were quite aware of the potential which cooperation would bring; they were simply several years ahead of their time.

Between 1921 and 1923 Congress passed a wagonload of agricultural bills, the first harvest of the Farm Bloc's efforts. There were the Packers and Stockyards Act, the Emergency Agricultural Credits Act, the Futures Trading Act, and two amendments to the Federal Farm Loan Act in 1922, the Capper-Volstead Act of 1922 (known as the "charter of liberty" for cooperatives) and the Intermediate Credits Act in 1923. Later bills which had Grange support included the Clark-McNary Act of 1924 which protected forest land and the Lenroot-Tabor Act of 1927.

This success also bred discontent. Big city newspapers blamed the farm interests for blocking legislation important to metropolitan interests and Congressman Martin C. Ansorge of New York even introduced a bill making it illegal and punishable by a $5,000 fine for a representative or senator to belong to any legislative bloc.

American farmers discover tractors

America's farmers in 1924 were about to enter another transformation of technology similar to those which been affecting them in waves since the mid-nineteenth century. Even though mass-produced tractors, most notably the Fordson, had been available since the eve of World War I, most of the machines were unreliable and ill-suited to the average American farm. International Harvester launched what has been called the "second revolution in

Mechanization of America's farms proceeded rapidly following World War I, bringing dramatic changes for rural families. Often, both traditional and modern horsepower worked side by side. (Cornell University Archives photo)

American agriculture" with its 1924 introduction of the Farmall, a small, dependable, general purpose tractor ideally suited for the majority of American farms. Other manufacturers quickly joined the parade, introducing their own innovations to ease the workload for farmers. John Deere offered its GP (general purpose) tractor, later replaced by the famous four-row John Deere A—complete with a lift to raise and lower implements with engine power. Farmers responded to the Farmall and its imitators, and between 1925 and 1928 tractors on farms increased from 549,000 to 782,000. Numbers climbed to over a million by 1932, with one in six farmers owning a tractor. The next major innovation occurred in 1939 when Henry Ford and Harry Ferguson unveiled the three point hitch, a feature which allowed implements to become integral parts of the tractor rather than being towed behind as horse-drawn machinery had been.

Although generally favorable, mechanization on the farm did have a negative impact as well. The need for manpower was greatly diminished with the introduction of machinery and it has been estimated that between 1909 and 1938 a total of 785 billion man-hours annually—about 10 percent of the labor required for crop production—were eliminated. The smallest farms also were hurt because they could not justify expenditures for machinery.

Louis J. Taber assumes national role

Christening of the Farmall was not the only event of 1924 which would impact American agriculture. The year began with a new master representing the National Grange, Louis J. Taber of Ohio, who had been elected at the November 1923 session. He would steer the organization ably until 1941. Taber's length of service as national master would be equaled only by that of Herschel Newsom, who also held the office for 18 years, between 1950 and 1968.

A college graduate, Taber was a successful Belmont County, Ohio dairyman. He participated in organizing Belmont Grange in Barnesville and was elected to offices there and in the Belmont County Pomona Grange. He advanced in the organization, serving eight years as lecturer of the Ohio State Grange and seven years as state master. Those years saw tremendous growth in the Grange in Ohio and elsewhere with his state's membership figures jumping from 40,000 to a high of 102,000 in 1921 when he left the state master's chair to become state director of agriculture. His name was frequently seen in conjunction with statewide and national efforts to improve agriculture, including service on the Hoover Wheat Price Committee in 1917. As national master he was appointed to President Coolidge's Agricultural Commission in 1924. He was the American delegate to the International Institute of Agriculture at Rome, Italy, in 1926. Following Taber's service with the National Grange, he went full-time for many years with the Farmers and Traders Life Insurance Company, the company he helped form and for which he had been president since 1938. In 1954 he represented the National Grange on a working tour for Radio Free Europe. Taber died in 1960.

Another event of 1924 which would solidify the agriculture forces in Washington was formation of the American Council of Agriculture, a group with input from the National Grange and other general farm groups. Spokesman for the new lobbying effort was George N. Peek, president of the Moline Plow Company and, later, the first head of President Franklin D. Roosevelt's Agricultural Adjustment Administration. The purpose of the group was to fight for a plan which Peek felt would bring farm relief and conditions of "equality" with industry for agriculture. Peek's proposal, introduced into Congress in 1924 as the McNary-Haugen bill, addressed the commodity surplus problem which kept farm prices low. The bill advanced the idea that surpluses be pulled out of domestic trade and sold internationally at world prices by a federal agricultural export corporation. This would allow domestic supplies to be sold at prices more advantageous to growers. Foreign sale losses would be recovered by a tax on each bushel or unit of

Louis J. Taber (1878-1960) helped the Grange secure even greater strength and national prominence during his long leadership. He is seen here with his wife Edna. (Cornell University Archives photo)

the commodity sold by producers. Such a plan, promoters argued, would place farmers in a better bargaining position with big business, ensure better prices and enhance their standing.

President Coolidge, his Secretary of Commerce Herbert Hoover and others in the administration strongly opposed Peek's idea and, with the death in 1924 of Secretary of Agriculture Wallace, his support also was lost. Farmers and farm organizations themselves had mixed feelings about surplus-control legislation but, despite those philosophical differences, the McNary-Haugen bill became a symbol of the struggle for farmers who desired to be treated equally with industry by their government. When it finally passed both Houses in 1927, President Coolidge reacted as expected with a stinging veto message. A revised measure the next year also was vetoed and the election of Hoover as president in 1928 killed any hopes of farm-relief legislation. Although the Farm Bloc had been effective in some areas, the McNary-Haugen disappointment brought them the mixed blessing of valuable experience which eventually would pay off. Farm representatives had finally come to realize, on the eve of the stock market crash of October 1929, that there was a role government could play to enhance the economic standing of America's agricultural producers.

The Grange grows, stabilizes

Not only was the agriculture gaining influence in Washington, D.C., but the Grange under Taber's guidance was undergoing dramatic organizational changes as well. Even though he operated during his entire term as master from his Columbus, Ohio, home, he had an interest in the Grange's presence in Washington, D.C. Atkeson was well established there and in 1924, feeling a hometown Grange would aid his legislative efforts, Atkeson attempted a reorganization of Potomac Grange at his National Grange office, then located at 630 Louisiana Avenue. This subordinate was originally organized by the Grange founders January 8, 1868, as a practice Grange for the emerging ritual work. After the ritual was well established, however, the group was allowed to slip into dormancy. In 1886 the group was reorganized again with Norman J. Colman, commissioner of agriculture, as its master. Founders John Thompson and William Saunders also were officers in the newly reorganized unit as was the brother of another founder, the Rev. John Trimble. The Grange met for about two years before another dormant period was encountered.

Atkeson's vision—and he was voted Potomac's master after the 1924 reorganization in order to execute it—was to enlist prominent members of Congress and other government officials as members. He was successful in this attempt and the subordinate Grange, which still meets at National Grange headquarters, has had many on its membership rolls over the years who played important roles in government. The combined expertise of its membership made the subordinate a logical choice for special research projects to help clarify complex issues under consideration by the national body. Over the years, dozens of lengthy, exhaustive reports have been issued by Potomac Grange committees which are then taken under advisement by delegates to the National Grange sessions.

In addition to the deepening involvement of the Grange in legislative matters, the fraternity was undergoing some structural modification during the Taber years. Charles M. Gardner, who had been serving as editor of the *National Grange Monthly* since its inception and who was high priest of Demeter from 1913 through 1947, engineered revisions in the degree work. Beginning in 1924 the sixth degree was turned over to state Granges, the fifth degree was designated as belonging to Pomona Granges and the seventh was reserved for use by the assembly of Demeter at the annual session of the National Grange. Two years later, changes were made and several new parts added to the sixth degree. Other meetings were livened with introduction in 1925 of *The Patron,* a new collection of songs for Granges. Attempts to strengthen subordinate Granges by promoting quality activities culminated in the 1927 establishment of Honor Grange awards for which subordinates competed. Significantly, community service work was incorporated into the Honor Grange specifications as a hallmark of local achievement. That community improvement spirit would evolve into a major driving force for the Grange in decades ahead.

Growing evidence of Grange interest in the vitality of local communities was becoming abundant. One of the first Grange scholarship funds, the Massachusetts Educational Fund, traces its origin to 1911. This fund, and the many which have appeared since, is an outgrowth of the importance attached to higher education by Grange members. In 1929, however, Grange members in both Massachusetts and Pennsylvania basked in the glory of accomplishments which would touch the lives of many more students than the scholarships ever would. That year Massachusetts Grange members, mostly women, were able to participate in dedication of the Home Economics Practice House at the state college in Amherst. Grange women had supplied all the furnishings for the building, which served an important function in the college's home economics program.

Further south, Grange Home Economics Committee members in Pennsylvania had long seen the need for women's housing at their state college and, in 1929, their response took the form of a beautiful four-story women's dormitory valued at the time at over $100,000. The project, commenced in 1923, was monumental. One of the principal fundraisers was a 40,000-copy edition of a cookbook from which the women earned $12,600. The project was under the guidance of Dr. Hannah McK. Lyons, chair of the state Grange's Home Economics Committee.

An increased stability of leadership was accomplished during the Taber administration. In 1927 James C. Farmer, New Hampshire State Grange master, was elected national lecturer, remaining in that post until 1947. It was Farmer who introduced the practice of Booster Nights for subordinate Granges in 1932. These programs, renamed Community Night in 1972, served as an

The Grange-sponsored women's dormitory at Pennsylvania State College was one of the most ambitious projects tackled by members in any state. It was dedicated in 1929. (Pennsylvania State Grange photo)

opportunity to invite non-members to a social event where they might be enticed to join the organization. At the 1928 national session in Washington, D.C., at which President Coolidge spoke to delegates, representatives elected Harry Caton as their secretary. Caton, who had succeeded Taber as Ohio State Grange master, was beginning a career which would shatter all National Grange longevity records long before his retirement from the secretary's station in 1965. Portraits of Farmer and Caton hang in an honored place in the National Grange headquarters building, a tribute to their long service to the organization.

Another personnel change, in 1927, saw Fred Brenckman, then secretary of the Pennsylvania State Grange, take the legislative representative spot previously held by T.C. Atkeson. With a personal agenda that was similar to Atkeson's, he gained immediate popularity. He continued in that capacity during the busy years of the Depression and war years, retiring from full-time lobbying and National Grange broadcasting work in 1945, when he was succeeded by Fred Bailey. Brenckman continued with the national body as a special consultant for some time after his retirement and, in 1949, his outstanding *History of the Pennsylvania State Grange* was published.

The new crop of National Grange leaders was careful to recognize that, as a new era was emerging within their fraternity, it was important to commemorate those who were responsible for the organization. Kelley and Saunders were both gone, but the Grange honored them by erecting a monument in 1926 to Kelley at his burial place in Washington's Rock Creek Cemetery, and one for Saunders (who had died in 1900) at Northern Illinois University in 1932. The University, located in Normal, Illinois, was chosen as the monument site because Saunders was responsible for the institution's landscape plan.

Perhaps the most lasting memorial to Grange origins is the 189-acre Oliver H. Kelley Farm near Elk River, Minnesota, which was purchased by the National Grange in 1935. Officially designated as a National Landmark, the property is now a "living history" exhibit where people can see demonstrations of farming, cooking and rural living skills as they were performed in the mid-nineteenth century. The National Grange turned the property over to the Minnesota Historical Society in 1961 and it is this group which maintains and operates the facility for thousands of visitors annually. The Kelley home has been restored and furnished as it would have

Grange delegates at the 1928 national session in Washington, D.C., posed at the White House with President Coolidge (standing, holding hat and paper, in front row, right of National Master Taber). This is only a small portion of the crowd captured in a panoramic photo.

been during the Grange founder's residence there. A large interpretive center has been built and crops popular during Kelley's time are grown. The women's activities department of the Grange continues to raise funds for the Kelley farm. In recent years this money has purchased teams of oxen and paid for outfitting of a Grange meeting room in the Kelley farmhouse, dedicated in May 1992.

Stock market crash turns thoughts toward banking

The stock market crash of October 1929 was foremost on Grange delegate's minds when they met the following month in Seattle for their National Grange session. At that meeting another strong statement against branch banking was issued: "Resolved, that the National Grange declare itself opposed to nationwide branch banking, and in favor of legislation which will increase the desirability of individual membership in the Federal Reserve System; and at the same time enable that body to impose restrictions upon the extent of reorganization and regrouping of banks at present individually operated, and upon the formation of new branches and chains." With the economy in shambles, the Grange leaders were more concerned than ever about the dangers of concentration of control of the nation's finances. Mistrust of "big money," evident in Kelley's appeals of the 1870s, was far from gone.

As the Depression wore on, its ravages impacted the operations of the National Grange as well. A direct result of the Depression, in 1933, was a listing of 1,043 subordinates and Pomonas which had not paid dues to their national organization because their funds were tied up in defunct banks. This situation, as well as the losses incurred by thousands of individual members nationwide, prompted an endorsement of the Federal Deposit Insurance Corporation (FDIC) plan at the 1934 Grange session. The "bank holiday" of March 1933, and permanent closures of financial institutions contributed to a surge of interest in credit unions within the Grange. California Grange members seem to have organized the most credit unions, embarking on the project in 1934 with the encouragement of the National Recovery Administration. Many American credit unions today can trace their origin to Grange halls where they were organized during the depths of the Depression.

Farmers were among those who suffered the most when the national economy slid. Total net income to farmers between 1929 and 1932 eroded from about $6.1 billion to approximately $2 billion. In 1932 the average net income for people living on farms had dropped to $74 a year. Foreclosures of farms due to unpaid taxes and mortgages skyrocketed and the onslaught of drought and the resulting Dust Bowl caused even more people to lose their holdings.

One interesting sidelight of the Hoover years was passage of the Brigham-Townsend Act in 1931, an attempt to regulate the use of oleomargarine in the United States. The Grange supported this measure, as it had previous laws, because "oleo" as a butter substitute adversely affected the incomes of dairymen. Grange members had been behind the first law to restrict the sale of butter substitutes in Pennsylvania in 1878. Manufacturers there were initially required to label their products as substitutes but subsequent legislation banned sales entirely. The cause was taken up in other states as well and West Virginia's law, under the guidance of T.C. Atkeson, called for all oleomargarine, artificial or adulterated butter to be colored pink. Congress passed its first margarine bill in 1886, because of Grange agitation. The oleo debate was not only a struggle to protect farm income by limiting competition, but it was in the forefront of Grange concerns about the purity and proper labeling of food products.

A Granger lives in the White House

The legislative groundwork laid by the Grange and other general

The farm once owned by Oliver H. Kelley, revered as the soil from which grew the Grange organization, was purchased by the National Grange during the Taber administration. The farm has been restored and serves as an interpretative center for thousands of visitors annually. The property, near Elk River, is now owned and operated by the Minnesota Historical Society. (David Howard photo)

farm organizations during the '20s served them well in Congress throughout 1933. And the inauguration of one of the Grange's most prominent members, Franklin Delano Roosevelt, as President that year didn't hurt either. Roosevelt had joined Chapel Corners Grange, near his New York home, in 1914 and he became a seventh degree member in 1930. His wife Eleanor was initiated as a Chapel Corners member in 1931 while her husband was governor of New York. In her syndicated newspaper column "My Day," the president's wife recalled the evening of June 26, 1939. "On Monday evening the President and I attended our Chapel Corners Grange meeting," she wrote, "and together with two ladies he was given his Silver Star certificate for 25 years membership.... When the President joined the Grange 25 years ago it was not a period of my life when I joined much of anything. For some years I spent most of my time looking after a family of children who were fairly near the same age.

"Later on I also joined the Grange," Mrs. Roosevelt continued, "so I was allowed to be at this meeting on Monday night, but only as a much more recent member. There were representatives from many other Granges in the county and even one or two from other counties. Everybody seemed to have a good time seeing everybody else, and my husband met a number of people he hadn't seen for a long time."

Franklin D. Roosevelt attended Chapel Corners Grange meetings on various occasions and spoke several times for the lecturer's program. "For many years I have been a member of the Grange," he said. "I have felt at home in it because it embodies the fine flavor of rural living which I myself have known and loved. Beyond this, it has been an instrument for expressing in useful activity the highest sentiments and deepest loyalties of Americans."

The Roosevelt home at Hyde Park, on the banks of the Hudson River, was often called an "estate." Roosevelt reacted negatively to that description and, exposing his affinity for the rural class, he is said to have responded, "call it by its right name, a farm. I don't like estates and I do like farms." Grange leaders found Roosevelt to be a man with an open mind and willing to try new ideas.

The New Deal moves down on the farm

Roosevelt, of course, entered the White House with domestic

economic problems which already had been festering for over three years. He took decisive, immediate action on all fronts with stabilization of agricultural production being one of his chief goals.

Originally coming out in support for McNary-Haugenism, Roosevelt later shifted his thinking and announced he would not endorse any farm program that did not include acreage control. Farm organization leaders, including those in the Grange, held a series of meetings in the fall of 1932 and the early months of 1933, trying to reach some common strategies for their upcoming legislative program. On March 10, 1933, Secretary of Agriculture Henry A. Wallace called the group together in Washington and, within two days, there was agreement on the basic outline of a farm bill which was introduced into Congress a few days later. The package would be passed May 12 as the Agricultural Adjustment Act with major provisions covering mortgage relief, inflation protection for consumers and arrangements for marketing agreements. As Gilbert C. Fite notes, "The legislation assumed that farmers as individuals were at a disadvantage in dealing with other economic groups and needed the centralizing power of government to place them in a stronger bargaining position." George Peek went to work immediately as head of the Agricultural Adjustment Administration to ensure swift relief for the farmers. Required reductions in production would bring government checks to the farmers and, perhaps, reduce national commodity surpluses. The overall goal was to return farmers' buying power back to the level it had been prior to World War I, a concept known as parity.

Understandably, there had been mounting impatience in rural areas as people had been losing their farms and income. One of the most widely publicized organized protests of the era was led by Milo Reno, a leader of the Iowa Farmers Union and son of enthusiastic Grange members. In May 1932 about 2,000 farmers massed in Des Moines to form the Farmers' Holiday Association and Reno prodded them to strike that summer. Followers responded by setting up pickets outside towns in Iowa and Nebraska, halting truck traffic of produce out of the communities. In some cases force was used or spikes were spread on highways.

In early 1933 protests and violence continued to erupt. Foreclosure sales were stormed by Farmers' Holiday members who often were successful in forcing the mortgage company to bid the full price of the mortgage. Another strategy involved farm equipment and livestock auctions of destitute farmers. Farmers' Holiday sympathizers kept bidding to pennies for their neighbor's property with items purchased being turned back to their original owners following the sale. In one case a group of Iowa farmers dragged a judge from his bench, threatened and assaulted him. Declarations of martial law were necessary in some Iowa counties in order to restore peace. Although it is unknown if any Grange members participated in the Holiday movement, agricultural interests nationally derived the benefit of greater awareness of the eroding economic conditions on America's farms.

Recognizing, as Grange members had pointed out for years, that the Federal Farm Loan Act of 1916 was not adequate for the needs of American farmers, the Roosevelt administration pushed for another part of its comprehensive package of New Deal legislation for agriculture, the Farm Credit Act. This act established the Farm Credit Administration in 1933, a cooperative long-term mortgage and short-term production and marketing credit system controlled by the farmers who used it. President Roosevelt promptly asked Washington State Grange Master Albert S. Goss to be commissioner of the Farm Credit Administration. Goss, who would later become master of the National Grange, had been present in 1916 as President Wilson signed the Federal Farm Loan Act. He went on to organize neighboring eastern Washington farmers, most of them Grange members, into a cooperative farm loan association with the goal of obtaining loans from the new Spokane Land Bank. In 1927 he was named president of the Spokane Land Bank, one of the 12 regional land banks set up by the 1916 legislation. His selection as commissioner was prompted by his many years of familiarity with the credit needs of America's farmers. It has been estimated that the Farm Credit System kept 1.5 million farms from changing hands through foreclosure within a two- or three-year period.

Poor farming and ranching practices were the root of the Dust Bowl that destroyed or reduced the fertility of millions of acres of American agricultural land. The spreading destruction had to be stopped, and the Soil Erosion Service within the Department of the Interior was set up in 1933 as the answer. Land resources were surveyed and farmers were encouraged to plant trees and grasses, terrace their fields and improve farming practices. This agency's function was absorbed by the Soil Conservation Service in the Department of Agriculture in 1935.

An additional important part of the New Deal for farmers was

FDR's October 1933 executive order establishing the Commodity Credit Corporation (CCC). Federal loans, under this plan, would be made on properly stored wheat and cotton (other crops were soon added), keeping price-depressing surpluses off the market. Only those farmers who were participating in acreage restriction contracts were eligible for these so-called nonrecourse loans. If prices soared above the loan level, the borrower could sell the commodity, pay off the loan and enjoy a profit. If the price fell below the loan figure, the CCC kept the commodity and the loss. This program placed a floor under the price of commodities which provided price protection for participating farmers.

The pivotal year of 1933 also saw establishment of the Tennessee Valley Authority and the Federal Surplus Relief Corporation. The TVA was a comprehensive plan to improve the quality of life for everyone in the upper South. Electricity production, flood control, improved agricultural practices, production and use of fertilizers and soil conservation were all part of the package. The surplus relief program, replaced in 1935 by the Federal Surplus Commodities Corporation, attempted to distribute millions of pounds

Louis J. Taber was active in national affairs throughout his life. In 1954 he represented the National Grange on a tour for Radio Free Europe. (Cornell University Archives photo)

of butter, pork, flour and other commodities to the nation's poor. Part of the package included federal assistance for school lunch programs. This strategy was part of the effort to control surpluses while, at the same time, feeding the growing numbers of undernourished Americans. A spin-off benefit to farmers, which would pay off in the farm bill and food stamp battles of the 1960s, was an improved attitude toward the agricultural sector on the part of poor consumers.

Gaining passage in 1935 were two monumental programs which have had longlasting effects in rural America. Establishment on May 11 of the Rural Electrification Administration with enthusiastic Grange support would have an almost immediate impact while enactment of Social Security would eventually help farmers when coverage was extended to them in 1954.

Cheap electricity was the farm family's dream

Despite introduction of the tractor, which eased labor for men, farm families in most of the nation were without the benefits of electricity—benefits which would lighten the workload for farm women perhaps more than for their husbands. Rural households were still mostly unelectrified at the dawn of the Depression because electricity distribution was under the control of large monopolies which refused to run lines through the countryside. The smaller number of meters per mile would not bring the profit they wanted.

The Grange had long been an advocate of public power. Members looked on in horror during the 1920s as massive holding companies concentrated ownership of the growing electricity generation and distribution system. The economic and political power of the holding companies was massive and their manipulation of Wall Street was one of the primary causes of the crash of 1929. Grange members in the Pacific Northwest were especially thrilled by the campaign speech made by Franklin D. Roosevelt at a stop in Portland in 1932. Besides promising to develop the power generation potential of the Columbia River, the presidential candidate announced that where "a community, a city or a county or district is not satisfied with the service rendered or the rates charged by the private utility, it has the undeniable right as one of the functions of government to set up...its own governmentally owned and operated service." This appealed to the Grange people nationwide, rural citizens with a belief that natural resources belonged to all people and that the people themselves—not trusts and monopolies controlled by the wealthy—had the right to control their own destiny.

Albert S. Goss, as master of the Washington State Grange, publicized the Grange's endorsement of public development of natural resources and public ownership of electric utilities. Several cities in the Northwest, principally Tacoma and Seattle, had superb municipal utilities and the rural Grange members felt the advantages of public ownership could benefit them also. Making use of the state's initiative, referendum and recall legislation passed by Grange action in 1912, members in Washington began an intense battle to bring public power to their state's rural areas. Initiative No. 1, the Grange's Public Power Bill, was passed by the voters in 1930 in spite of dirty attacks from private power interests. The hard work was still ahead, though, and Grange members and others across the state immediately went to work organizing quasi-governmental public utility districts which finally brought power to their farms. The efforts of Goss and his chief Grange power campaigner, Fred J. Chamberlain, paid off and most of Washington state is still effectively served by their large network of PUDs. A similar structure was adopted in neighboring Oregon, but a limited number of districts were formed there.

Grange activists in other states (and in some areas of Washington and Oregon as well) followed different avenues in order to achieve the same purpose, and activation of the Rural Electrification Administration in 1935 gave them the inspiration and financing they needed. Across the country, many times in Grange halls, electric cooperatives were formed and low-cost loans secured from REA. The REA plan included a feature called "area coverage" which required a cooperative to serve everyone in their jurisdiction regardless of location. Another popular facet was the ability of cooperative members to work off a portion of the total expense through providing labor on line construction and home wiring. Tens of thousands of farmers left their fields to join neighbors in putting up power poles and stringing wire—a modern day equivalent to pioneer barn-raisings. Their hard work paid off, much to the surprise of the private power companies who were waiting for the co-ops to fail so they could, in the words of one executive, "buy them up at ten cents on the dollar." In 1934 only

744,000 farms had electricity; in seven short years the number had climbed to 2,351,603, 40 percent of the nation's farm families. The rural electrification program slowed during the war years but commenced shortly thereafter. Within a few more years, virtually all farms were receiving the benefits electricity provided.

A related victory for the Granges of Washington and Oregon was the fulfillment of Roosevelt's promise to develop the Columbia River. This formidable goal included a network of dams which would be used for generation of electricity, navigation and irrigation. Long a dream of Northwestern Grange people, the dam construction finally commenced in 1933 at Grand Coulee—"The biggest thing," songwriter Woody Guthrie penned, "that man has ever done." Work on Bonneville Dam was conducted simultaneously. In 1937 the Bonneville Power Administration was set up to handle distribution of electric power generated by the federal facilities with preference being given to the public power utilities that had been formed. The BPA was strongly supported by both the Oregon and Washington state Granges. Through the years, irrigation water from Grand Coulee Dam has brought tens of thousands of acres of rich farmland into production in eastern Washington and parts of arid Oregon.

Cooperatives regain popularity for Grangers

With passage of favorable laws, particularly the Capper-Volstead Act of 1922, interest in organizing supply and marketing cooperatives again began to surface within Grange circles. Attempting to avoid the mistakes of the 1870s, Granges did not directly form these business ventures but, rather, provided sponsorship in the form of member manpower and assistance.

Cooperatives also were being formed by the other general farm groups. One of the earlier examples of a cooperative which bridged organizational lines was the GLF. Exchange, (Grange League Federation Exchange) organized in 1920 in Ithaca, New York, with the joint sponsorship of the Grange, Dairymen's League and the Farm Bureau. National Master Lowell was an active factor in organizing the New York State Grange Exchange, a precursor to GLF., and he became one of its directors. Many other supply cooperatives appeared across the country during the '20s and '30s.

Albert S. Goss played an important role in developing perhaps the largest system of Grange-connected cooperatives in the country. Across Washington state there were, in 1918, 50 or more small, independent Grange supply cooperatives. Centralized purchasing would, it was felt, help keep costs low for members, and the Grange Wholesale Warehouse Company was organized to bring this about. In 1920 Goss assumed managership of the wholesale cooperative. In the 1930s cooperatives were helped with the rapid expansion of tractor use and the new need farmers had for petroleum products. A fleet of co-op tanker trucks was soon seen on the highways, transporting fuel to storage tanks at Grange Supply stores throughout the state. The network survives as part of the massive CENEX cooperative, the Farmers Union Central Exchange formed in Minnesota in 1931.

Washington Grange cooperative ventures of the 1920s and 1930s included a plant to manufacture stumping powder to dynamite stumps, the Grange Milling Company producing Pomona brand flour, the Grange Cooperative Livestock Marketing Association and the Grange Cooperative Printing Association. The latter survived the longest, until the 1980s, getting its start printing *The Grange News,* the official newspaper of the Washington State Grange, and the Oregon State Grange *Bulletin.* Grange people, in Washington, and in most other states as well, worked diligently with others in forming grain, milk, poultry and egg marketing cooperatives.

A couple of novel cooperative ventures, again in Washington state, attempted to deal with two basic human needs, health and burial. Appearing later, the Group Health Cooperative of Seattle began as a small clinic in 1945. King County Grange members were prominent among the early group of organizers, and now the cooperative has hospitals and clinics statewide.

The high cost of burial during the cash-short days of the Depression prompted Grange members in eastern Washington to start a movement which, more than 50 years later, is still gaining in importance. *The Grange News* of March 5, 1938, reported that, "Adhering again to the principles of Grange cooperation, Okanogan County has extended to its members the hand of group assistance and sympathy in time of sorrow and bereavement, and have joined together in an association known as the Funeral Aid Association." The article continues to outline a contract which had been negotiated between the Grange association and a local mortician which guaranteed specific funeral services for members at an agreed price of $115. The sum was paid for in full by the association. Grange members interested in joining the association paid a $2 membership fee and, upon the death of a member, each living member was assessed a minimal amount creating a fund responsible for paying the funeral director. The plan caught on and, with some modifications, it survives in the form of memorial societies located in over 200 communities across North America.

Another Grange insurance endeavor, Grange Mutual Life Company of Nampa, Idaho, had its origins at this time. The mutual life insurance company was formed in 1935 and it has grown since. Initially writing insurance only for members, it later opened its benefits to non-members as well. It has been known since 1991 as United Heritage Mutual Life Insurance Company.

National Master Taber was approving of the Grange's renewed, and this time cautious, entry into cooperative enterprises. Each was designed to provide financial benefits to Grange members, and that attraction also helped bring many new members into the fraternity. When Taber became master at the 1923 Pittsburgh, Pennsylvania, session, national membership stood at 601,086. Although numbers shrunk somewhat through the worst years of the Depression, he left office in 1941 with 638,650 on the rolls. Stability within the organization had been achieved despite competition from other general farm groups.

As the dampening effects of the Depression lingered on, Congress and the Roosevelt administration continued to transform the agenda of American politics. Many times the National Grange was a willing partner; at other moments the organization remained skeptical or uninvolved.

Social Security is one illustration of the wary stance of the Grange. When the revolutionary program was implemented in 1935, the Grange had nothing to say. By 1937, however, Taber was telling national session delegates that "Every right-thinking American should favor legislation of this type" even though Social Security needed some "improvement and simplification." It took another six years for the national organization to jump on the bandwagon already being pulled by several state Granges urging expansion of Social Security to cover farmers. As the average age of members appeared to grow older during the 1960s through the 1980s, the number of resolutions and policies relating to Social Security would grow.

Farm programs become a permanent fixture

In January 1936, the U.S. Supreme Court declared unconstitutional some of the provisions of the momentous Agricultural Adjustment Act (AAA) passed in the early days of the New Deal. Within one hour of the pronouncement, the National Grange issued a statement outlining a series of initiatives that would resolve the problem for America's farmers. The recommendations were for farmers to be paid for all uncompleted contracts entered into in good faith; shifting emphasis to a soil conservation program; and urging no tampering with the U.S. Constitution to alleviate the crisis. Weeks later Congress acted upon the suggestions and passed the Soil Conservation and Domestic Allotment Act. The new act was designed to do the same thing done by the AAA—restrict acreage and make benefit payments to cooperating producers. The legislation, however, allowed payment to producers ostensibly for conserving soil, not cutting production. Two years later the Agricultural Adjustment Act of 1938 was passed and this became the basic law for future years.

Largely because of federal programs, farm income slowly expanded during the 1930s. Average net income per farm more than doubled from 1932 to 1939, jumping from $304 to $685. From 1934 to 1940 inclusive, direct federal payments to farmers totaled $4.5 billion (exclusive of farm security-type expenditures). Prices, however, remained low for farm commodities, primarily because of persistent surpluses in spite of acreage reductions.

Unfortunately, federal farm legislation had a disastrous effect upon the hundreds of thousands of tenants, sharecroppers and small acreage farmers of the South. Their plots of farmland were too small to allow them to remove acres from production and thus receive government benefit checks. Those who were tenants or sharecroppers found their plots removed from production by their landlords, instead, and they were forced off the land, many of them gravitating to crowded cities of the Northeast looking for work.

President Roosevelt responded to the needs of the poorest of America's farmers by establishing the Resettlement Administration in April 1935. Limited loans were made available to allow poor farmers to move to better acreages, obtain equipment and make a new start. Model cooperative communities were attempted and, by 1936, more than half a million poor farm families were being assisted. The Resettlement Administration was absorbed in 1937 by the Farm Security Administration, set up by the Grange-supported Bankhead-Jones Farm Tenant Act. While many poor families were given a measure of opportunity through these efforts, the success of the initiative was limited. One obstacle, which the Grange would address again and again in the years ahead, was the marriage which had been effected between the American Farm Bureau Federation and the USDA Extension Service. Many county extension agents, who were for all practical purposes business agents for the Farm Bureau as well, were never convinced the programs of the Resettlement Administration and the Farm Security Administration had value. These agents were charged with the task of implementing the provisions of the Bankhead-Jones Farm Tenant Act and, because of their prejudice against the program, their attempts to make it work were half-hearted at best. Finally, disillusionment set in and even the Grange, in 1943, testified against additional funding for the Farm Security Administration.

The Grange, even though it had lost the power of a solid membership base in the South, took a concrete interest in the tenant farmer problem. As far back as 1916 the Grange had issued a warning about the mushrooming of poverty in the rural South and culminated its concern by adopting a statement at the 1948 session branding the tenant problem as "one of the most, if not the most, important questions of the present, affecting the interests of agriculture and the future of the Republic..." Nevertheless, the FSA, in the words of Gilbert Fite, "became one of the victims of a growing conservative opposition to Roosevelt and the New Deal" and the fight to alleviate rural poverty would not erupt again until the presidency of Lyndon B. Johnson.

Legislation affecting farmers continued to be drafted and Grange input was consistent. Additional legislative battles were entered into which, at the time, perhaps had only marginal effect upon rural America. In a broader perspective, Grange leaders pointed out, New Deal labor legislation was one example of significant change in the structure of America's workforce which inevitably would have dramatic impact upon everyone in the country. One notable labor law which had mixed Grange support was the National Labor Relations Act of 1935. While the Grange agreed with the provisions for collective bargaining contained in the act, there were other portions which did not secure Grange support, particularly references to unionization of workers on farms or farmers' cooperatives. These perceived discrepancies led to the later passage of the Taft-Hartley Act in 1947, another piece of labor legislation receiving partial Grange support. The organization strongly approved of the equal playing field created by the laws for employers and workers but came out in opposition to secondary boycotts, unionization of farm laborers and some other union policies.

Other Grange-endorsed legislation of the latter part of Taber's administration included the Purnell Act of 1938 which set up large agriculture research laboratories, the Pure Seed law of 1939 and the Wool Products Labeling Act of 1940. The Grange also came out, on the eve of World War II, in favor of the Alien Registration Act of 1940. This was consistent with its policy announced in 1924 when it supported the alien quotas inherent in the Immigration Act of that year.

Even though one meaning of the word "Grange" was a feudal estate under the ownership of one person, the organization had long backed legislation which would discourage accumulation of massive tracts of farmland. That attitude dictated Grange backing of the acreage limitation in the 1902 Reclamation Act and it also led to enactment at the 1937 National Grange session of a resolution favoring a graduated land tax. Such a measure, the Grange delegates felt, would "discourage excessive land holdings and

Farmers and Traders Life Insurance Company, a Grange-affiliated firm which received Louis Taber's dedicated labor for many years, continues to serve Grange members.

promote the interest and home ownership of the family-sized farm." Already, the Grange leaders had seen the decline in these medium-sized farming operations under the control of one family. The Depression had forced many farmers off the soil which had been in their families for generations and that trend would continue at an increasingly rapid pace.

Grange vigilant on railroad and highway issues

Transportation issues continued to occupy the Grange during the Taber era. In 1931 railroads petitioned the Interstate Commerce Commission for a blanket 15 percent increase in freight rates. The Grange was the first farm organization to register its opposition, pointing out that such a jump in rates would cost farmers $150 million annually. The commission concurred and refused to boost rates on agricultural commodities.

Highway transportation was becoming more important to all Americans and the Grange responded by assisting in the formation of the National Council of Private Motor Truck Owners in 1928 and the National Highway Users Conference in 1932. These cooperative alignments sought to enhance the lobbying power of participating groups for highway-related issues.

An example of action to improve road transportation was the State Grange's 1930 "Get Connecticut Out of the Mud" campaign which resulted in the appropriation for several years of $3 million annually for the improvement of dirt roads in the state. A significant piece of federal legislation, the Motor Carrier Act of 1935, contained exemptions for certain agriculture products which greatly helped farmers move commodities to markets in the least expensive manner. The exemptions were the direct result of Grange lobbying, but the organization would have to fight for these benefits again in the 1970s as truckers and railroads worked for their elimination.

After 18 years at the helm, Louis J. Taber stepped down as master of the National Grange to assume full-time responsibility in the insurance firm he helped establish. During his administration the Grange had transformed itself into an organization that was openly involved in lobbying for good rural improvement legislation. Legislative goals often were achieved through cooperation with alliances of other farm groups working in conjunction with powerful leaders in Congress, the USDA and the White House. Many times, especially during the New Deal years, the stage was set in back rooms with Congressional action being swift and decisive. Taber oversaw streamlining of organizational activities and membership stability was finally achieved. However, it would be Taber's successor who would move the organization on to its zenith during the turbulent years of World War II and the administration of another Grange president, Harry Truman.

10

Gaining Honor and Permanence

1941-1950

LOUIS J. TABER left the highest seat in the National Grange at a point when the world was reeling from armed aggression in Europe and the Orient. Within days after the election of Albert S. Goss as national master, the aggression reached American soil with the attack on Pearl Harbor, December 7, 1941.

At the 1941 Worcester, Massachusetts, session where Goss had been elected, Henry Morgenthau Jr., FDR's secretary of the treasury, had received his 25-year membership pin and then addressed Grange delegates about "The Farmer, Taxation and Defense." With a major world war still lingering heavy on the minds of many within the Grange, the assertion that farmers played a major role in ensuring victory for our troops was an unmistakable conclusion. For at least the second time in its history, the Grange had to set aside its pacifist position and support the country's decision to confront armed force with armed resistance.

Even though Pearl Harbor had been a shock, events around the globe had been preparing America for war. Nine months before Pearl Harbor, on February 8, 1941, Potomac Grange had been instrumental in securing a nationwide CBS radio hookup for a broadcast on "Agriculture in National Defense." The program was a symposium with eight freshman U.S. senators as guests, all introduced by Potomac's Master Chester H. Gray. The senators from both sides of the aisle agreed that agriculture played an indisputable role in the defense of the nation because food was just as important—or more so—as the tools of war. The broadcast was part of Potomac Grange's effort to highlight the 75th anniversary of the National Grange, celebrated in Worcester.

Goss was well-equipped to meet the challenges posed by the war effort and he skillfully used these abilities to build the Grange as an even more powerful force in American life. He came to the National Grange with a unique combination of leadership, business and finance skills acquired from his years of service as master of the Washington State Grange, Grange Cooperative Wholesale, the Federal Land Bank at Spokane and, most recently, as national land bank commissioner for President Roosevelt. In that position, which he held for seven years, he was a champion for the cooperative approach to farm finance, decentralized and under local control. His outspoken view was that the federal role was to supervise rather than control.

Albert S. Goss (1882-1950) gained the respect, love and reverence of those inside and outside the Grange because of his dynamic, capable leadership. Under his guidance the fraternity reached its peak in membership and achieved international prominence.

In extending credit to farmers for land and equipment, lenders had to be assured that borrowers possessed the ability to pay back their loans. During the Depression years that was often a difficult conclusion to reach because farm income necessary for loan repayment had to come from crops sold at decent prices. A basic assumption of the AAA (Agricultural Adjustment Act) was that reducing surpluses by taking land out of production would allow commodity prices to return to levels favorable to the farmers. The surplus problem was not solved by AAA and, consequently, prices did not edge upward as quickly as anticipated.

The debate about commodity prices and land bank loan repayments during the 1940 presidential campaign increased pressure for outright subsidies to farmers and writing down of loans. Goss termed these strategies "abolition of personal responsibility" which would shift the burden to other cooperative members. He wanted to keep the problem of farm price parity separate from the farm credit system; if farmers received adequate prices for their crops, he insisted, other farmer bail-out tactics would be unnecessary and loans could be repaid easily. Goss dissented from the prevailing belief in vain and finally resigned in protest from his federal post June 16, 1940.

As the U.S. entered the war there were burdensome surpluses of agricultural commodities. Within the decade of the 1930s overall farm production jumped 10 percent despite the fact that 38 million acres had been pulled from production. Introduction of new crop varieties such as hybrid corn, amplified use of machinery and the emerging benefits of farm chemicals all contributed to the efficiency that produced the stockpiles. Technology also reduced the number of workers in agriculture between 1920 and 1940 from 25.6 to 17.5 percent of America's labor force. The overall population of people living on farms remained about constant, however, causing a population surplus in rural America.

World War II solved several farm problems simultaneously. The need for troops and employees in war-related plants drew about five million people away from farm regions during the first half of the 1940s. The wartime need for food and fiber eliminated the price-depressing surpluses almost instantly. And, finally, with increased demand, farmers began to enjoy better prices.

The new Secretary of Agriculture, Claude R. Wickard, a seventh degree Grange member, was in a position to realize better times on the farm were only temporary and any gains made during the war would soon evaporate unless farmers organized and worked together to achieve common goals. "In the face of the tremendous problems that confront us today," he said, "division and bickering among the farm organizations and the farm groups would be stupid and dangerous." He then added that farmers would need to enlist the help of other groups because they were quickly becoming a "minority" and did not have the power to achieve their objectives on their own. Goss had formed such alliances in Washington state and was eager to do the same in Washington, D.C.

Goss was a strategist. The war provided a golden opportunity for the rural residents in the Grange to boost their public image by promoting popular war-related projects. Although some called for the Granges to curtail regular meeting schedules because of gasoline rationing, leaders, instead, urged continued organizational activity. Actually, members gathered even more often during the war because gasoline and tire rationing had the effect of curbing longer trips, making shorter jaunts to Grange gatherings more practical. During crisis situations, friends derive comfort from being together, and in thousands of Grange halls nationwide the pain and hardship of the war seemed a little less intense for members who shared Grange events. There were Red Cross campaigns, salvage drives, blood donations and bond sales in virtually every Grange. An enlarged force of deputies in the field enlisted new members, and the Grange prospered. Goss was one of the first within the Grange to announce that the organization would be best served by strengthening its weaker Granges, putting the most organizing effort into regions where the fraternity already had a presence rather than advancing into new territory.

The war caused some interruptions in local Granges, nonetheless. Typical of these disruptions was the Clallam County Pomona Grange hall, the only Pomona Grange in Washington state with its own building, being taken over for military purposes. So, too, was the spacious New England Grange Building at the Eastern States Exposition grounds in West Springfield, Massachusetts, which was outfitted as an infirmary. The space-consuming Hanford project in the Northwest, eventually instrumental in the development of the atomic bomb, took the halls of several Granges, forcing the members to transfer to other subordinates.

Goss opposed the concept of government-enforced price controls, but when wartime inflation conditions dictated their necessity, he joined with other farm representatives who felt agriculture should have its interests protected along with other industries. As a result of agricultural pressure, the Emergency Price Control Act of 1942 gave some special consideration to the needs of farmers, angering consumer and urban groups. The term "Farm Bloc" was again being used, and the *New York Times* accused Congress of taking advantage of "the national emergency to grab everything possible for agriculture while the getting is good." Later that year, President Roosevelt pushed for even stronger controls on farm prices in exchange for government assurances for good prices following the war. The Grange was among those in the farm coalition who called for an all-out grass-roots lobbying effort and in October the act was amended in a manner that pleased the administration as well as the farm groups. Wickard's admonition for farm groups to cooperate was being taken seriously and, with the conspicuous exception of the more liberal Farmers Union under the leadership of Grange member James Patton, they presented a solid front.

The Grange's policy on price control had been nurtured in 1941 under the guidance of Indiana State Master Herschel D. Newsom, chair of the session's agriculture committee and later national master. "Equality" was a word used several times in the forward-looking statement which cautioned that all sectors of the economy should be treated fairly if price controls ever became necessary.

Finding a home

The Grange had maintained an office for legislative affairs in the nation's capital since Atkeson moved there in 1919. Goss, of course, lived there for years before his election as national master. Although there had been occasional resistance from some of his predecessors about locating permanent administrative headquarters in Washington, D.C., Goss felt it was essential to the future of the Grange that a national office be acquired there. His own Washington State Grange had started a trend in 1935 when it was the first state Grange to build its permanent office building. A strong central headquarters was a decided advantage to the work of the fraternity in that state and Goss knew the pattern would be repeated on a national level as well.

In 1943 the decision was made to purchase an eight-story building at 744 Jackson Place Northwest, fronting Lafayette Square (located across Pennsylvania Avenue from the White House). The

The first Grange-owned national headquarters building, 744 Jackson Place Northwest, Washington, D.C., was secured in 1943. The eight story structure was a visible testimonial of the Grange's permanent role in the nation's capital.

purchase price of $292,000 was quickly seen as a bargain and rental of much of the space helped pay the mortgage payments.

There had been an undercurrent for a national headquarters

since the early days of the Grange. A fund had been initiated in 1883 as an attempt to secure finances to build a "temple to Ceres" in the nation's capital, but the 1920 session officially dropped that project and instituted in its stead the Washington Building Fund. A transfer of $5,000 each year from the National Grange's general fund was made into this account and a special fund-raising push for the organization's diamond anniversary in 1941 brought additional money for this purpose. The accumulation allowed a sizeable downpayment on the Jackson Place building, leaving a balance due of only $125,000. The National Grange Mutual Liability Company of Keene, New Hampshire, offered to loan this amount. The permanent headquarters, owned by the organization, gave added credibility to the group; locating in Washington, D.C., placed it right where Goss and others felt it best belonged. The fraternity had finally evolved into the institutionalized legislative force Kelley envisioned, even though its policies and strategies were closer to those recommended by the less ebullient Saunders.

Influencing social policy

Goss, perhaps more than any previous national master, was interested in seeing the Grange become profoundly involved in emerging social issues. There was a rich heritage of that involvement within the fraternity and the struggles for woman suffrage and prohibition were often cited as outstanding examples of Grange social consciousness. The achievement of prohibition, of course, was put aside with its repeal in 1933. Reflecting on the prohibition experiment in 1948, Goss admitted, "We probably made a serious mistake when we attempted to substitute government control of liquor for a continuing and intensive campaign in temperance and individual responsibility." Apparently, the membership agreed and education took the place of a legislative approach. A National Grange Interim Committee on Liquor issued a long, instructive report at that 1948 session, of which 15,000 copies were later reprinted and distributed. Delegates also began pushing for more austere drunk driving laws while Goss, speaking on what he labeled a related health issue, bemoaned the 120 percent per capita increase in the use of cigarettes since 1935.

In 1943, at the national session in Grand Rapids, Michigan, delegates authorized two special studies which would have far-reaching effects. The first study was to investigate the possibility of extending Social Security coverage to farmers. After delegates endorsed the idea the following year, Grange lobbying would be instrumental in securing this benefit in 1954. The second study would later be seen as the foundation stone of the Grange commitment to improving the health of rural Americans.

The initial purpose of the health study was to investigate the possibility of securing group hospitalization for farmers. Medical insurance was becoming increasingly important to urban residents, but self-employed farmers had little access to affordable coverage. The committee's extensive report at the 1944 session outlined a number of steps which could be taken to not only help farmers obtain insurance, but also secure more accessible, improved health care. Granges were admonished to use their group status to negotiate hospital plans with Blue Cross and other carriers which then could be purchased by their members. This recommendation was acted upon across the country and for the first time in many localities, because of ties formed between the Grange and Blue Cross, rural residents had access to health insurance. In many Grange states, the organization had to secure legislative approval before the hospitalization plans could be offered to members.

Insurance would do the Grange members little good, however, if adequate hospitals and clinics were not available nearby. Another committee recommendation asked for expanded federal and state aid "for the erection of hospitals, supplying of medical equipment and training personnel for medical care so that the cost of these may be reduced as well as making more of them available." In 1944 nearly 40 percent of the counties in the nation were still without any hospital. The report recognized "the moral and social responsibility of the nation in the field of human welfare" and Grange leaders believed that government had "the right to try to prevent unnecessary suffering and death due to a scarcity of services that people cannot afford." Nonetheless, the lifelong Grange insistence on local control surfaced and the resolution passed with the provision that the federal government should not use this universal right of medical care as "a pretext to assuming control of our medical services" or as an excuse for establishing any national health insurance program. The final report concluded with a medical consumer's "bill of rights" outlining minimal standards for medical and dental care.

This elevated interest in rural health prompted renaming of the Grange's national Committee on Education as the Committee on Education and Health in 1944 with the intersession Special Committee on Group Hospitalization still functioning through 1946. An interim committee on health was formed after the 1946 session and several members of the group hospitalization committee appeared on the new committee. It was reported at the 1945 national session that most state Granges had either secured health insurance plans for their members or were in the process of doing so. Plans differed but a typical example was the one offered Connecticut Grange members. It provided full hospital coverage for 21 days and half coverage for an additional 90 days for 90 cents a month for an individual, $1.75 a month for a couple and $2 per month for an entire family. Fees were paid semi-annually to a subordinate Grange insurance representative and the Grange transmitted the collective premiums to Blue Cross. This health insurance benefit was undoubtedly responsible for some of the gains in membership during the 1940s and one unnamed state master was quoted as saying, "The Blue Cross program has practically made some of our Granges."

The new Interim Committee on Health took its assignment seriously. Committee chair Joseph W. Fichter, master of the Ohio State Grange, was appointed by the surgeon general as a member of the Federal Hospital Council and state Granges across the country became involved with the assessment activities promoted by the Hospital Survey and Construction Act. The National Grange cooperated with the American Medical Association and other farm groups in conducting a conference in Chicago on rural health. The coalition, named the Conference Committee on Rural Health, had Fichter as its chair. Soon, regional conferences were being conducted in an effort to spread interest in rural health problems. One solution proposed to the Granges by the American Public Health Association was enactment of state laws authorizing creation of "county-wide, city-wide or multi-county units of health jurisdiction covering not less than 50,000 persons," supported by modest taxes and governed by community health councils. Rural hospital districts emerged from this model. The Intersession Health Committee's last report was made in 1950 with the chairman indicating continued attendance at the annual American Medical Association's Rural Health Conference and the Farm Organization Conference Committee on Rural Health Services. Educational materials about health were being distributed to Granges, and the Grange endorsed the hospital construction program authorized by the Hill-Burton Act.

Goss was always a strong supporter of the Grange concept that control of institutions should be at the level where services are performed. That was the guiding principle in the Farm Credit System and it also was prominent in Grange education policies. Noting the vast differences in the quality of education between districts and from state to state, Goss said at the 1948 national session that "the need for Federal aid for equalization purposes is just as strong as ever." The fear was that aid would diminish local control of schools, a right the Grange jealously guarded. "With reference to the danger of Federal control," Goss continued, "I believe that the Grange should change its policy from an indefinite negative approach to a definite positive approach with a clear-cut program which will achieve the results we desire to attain." He apparently was referring to the 1946 resolution stating that "Because we are against bureaucracy and all the evils that go with it, and because we are opposed to Federal control of education and in favor of continued state and local control of our public school system, we must oppose Federal appropriations for elementary and secondary education except the already existing vocational educational program."

Goss was a practical man with the ability to see the logical consequences of current conditions within American schools. Inflation was hitting teachers especially hard in the post-war years and salaries were not keeping up with the cost of living. Educators were walking away from their schools to take up better paying careers and many districts could not staff their classrooms adequately. Americans were becoming acquainted with teacher strikes for the first time and they were still stunned with Census Bureau reports revealing that 2,800,000 American citizens over 14 years of age could not read or write. Conceding that this rate was the lowest in America's history, Goss added that "it is nevertheless shocking to find that our public school system in which we take so much pride, has failed to reach these millions of people. It is particularly shocking for farmers to find that the rate of illiteracy in rural areas is twice as great as elsewhere."

Delegates could see the point made by Goss and passed a statement approving federal aid to equalize educational opportunity between states. Grange conditions placed on potential federal handouts included requiring states receiving aid to meet minimum educational standards and total noninterference from the federal government in the use of those funds. The concept of a bipartisan federal education commission advanced by Goss was tabled for further study by the delegates and adopted in 1947.

The Grange had always expressed a somewhat less than tolerant attitude toward publications and forms of entertainment which did not meet certain standards of decency and morality. Early expressions of these attitudes had been evident in the era when the Women's Christian Temperance Union and Grange women had worked together to achieve the goals of Francis Willard's social purity movement. When radio and motion pictures became common, Grange members vocalized again the need for adherence to minimal standards. An interim committee on movies was set up and an extensive report of their findings and recommendations was adopted by delegates at the 1947 session. Recognizing the power of entertainment upon children, the report urged cooperation with other groups who were encouraging production of only "clean, wholesome and constructive movies." Furthermore, the Grange was instructed to communicate to movie producers the types of scenes and movies it considered objectionable and "if the movie industry will not voluntarily stop the production of films contributory to moral breakdown, the only alternative is federal censorship with all its dangers." The radio industry was asked to "eliminate programs which build up in suspense or otherwise an act of crime as distinguished from the apprehension and conviction of criminals. It is especially important that such programs do not come on at hours when the juvenile and adolescent audiences are appreciable."

The next year, however, delegates apparently set aside apprehension about the dangers of censorship voiced by their committee and voted in favor of "a strict censorship" of "so-called comic books, some types of movies and radio programs" which were deemed "detrimental to the thinking of American boys and girls." Similar calls for censorship appeared at subsequent sessions and the media of television was added, but by 1959 the policy had jelled into a non-censorship statement voicing opposition to "objectionable movies and TV programs" and a non-confrontational encouragement of "the use of clean, moral, and wholesome programs."

There also was broad-based Grange concern about the increase in crime and delinquency. Although it was pointed out that much of this could be related to alcohol use, Goss felt lawlessness was furthered by "inadequate sentences for serious crimes," releasing criminals from overcrowded penitentiaries and "the sentimentality of social and welfare workers" which often swayed the thinking of those sitting on parole boards. Problems of youth, which troubled Goss continually, included lack of adequate recreational facilities, inadequate parental supervision and packed school activity schedules which took children out of their homes more often. His response to these concerns was appointment of Wib Justi, then the National Grange publicity director, as director of youth activities in 1949. This was a new post within the Grange structure and Justi would continue active promotion of alternative Grange youth projects until 1966.

An evolving world view

In the post-war climate, one overriding issue for young and old alike was world peace. There was admission of the possible necessity of the draft during wartime but the old Grange opposition to compulsory military training during times of peace came to the surface again. The Grange did not want military training to become part of the schools as many others proposed, nor did members want military training to become universal in scope, requiring all citizens to participate. It was felt volunteers would normally be sufficient to supply manpower needs of the armed forces. A bitter Congressional fight in 1948 saw the Grange view emerge triumphant although it appeared at times that this might not be the case.

Internationally, the Grange had been a firmly behind the League of Nations, but its failure to avert World War II revealed its weaknesses and ineffectiveness. A new organization with more authority must take its place and when the United Nations was formed, the Grange became a zealous supporter. When the young U.N. encountered a credibility gap due to its inability to negotiate a permanent world-wide peace treaty within its first three years, Goss jumped into the debate. "While the United Nations has not achieved all we might wish," he told delegates in 1948, "it is far from a failure. It is the greatest forum for holding the purposes and ambitions of nations up to public view the world has ever seen." He admitted that "probably the greatest mistake made" by the United Nations "was when the United States and Russia joined in an effort to use the United Nations to force the partition of Palestine," an action resulting in the formation of Israel. In spite of some errors of judgment and slow progress in effecting world peace, Goss thought the U.N. deserved unified endorsement. "Our [Grange] policy then should be one of wholehearted support of the United Nations and to do everything in our power to build it and strengthen it as an instrument of peace. If we can make a success of this, time will show how it can be used to improve international relations in many ways until it develops a world leadership which will affect the welfare of all nations for good." Delegates agreed, and Grange policy was adopted which stated that American national security "must rest fundamentally on: (1) a strong, educated, healthy population; (2) an increased emphasis on scientific research; (3) faith in and vigorous support of the United Nations." The power of example was seen as America's best tool for "our best defense lies finally in an effective demonstration of what a free people can do in helping others while remaining strong at home." At the 1950 session, several United Nations flags were presented in lieu of plaques or certificates to individuals receiving recognition for service.

World leaders had long thought of the food supply in global terms. President Roosevelt had anticipated war-related problems with international food supply in 1943 and had organized a conference of nations to discuss the problem. Unfortunately, he did not involve farm groups or the well-established International Institute of Agriculture at Rome. Farm leaders felt snubbed and when a second conference was set up at Quebec in 1945, independent farm group officials, including Goss, were invited as advisers. Goss insisted the work of the institute be considered and an outcome of the Quebec conference was consolidation of the institute with the newly-formed Food and Agriculture Organization (FAO) of the United Nations. Sir John Orr of Scotland, director of the FAO, was a featured speaker at the 1947 session of the National Grange.

One of the early initiatives of the U.N. was the United Nations Relief and Rehabilitation Administration headed by former New York Governor Herbert Lehman. Shortly after the war, Lehman and others were warning about impending famine in Europe and Lehman's efforts were instrumental in obtaining relief foodstuffs for a young organization with which the Grange would later become integrally involved, CARE. The war had greatly curtailed means of production for Europe's industry and agriculture, provoking widespread suffering. Goss later lamented that even after two years following the fighting, a large part of Europe was still stagnating and that "the people have less to eat and less to wear than at war's end."

On June 5, 1947, Secretary of State George Marshall outlined a plan, ultimately known by his name, which would involve the U.S. government in rehabilitating Europe. Goss viewed the Marshall Plan as a "badly needed ray of hope" for the suffering, unemployed masses of Europe. They needed economic recovery in order to again become self-sufficient. Perhaps as important to Goss was the postwar battle being waged for European's minds. "Propaganda and infiltration" were being used by our former ally, the USSR, "with the apparent intent of seeking dictatorial control of all Europe and Asia." Rebuilding of Europe under the Marshall Plan would help curb the growth of communism, Goss felt.

Goss had some words of instruction, however, which he felt would ensure maximum use of American dollars. He labeled the Marshall Plan as "basically a self-help plan" which was "exactly what Europe needs.... Congress should see that no Marshall plan is accepted unless it is based on good honest self-help." He expressed the most concern about shorter European work weeks and said there was "no justice in the American people working from 40 to 70 hours a week to create the wealth to feed and clothe a people who refuse to work over 30 or 35 hours a week." He stopped short of insisting that Europeans be forced to change their labor laws, however. "To insist on such governmental changes would be to interfere in the political affairs of a foreign nation—the very thing which caused the war." By 1949 Goss was writing in *The National Grange Monthly* that many European nations had, because of the Marshall Plan, achieved record gains in production and many of them were manufacturing more than they had prior to the war.

The threat of communism was a very real one for Goss and most other Americans in the late 1940s. He saw the conflict between communism and democratic capitalism as "a war of gross materialism as opposed to ideals based on a spiritual foundation," the "idea of the supremacy of the state" as opposed to "the supremacy of the individual." Democracy, Goss said, "can live only when founded on equality, justice, mutual trust and good will. When these fail, government by compulsion must follow." Europe's solution rested ultimately not in economic restructuring and rebuilding of farms and industries, but in "a spiritual renaissance" which would move the people beyond materialism.

Inflation worries farmers worldwide

Material gain, however, was an essential part of the capitalist formula and, for America's farmers, international trade was seen as crucial for holding onto slight economic gains made during the war years. Goss was convinced that the Grange had an important role to play for farmers in the international arena and that conviction drew him to participate in the first meeting of the International Federation of Agricultural Producers (IFAP) held in London in May 1946. The IFAP was an outgrowth of discussions held the previous year at the Quebec conference and the commitment Goss displayed to its mission was recognized when the other participants elected him to the group's executive committee. At the second annual IFAP conference in Holland, Goss was elated that many of his proposals were incorporated into the group's charter. That year the president of the IFAP, James Turner of London and an international seventh degree member of Potomac Grange, would be a featured speaker at the National Grange session in Columbus, Ohio. Grange participation in the IFAP would be vigorous for many years.

Commercial farmers around the world, but particularly those in the Grange, were becoming increasingly alarmed about the problems of inflation. Goss, of course, was eminently qualified to speak about finance and economic questions because of his extensive background in the field of farm credit. His predecessor, Louis J. Taber, had also secured a good banking and finance background and it was he who warned Grange delegates in 1941 that "Wild inflation means economic disaster. Inflation endangers all forms of wealth, every bank deposit and all the established accumulations of generations...." Herschel Newsom's agriculture committee was especially busy that session and the group turned out a six-point plan for controlling inflation. Among their recommendations were increased savings on the part of individuals, increased income taxes "coupled with efficient and economical administration of government," maximum production of consumer goods, restricting credit to "productive purposes and sound investments," and voluntary reduction in prices. The nation continued to suffer from inflationary forces, however, and price controls became necessary.

Following the war, Goss continued to educate about the

problems of inflation. He urged, in 1946, a gradual easing of ceiling prices so supply and demand could again dictate farm prices. The following year he complained about labor's attempts to increase wages and in 1949 the largest portion of his massive master's address concerned economic problems. He cautioned that "America is fast approaching a surplus problem similar to that which led to the collapse of 1929-32."

To further illustrate his economic approach, Goss condensed Grange principles into three "Grange Guide Posts" which he said would "help guide labor, management and agriculture" as they consider complex economic problems:

1. All prosperity springs from the production of wealth.
2. The compensation of each should be based on what he contributes to the general welfare.
3. The prime purpose of government is to protect its citizens from aggression both physical and economic.

The three guideposts Goss advanced are reminiscent of those advocated by Saunders 76 years before in his Preamble to the National Grange Constitution. Saunders stated that "Individual happiness depends upon general prosperity," an assumption to which frontier American farmers eagerly subscribed. National prosperity, Saunders continued, "is in proportion to the value of its production." Unlike Goss, however, Saunders went on to say that agriculture was the source of all wealth. In the Goss interpretation, voiced at a time when agriculture was definitely recognizing its minority status in America, national prosperity depended upon teamwork between a variety of affected groups. Labor, industry, transportation, finance, agriculture and government must pull together to make democratic capitalism function properly. Negotiation and compromise as well as a strict adherence to the three guideposts would be necessary for prosperity to continue following the war.

Although it was depressing to most Grange people, the governmental stop-gap measures of the war years continued in place following the declaration of peace and little agreement between farm groups was forthcoming. Surpluses were mounting again and the fear was that the delicate balance between supply and demand for agricultural products would be lost as it had been in the manufacturing sector.

An example of the frustration developing as a result of ineffective farm programs was the so-called "potato scandal." Potato production was excessive in 1946 causing the Commodity Credit Corporation to buy 108 million bushels to support the price. The following year acreage was cut back drastically but farmers simply planted rows closer together and implemented other farming practices which produced another bumper crop. Further acreage cutbacks were made in 1948 without noticeable effect on the surplus problem, and the CCC had to buy 139 million bushels. Potatoes were given to school lunch programs, burned, dyed to keep them off the market and used as fertilizer. Between 1946 and 1949 about $350 million had been spent on potatoes and the problem remained. Congress and the farm organizations felt pressured to come up with some better solutions because public opinion was anything but positive. Solutions tended to evade the farm leaders and policy makers alike.

In 1945 Secretary of Agriculture Claude R. Wickard moved to the top post in the Rural Electrification Administration at the request of President Truman and was replaced with another seventh degree Grange member, Clinton P. Anderson. Wickard's deputy administrator at the REA was William J. Neal, former master of the New Hampshire State Grange (1938-43). Another Grange member, Charles F. Brannan, replaced Anderson in 1948, and it was his proposal to Congress the next year which created more controversy in farm circles nationwide than anything since the McNary-Haugen debates of the 1920s.

The basic provision of the "Brannan Plan" was support prices for basic commodities at 90 to 100 percent of parity but the support was limited to the first $25,700 worth of products per farm. The idea was that small family farms would benefit most from this approach. Brannan also proposed the supports be extended to perishable commodities but there would be no production controls imposed on these crops. With perishable commodities, farmers would be paid by the government for the difference between the market price they received for their production and the support price. Brannan felt this overall approach would mean good prices for farmers while consumers could continue to enjoy low food prices.

Brannan's proposal was immediately endorsed by the Farmers Union, the group for which he served many years as general legal counsel after his departure from the Department of Agriculture. Labor and some urban groups also supported the plan but most criticism was negative. He attended the 1949 National Grange session in Sacramento, speaking to 3,000 members on the food needs of people around the world and the unsatisfactory situation of agricultural surpluses existing in the U.S. A blueprint needed to be drawn to move this excess food to those who desperately needed it, he said. Delegates six days later, however, conceded that while Brannan's plan contained some objectives which were sensible, the "proposed means of reaching these objectives are unsound." The guideposts advanced by Goss were worked into the Grange's anti-support statement when the delegates said farmers needed to be compensated in accordance to their "contribution to the general welfare." Producers should receive a "fair price" in the marketplace and not come to depend upon any form of subsidy. Subsidies would create a "tax liability which would raise all costs of production thereby lowering purchasing power and ultimately leading to a lower standard of living for the rank and file of consumers," the resolution continued. Subsidies also would "place farmers at the mercy of congressional appropriations for their income." The lengthy resolution was moot, however, since the Brannan Plan had been squashed by Congress shortly before the national session.

Goss had already testified in Congress in opposition to the subsidy part of Brannan's plan, stating the Grange "did not believe that the government should furnish food to the public below cost as a means of holding down living costs and the general price level." He also proposed a bi-partisan or non-partisan marketing commission or advisory board composed of representatives of producers, processors and distributors. This group, appointed by the president, would monitor supplies of commodities and make recommendations regarding commodities to push in the marketplace and those to withhold. Such advice, Goss felt, would enable the market to function at optimum levels without interference.

The heart of the Brannan Plan, though, was to aid the struggling mid-size family farm operation. The Grange had situated itself as a representative of that constituency, a role which was being challenged by the more liberal Farmers Union. The Farm Bureau tended to represent the larger, more prosperous commercial farmers. Brannan was aware that the smaller commercial farms were being squeezed more and more but he had the unfortunate experience of devising a proposal which met with little acceptance.

Leaders within the Grange were showing alarm about some trends which contributed to the squeeze family farmers were experiencing. Initial inroads into agriculture were being made by corporations and wealthy investors who were using farming to offset tax liability on other business operations. This practice prompted the Grange policy which held that "losses on agricultural operations should be deductible only from income derived from agricultural operations" rather than being deferred to other business activities. Likewise, the move to larger farm units was creating tension with the 160-acre limitation contained in the 1902 Reclamation Act. Forsaking the limitation "would open the door for tremendous corporation and commercial farms," Goss warned, "and in many instances might result in the control of vast reclamation areas, and make it hard for the family sized farm."

Goss also strongly believed that conservation made better farmers while it protected the land. The right of land ownership, he said, "should not carry with it the right to destroy the land which future generations will need to produce food." Destructive farming practices had to be altered but, he added, newer techniques often involved "action beyond the capacity of an individual land owner to carry out." Local initiatives would be best but Goss conceded the extent of the erosion problem meant that "Federal aid is frequently justified." He expressed little concern about complaints about duplication of services between the Soil Conservation Service (SCS) of the USDA and the Extension Service. Goss opposed transferring the SCS to Extension and felt the duplication would be resolved when SCS had more time to finalize its programs.

Another looming threat to family farmers was an insidious attack on their farm cooperatives. "Reactionary forces are trying to destroy cooperatives," Goss warned, and the Intermediate Credit Bank which made loans to cooperatives had its appropriations "drastically cut." Goss pointed out that the cooperatives were self-supporting, but financing was obtained from government capital. When the Federal Land Bank System underwent a similar attack in 1940 the Grange fought to keep it an independent cooperative system free of government control. "I believe that the time has come when borrowers from the Production Credit System and the Banks for Cooperatives should begin a more effective program of retiring Government investments," Goss advised, so they could also enjoy greater freedom. In the days of the Cold War, some Americans thought of cooperatives as un-American business structures and the "reactionaries" singled out by Goss would spend several years campaigning against co-ops. Although Grange members were not called unpatriotic for their support of co-ops as they had been in the 1870s by Southern Pacific boss Collis P. Huntington when he said "Grangers are a pack of communists," there were many subtle pressures which caused discomfort for co-op leaders.

The Grange had positioned itself as an integral part of the Farm Bloc which the *New York Times* would describe in 1951 as "the single greatest force on Capitol Hill." But the organization, unlike the Farmers Union and the Farm Bureau, was much more than a special interest lobbying effort or insurance benefit provisioner. In 1947 Albert Goss ushered in the best example of that extra level of activity, making the Grange a true leader in local rural American affairs. It was then that he unveiled the community service contest—underwritten by the Sears Roebuck Foundation—the competion that was dubbed in 1957 as "The Contest Everyone Wins." The Grange-Sears marriage would produce the most visible expression of fraternal goodwill the Grange had ever known.

Grange, Sears join to promote service

Some state Granges had already formalized community service projects as an approved subordinate activity. Those states reported "Grange membership, Grange interest and prestige have been advanced" as a result of organized volunteer efforts to "improve community conditions" and projects to "make undesirable places attractive." The national home economics committee took credit for initiating the concept two years previous to the Sears program, but the new contest format would involve all members, not just Grange women.

On the eve of adopting the offer from the Sears Roebuck Foundation, the *National Grange Monthly* had reported a typical example of Grange fraternalism and service. In the September 1947 issue readers learned about John Knoebel, a farmer and member of Shiloh Valley Grange in St. Clair County, Illinois. Knoebel had been quarantined for diphtheria and his 42 acres of wheat needed to be harvested, 12 acres of soybeans were yet to be drilled and 70 acres of corn demanded cultivation. Unknown to him, fellow members had discussed his predicament at their Grange meeting and a few days later 35 of them showed up with their farm equipment, making quick work of Knoebel's chores. That same day another Shiloh Valley Grange member was killed in an auto accident and the same crew moved over to his farm the next morning to harvest his wheat and oats for the family. Grange women provided hot lunches for the workers and families of those being assisted. This type of activity was typical of the spirit of helpfulness seen within the organization since the 1870s. The community service program attempted to formalize that attitude, encourage an expansion of service projects and, in the process, increase the participation of members.

Linking up with a prosperous foundation allowed the contest to start off with impressive prizes. The entire nation listened on NBC radio when E.J. Condon, president of the Sears Roebuck Foundation, announced the winners of the first awards. The 64 members of Schley Grange, North Carolina, would enjoy a new, fully outfitted Grange hall for taking first place. Green Valley Grange, New York, was given $1,500 worth of Grange hall equipment for placing second and $1,000 in Grange equipment went to Indian Trail

Judges for the National Grange-Sears Roebuck Foundation Community Service Contest personally visited the top 10 subordinate Granges each year as part of the judging process. The marathon visitation schedule, taking the team to all corners of the nation, was made possible by the Sears airplane. Below, judges compare impressions on a flight between two of the contestants.

Albert S. Goss believed in the importance of youth to the Grange and to the nation. He promoted youth activities within the Grange and supported other youth initiatives such as scouting and 4-H. Above, Goss, seated in the center, confers with national FFA officers and advisers at National Grange headquarters. Herschel Newsom, successor to Goss as national master, is standing at the far right.

Grange, Indiana. Condon noted that approximately 1,400 Granges scattered throughout 37 states had taken part in the contest.

Guidelines for participation in the contest stipulated that projects be planned and carried out to the benefit of the entire community. Different types of goals would include those which "increase employment and income" such as the "expansion and development of rural industries and more productive agriculture." Other projects would "aid in serving your young people with better schools, health, sanitation, communication, protection, and recreation, and old age comforts." Some Granges worked to "improve the living environment, appearance, and culture" of their communities or initiated efforts which focused on youth development or assisting the disadvantaged. Interest continued to grow and the top prize of a new hall was replaced with a $10,000 cash award. In the Grange's 1967 centennial year the contest booklet noted that in one year it was calculated the contest had generated volunteer involvement by 275,000 members who contributed four million man-hours of labor—"enough, if concentrated, to build an entire city of 2,000 homes." One national judge said the program had been called "the rural counterpart of the urban rehabilitation movement."

Granges participating in the contest were required to submit lengthy reports of their successful projects for judging on the state level. Winning entries advanced to national judging where the top 10 were selected for further examination. A panel of judges was selected each year, always with representation from the state Granges. Other judges came from national food companies such as Pillsbury or Quaker Oats and other companies; the media and agriculture-related firms were also represented. These judges would board the Sears airplane and personally visit the "top ten" finalists, viewing first-hand their accomplishments. They were always greeted by excited crowds of Grange members, feted to a traditional Grange program and potluck dinner and escorted to the site of their labor. Judges saw complete telephone systems which had been installed by Granges, they entered recreational pavilions and parks put in place by Grange labor and funds, and they heard about countless projects to advance rural health, safety, education, employment, and the general quality of living conditions. The Sears Roebuck Foundation would continue to demonstrate its faith in this rural self-help effort by financially backing the Grange community service contest for 20 years.

The traveling community service judges, who took at least 10 days to make the rounds to Granges across the nation, gave insightful reports of their experiences. Kenneth Kendrick, a wheat farmer from Stratford, Texas, reported on several heart-warming encounters in Granges when he was a judge in 1956. He told of one lady who informed the judges about her Grange's home improvement project. Her committee pointed out to area residents that Grangers would be willing to assist families with planning and much of the work, but most of the labor could be done easily by family members. The Grange people eventually got one family to participate and, before long, "a neighbor noticed what was being done and decided they would like to have the Grange committee help with their plans." Kendrick said that at this point of the lady's report one of his fellow judges asked if the committee found that "after two or three homes had been improved" it "became easier to get cooperation of the neighbors." The woman turned to the judge and said, "Mister, it was just as catching as the itch!"

The idea of community service and its benefits did catch on and Grange members everywhere began to agree with Kendrick when he said it made him glad he was a member, "proud indeed to be associated with this great farm organization." The contest was a dramatic plan for encouraging rural improvement and during the life of the program the benefits to the nation have totaled hundreds of millions of dollars.

The flurry of legislative activity, addition of member benefits like Blue Cross and expanded Grange insurance programs, wartime activities and the community service contest all combined to create an atmosphere of phenomenal growth for the Grange in most parts of the country during the Goss years. The strong leadership ability of Albert S. Goss was recognized internationally as one of the National Grange's greatest assets. Other organizational activities also contributed to the swelling of interest in the organization.

Women retain vital role

The national home economics committee was an established, hard-working segment of the Grange throughout the nation following their victories with woman suffrage and prohibition. As a group they were also proud that, largely due to their efforts, the field of home economics had been finally recognized as subject matter fit to be listed on the curricula of high schools and in the catalogs of colleges and universities. They had discovered contests as a means to promote excellence in sewing and they were beginning to secure corporate sponsorship for prizes.

However, Ora L. Dykes, chairman of the National Grange home economics committee, admonished female members in 1949 to recognize that "Home Economics in the Grange is the science of better living and includes more than the necessities of life—food, clothing and shelter. It has to do with all phases of our home life, including our family relationships and our social, educational and moral responsibilities to society." Women could derive benefits from participation because through committee projects they would

The New England Grange Building at the Eastern States Exposition Grounds, West Springfield, Massachusetts, was built in 1938 and is still in use. In the top photo, taken in 1954, Eleanor Follensbee, junior achievement queen of the Connecticut State Grange, trims shrubbery. The bottom photo shows part of the 3,000 voice Grange chorus assembled at the exposition in 1941. The chorus director was Homer Rodeheaver (inset) who gained fame as song leader for evangelist Billy Sunday. The musical event was broadcast nationwide by CBS radio.

NEW ENGLAND GRANGE BUILDI

CBS
24

be prepared "to meet any emergency and to perpetuate those activities and services which contribute to community welfare, help to yield a more serviceable and worthwhile Grange and expand the higher values of rural life."

Grange women were still the driving force of the juvenile Granges. There had been steady increase in interest in the juvenile programs but, as noted by National Juvenile Superintendent Alice L. Pearson in 1949, only 1,690 of the nation's 7,094 active subordinate Granges were at that time sponsoring a unit for children. Pearson cited many benefits of juvenile work, paramount of which was the pool of young members who could "graduate" from the juvenile Grange into regular subordinate membership. The young members also were involved with community service on their own level, raising money for the Salvation Army, Red Cross, crippled children, and the polio drive.

One of the outstanding projects of the juvenile Granges named by Pearson in her report was the Taber Memorial Forest in Ohio, home state of the former national master. After Louis Taber left his National Grange post, National Juvenile Superintendent Margaret H. Caldwell developed the idea of a national project to stimulate interest of children across the nation. She discovered that, as a farmer and as director of agriculture for the state of Ohio, Taber had a strong interest in forest conservation. Arrangements were made with the U.S. Forest Service to set aside a portion of the Wayne National Forest in southeastern Ohio for juvenile Granges to replant. The 200-acre plot was the focus of Grange children for many years as they raised money to pay for baby trees in their Louis J. Taber Memorial Forest. The forest was dedicated in 1947 by National Grange convention delegates who traveled from Columbus, Ohio, to the site. A plaque was unveiled and remarks were made by Taber, Forest Service officials and Albert S. Goss. By 1957 the young Grange members had raised funds to replant 370 acres.

Goss had been responsible for placing the Grange organization in the national eye and public leaders were responding by getting involved themselves. President Harry Truman became a charter member of Heart of America Grange in Kansas City, Missouri, in 1945 and State Master and Vermont Governor Harold J. Arthur held both jobs simultaneously for several years. Past North Carolina State Master W. Kerr Scott was elected governor of his state in 1949. In 1948 Oregon's Governor Snell called the Grange

"America's great stabilizing influence."

The Grange organization was about to lose its most stabilizing internal influence, however. On October 25, 1950, Albert S. Goss addressed a large crowd at the New York Herald Tribune Forum, and returned to his room at the Waldorf-Astoria Hotel. Moments later he was dead. He had most recently been appointed to serve on the Agriculture Research Policy Committee and to the National Security Resources Board. Besides his Grange duties, he had risen to the post of third vice president of the IFAP, was a trustee of the American Institute of Cooperation, a director of the Farmers Insurance Exchange of Los Angeles (now called Farmers Insurance), a director for Rural Scouting for the Boy Scouts of America and was a director of the National Highway Users' Conference. The *National Grange Monthly* noted, "The late National Master was tireless in his devotion to Grange duties, frequently jumping from one section of the country to another to fill speaking engagements with complete disregard for his health."

Speaking before the National Grange assembled less than three weeks after the sudden death, Past Master Taber said Goss had given "a full measure of devotion" to the Grange, agriculture and the nation. "He walked with presidents," Taber added. "He was the counselor of administrators; he was consulted by the wisest and most influential and the best in the land, and yet the humblest Patron found in him a defender and a friend."

Tributes to Goss flooded in from around the world. "I thought very highly of Albert Goss," wrote President Truman. "He was a fine man and a fine citizen. He was always interested in the welfare of the farmers of our country, and he devoted his life to it." Secretary of Agriculture Brannan said Goss "built many close friendships, including one which I valued personally." Calling Goss one of American agriculture's "great statesmen," John H. Davis, executive secretary of the National Council of Farmer Cooperatives, predicted that the nation's "farmer cooperatives and progressive rural institutions in general will miss his unwavering support and guidance." And the editor of *Country Gentleman* said the Goss name "stood for honesty and integrity."

Goss had presided over the National Grange as it experienced its most substantial growth since the great enrollment of membership in the early 1870s. He engineered its legislative message in such a way that the organization was respected by all and effective in most causes it undertook. He helped open the doors of its first national headquarters building and for nearly nine years he crisscrossed the nation and journeyed around the world telling all who would listen about the farm fraternity he loved.

The passing of Albert S. Goss was more than the loss of a great Grange leader. His portrait would eventually hang in a place of honor in the National Grange building and in Grange halls around the country. But in the minds of thousands of Grange members would be memories of the man alongside memories of the energetic, prosperous and influential Grange he led. Challenges immediately ahead would tend to make many Grange members remember even more fondly and more often the days of Goss. The world at large was entering another era, an era when agriculture and the Grange would soon find themselves radically transformed from what had been before.

11

Equality for Rural Americans

1950-1968

THE NATIONAL GRANGE IN 1950 again found itself at a crossroads of leadership at the same time the United States was again preoccupied with war. Albert S. Goss had become master on the eve of World War II, and now his untimely death just four months after President Truman sent American troops to South Korea meant another transition at a difficult time.

Goss was the second national master to die in office. Following the death of Putnam Darden in July 1888, National Overseer James Draper was named master until the session in November. At a special executive committee meeting October 26, 1950, at headquarters in Washington, D.C., Past Master Louis J. Taber followed that pattern by installing Overseer Henry D. Sherwood to serve as master until an election could be held the following month at the session in Minneapolis, Minnesota. Sherwood had been national overseer since 1945 and had been serving as master of the New York State Grange since 1944.

Sherwood was fortunate in that Goss had completed his massive master's address before his death. At the commencement of the session in the Minneapolis Radisson Hotel, Sherwood read the speech which began with a tribute to Minnesotans O.H. Kelley, his wife Temperance and her niece Caroline Hall who "carried on the discouraging pioneering work" of the Grange. Goss wrote on that "In those early days Minnesota was a land of pioneers, and it was the independence and pioneering spirit of its citizens, and those who joined with them, which gave to the Grange the progressiveness and initiative which have characterized its leadership in national and civic affairs for three generations."

Goss had one year remaining in his two-year term so whoever was elected in Minneapolis would need to face another ballot in 1951. The victor was Herschel D. Newsom, master of the Indiana State Grange since 1937 and chair of the National Grange executive committee since 1948. A farmer with a bachelor's degree in chemistry from Indiana University, Newsom would lead the National Grange through 18 of its most difficult years since the adverse days of the late 1870s.

One piece of unfinished business tended to at the Minneapolis session was placement of a bronze memorial tablet honoring Caroline A. Hall at Lakewood Cemetery in Minneapolis. Several of Hall's relatives were present to read the tablet, which said, "Her name is held in grateful remembrance because of her devoted and unselfish labors in association with others in the founding and early development of the Grange." The person who played a predominant role in granting American women their first major equality victory was finally granted a permanent physical

Herschel D. Newsom (1905-1970)

memorial.

The afternoon before, national delegates had visited the Kelley farm near Elk River, just a few miles upstream from Minneapolis, and attended a banquet and program hosted by Minnehaha Grange at Edina. It appeared almost providential that with the unexpected passing of a popular, dynamic leader, Grange people nationwide were afforded the time together at the actual birthplace of their order. In unison they could look back at the legacy of A.S. Goss while standing on the soil tilled by O.H. Kelley.

Present at Minneapolis was Secretary of Agriculture Brannan who paid tribute to A.S. Goss. He went on to stress the importance of the family owned and operated farms which were beginning to disappear at an alarming rate. Such farms, Brannan said, and the rural communities where they were located were an essential bulwark of our democratic system.

Membership growth chosen as Goss memorial

Delegates at the session expressed a strong desire to memorialize Past Master Goss in a way which would go far beyond verbal tributes. They recognized his burning desire was to see the Grange grow in influence both nationally and internationally. They also knew his ambition was to lead the organization when its membership passed the million mark. Since his premature death had made that goal impossible, delegates reasoned that a concerted effort to swell membership past the enchanting million member level would be the most fitting honor they could pay to Goss.

The new member plan was enthusiastically adopted with a deadline set for June 30, 1952, and a Goss Grange membership memorial advisory committee was appointed to ensure success. Each subordinate Grange would have to show only a net increase of 10 members for the goal to be reached. But the plan also called for each Grange insisting on "greater Grange service in ritualism, lecturer's work and community service to the end that these new members become active members in our great fraternity which Albert S. Goss loved, lived and died for in order to build a stronger rural America and a World in which the freedom and dignity of the individual is supreme."

The idea was apparently doomed from the start. In 1951 national membership gains were less than 10 percent of what they had been in 1950 and, beginning in 1952, numbers began a decline which continued uninterrupted for 40 years.

Almost prophetically, Charles M. Gardner had spoken on "Facing Grange Weaknesses" at the 1950 Grange Leaders' Conference held in Boston, Massachusets. Gardner, former longtime editor of the *National Grange Monthly,* author of *The Grange—Friend of the Farmer* (released in 1949), high priest of Demeter from 1913 through 1947 and then high priest emeritus, had a unique perspective which prepared him to speak on this touchy subject. Goss had felt Gardner's observations pertinent enough that he had them reprinted in a special pamphlet just before his death.

Gardner began his address by pointing out that each Grange has two sides: "One expresses its relation to the home community—the service it can render to individual lives and homes and improvements." The other side builds the organization on state and national levels "into the powerful fraternity that throws all its influence in support of the principles that have made America great." Gardner felt many of the members did not understand this broader vision and called it a "weakness of actually serious character." He noted the establishment of national headquarters in Washington had "gone a long way in creating an expanded view of our Order," but many subordinate members did not see the collective Grange organization as one having a mission to fulfill on the national level. It would be said many times in the next few years that lack of communication from the National Grange to each Grange family was a principal cause for this paucity of awareness and commitment. The national publication had always been circulated to those who subscribed and was not universally read by all members.

Small, struggling subordinate Granges also drew Gardner's concern. Many subordinates had few members and were fighting for their existence. Changing demographics made the problem even greater because the rural population base from which new members came was shrinking, as Brannan had warned. Grange leaders were encouraged by Gardner to attend meetings of these struggling units, even if they were "unenthusiastic" or "uninteresting," because those Granges needed to catch the vision that they were "a vital part" of the bigger picture. "Whenever new courage can be put into a faltering subordinate, actual strength is added to the entire Grange structure."

The "danger of mechanization" cited by Gardner has been repeated ever since. He told how the home-spun lecture hour had been used for generations to promote "free and full discussion of timely issues" with the goal of promoting "enlightenment and understanding." Now, newer mechanical means of entertainment—"the juke box, the radio, and now television"—were diminishing the desire of members to promote activities which helped them "learn by doing." This was a dangerous trend, Gardner felt. Local Granges which emphasized only the social and entertainment features of the organization were also missing the opportunity to attract the many commercial farmers who were not being enlisted into membership. A change in tone was suggested; the Grange should be promoted as an opportunity for farmers and others to make an actual contribution to their communities. Youth, too, should have a role within the organization, Gardner emphasized, and be made to feel "they are as definitely responsible for Grange success as their elders."

Grange youth given arena for involvement

Goss also had seen the wisdom of enlisting the involvement of young people in the Grange. Juvenile Granges occupied small children through early teenage years but high school students and young adults needed other avenues for expression, he felt. A special juvenile Grange "graduation" ceremony had been implemented in 1930 to make passage into full subordinate membership significant for these young people. But there was a need for more in the changing society of the postwar years. A "Young Peoples' Committee" had been mentioned in 1934 but it wasn't until the 1943 Grand Rapids, Michigan, session that an intersession youth committee appeared. A youth advisory committee was later added so young members could have input into planned youth activities. With the placement of Wib Justi as a staff person responsible for youth activities in 1949, the structure was in place to expand these services.

Justi and the committee went to work and one of the first visible accomplishments was the rural teenager exchange project started in 1950 in cooperation with the U.S. State Department. During the next five years, about 500 German and Austrian teenagers would stay in Grange homes, learning about America from rural American families. Justi noted in his 1952 report that some newspapers and magazines had begun calling the organization the

"International Grange" because of widespread interest in the youth exchange program. The exchange program arranged for a total of 375 young people to live in America for one year and the young farmer project saw 131 people from eight countries living on Grange farms from six to 12 months each. This international exchange terminated in 1960 along with the young farmer project due to funding problems.

An interstate exchange was implemented a couple of years after the international exchange started, allowing Grange young people to visit with Grange families in other regions of the country.

All told, the Grange arranged for over 1,700 people from 39 countries to spend time with American Grange hosts. In 1954 a youth public speaking contest was implemented, a competition which has proven popular for nearly 40 years. Another competition, the young couple of the year contest, started in 1956 under the sponsorship of the Sears Roebuck Foundation. A host of other projects including a network of youth committees on the subordinate, Pomona and state levels, were promoted with the objective of developing "a fine type of leadership and experience, with excellent moral and spiritual character."

Young people from Europe were not the only ones traveling to Grange homes in 1950. North Carolina Grange members hosted 13 German farm leaders for one week at the request of the U.S. Department of Agriculture with one of those returning for an additional month later in the year. During 1950 a total of approximately 200 farm workers and teenage students were placed in Grange homes.

The 1951 Atlantic City, New Jersey, session was the first to hear Newsom report as national master. He spoke in a lofty tone, reminding Grange people about their noble heritage. "The Grange was born in 1867," he said, "because of a tremendous need for the kind of an institution that would promote understanding and encourage cooperation and teamwork, and develop a feeling of unity rather than dissension, strife and chaos. Its early successes attested the need of just such an institution." Newsom saw greater achievements ahead for the organization he led. "The Grange has a vital role to play in the current and future history of America," he instructed. "To the extent that the Grange meets that challenge, America will be enriched."

Unknown to Newsom at that point, Goss had led the Grange to its second high water mark of participation. There was still much to be accomplished but those gains would be made with fewer resources. Ironically, this second membership decline would be more the result of external conditions than of actions or failures on the part of the organization.

American farmers dwindle into minority status

General Dwight D. Eisenhower was inaugurated president January 20, 1953, at the very end of what Gilbert Fite calls "the longest period of sustained prosperity in American agricultural history" (1940-1952). A combination of economic conditions and government actions would create intolerable conditions for marginal and near-marginal farmers, causing many of them to be forced out of business. At the end of the decade, there would be 1,677,934 fewer farmers than in 1950 with the result that farming would become even more concentrated in the hands of fewer operators.

The poorest of the farmers created a difficult situation for agriculture and government. As it had been seen since the 1930s, government programs designed for commercial farmers held no hope for these small operations, and the Farmers Home Administration, structured to help tenants become landowners, would require two centuries of work at its current level of activity in order to solve the problem. Clearly, according to most contemporary agricultural economists, there were too many farmers, and many of them should be encouraged to leave the business. President Eisenhower's Secretary of Agriculture, Ezra Taft Benson, agreed, and at the 1953 National Grange convention in Burlington, Vermont, he alluded to his philosophy of diminished government involvement by stressing "self-help" programs for farmers. And in 1954 Newsom joined in by admitting that since "roughly 90 percent of the nation's food and fiber is produced by about 50 percent of the farm families, it seems clearly obvious that it will never be possible to completely and adequately meet this particular problem of these low income families *within the business of agriculture*" (emphasis added). The general public, however, was reluctant to endorse farm programs which would have the appearance of forcing low income farmers out of their livelihood even though the government goal of acreage restriction to reduce output and keep prices fair had that effect anyway.

The American institution known as the family farm was becoming a less recognizable part of our national landscape. In its place Americans were seeing more of what former Assistant Secretary of Agriculture John H. Davis in 1955 called "agribusiness." This term described, Davis said, "the sum total of all operations involved in the production and distribution of food and fiber."

A potent example of industrial agriculture replacing "folksy" family farms was "vertical integration," or the control of all production, processing and marketing of a particular agricultural product. One of the best examples of vertical integration was the control being gained in the poultry industry by the feed companies during the 1950s. Those companies would contract with farmers, particularly in the South, and all the farmer would supply was the land, labor, equipment and broiler houses. The feed company furnished everything else and promised to buy the production at a specified price. By 1963 such growers controlled 75 percent of the broiler industry, with 20 percent accounted for by company-owned operations. Poultry raising was no longer an option for general farmers. In 1967 Newsom would touch on this issue by cautioning, "Within this modern America of ours...we must understand that 'of 31,000 companies processing food, the 100 largest of these own 60 percent of the assets and earn 70 percent of the profits' as William F. Mueller, Director of the Bureau of Economics of the Federal Trade Commission, pointed out...."

The Grange reacted to this alarming trend by restating its dedication to the family farm. In 1956 delegates asserted that "room must be preserved in American agriculture for families to engage in gainful work as their own masters, on economic-sized units of land, and...be able to make a decent living justly comparable with that of any other part of our society." Nearly everyone else agreed because, in the American mind, the family farm represented much more than a unit of agricultural production. Family farms also were homes, the homes of good, hard-working, honest people—the backbone of America. The Grange felt that in the atomic age it was even more important to support its policies because they reflected "balance and stability, traditional with rural people."

But the scene was changing faster than most people recognized. "The gap between image and reality, the difference between what many people thought conditions should be in rural America and what really existed, was ever widening," Gilbert Fite wrote. "Technology, science, and modern management, assisted by government policies, were rapidly creating a new agriculture. Farming could not escape the same trends that were affecting nearly all aspects of the economy. The modern farmer, larger and more efficient, viewed farming more as a business than as a way of life. That phase of American life where millions of small farms dotted the countryside was disappearing." And with its disappearance went rural schools and churches, small communities and the businesses which depended upon the farm families. The rural Granges did not escape the transformation, either.

At the heart of Newsom's approach to the changes that were only then becoming evident was public relations. In his first master's address he talked about the necessity to educate the masses of Americans about the needs of agriculture. Decisions of government were "certain to be responsive to that public opinion," he confidently told the Grange audience, and if the Grange did not do its best to tell the story, then "we fail in our civil duty. To thus fail is to invite erroneous, unworkable and unjust decisions."

One example of the Grange's effort to improve communications nationwide about the needs of agriculture materialized in the mid-1950s. After 18 months of study, the National Grange released a comprehensive report in early 1955 called "Barriers to Increased Consumption of Fluid Milk." The lengthy account, printed in book form, detailed problems being faced by the dairy industry and advanced some potential solutions. A Grange representative presented findings of the study to the dairy subcommittee of the House Committee on Agriculture and copies of the book were distributed nationally.

Communications seen as key to boosting Grange

On an organizational level, Newsom looked to public relations and communications as the keys to solving internal problems which were, in the years following Gardner's speech, becoming increasingly evident. In 1953 Newsom lamented the many active Grange members who had no conception of state or National Grange programs. This, he said, was inexcusable in that many outsiders envied the Grange and called the organization "a great medium for molding as well as expressing rural opinion." But the Grange had "missed the boat" in hundreds of subordinates, he added, because it had "failed to use effectively the tremendously important medium of improved communications throughout the whole organizational structure." One answer, he felt, was increasing the readership of the *National Grange Monthly.* Other communication mediums should be employed and the national lecturer must become a full-time in order to adequately meet the needs of subordinate lecturers. The transformation of the national lecturer's job into a full-time responsibility took place in 1956.

Newsom took every opportunity to get the Grange into the public eye in the most impressive way possible. The resulting image enhancement would be beneficial for the organization by building its prestige with both members and nonmembers. During the Newsom years, national session agendas were filled with names of prominent speakers and Newsom himself carried the Grange message even more widely than his predecessor Goss had done. At the 1953 session alone, speakers included American Federation of Labor chief George Meany; Senator George D. Aiken, a Grange member from Vermont; Governor John Lodge of Connecticut, another Grange member; Harold E. Stassen, director of the Foreign Operations Administration and longtime Republican presidential hopeful; Paul C. French, executive director of CARE; and Secretary of Agriculture Benson. Additionally, a portrait of Newsom painted by Vermont Grange member Norman Rockwell was presented to the national master.

Over the years, Newsom was appointed to many special committees and commissions by presidents Truman, Eisenhower and Kennedy. \ He served on the boards of numerous groups for agriculture, transportation, social concern programs, and business interests. At every opportunity, he attempted to make the Grange organization a visible part of American national life.

While changes were transpiring on America's farms, other organizations representing the farmers were shifting gears along with the Grange. General farm organizations still had a powerful presence, but newer groups representing specific commodities began to set up offices in Washington during the 1950s. These commodity groups had the ability to build product-by-product coalitions and mount surprisingly effective lobbying efforts in Congress. Organizations began competing for the allegiance and membership dollars of farmers while governmental decisions were increasingly being made in more bureaucratic, decentralized environments. The old Farm Bloc—the group of senators and congressmen primarily from the farm states in the Midwest and South and the corresponding coalition of farm groups—was beginning to disintegrate. Dr. Lloyd C. Halvorson, economist for the National Grange, admitted this in his 1954 legislative report, noting that rural America's minority status made it imperative that there be "public understanding" of the rural problems and the Grange's legislative solutions.

By the end of the decade, Congressman Harold D. Cooley of North Carolina, chairman of the House Agriculture Committee, expressed the opinion of many of his colleagues when he said, "I would like to believe that the leaders of these four organizations [the Grange, AFBF, Farmers Union and National Council of Farmer Cooperatives] could sit down and agree on a major farm program. I am not optimistic." North Dakota's Senator Milton Young blamed "the stubborn and self-righteous attitude of many farm leaders" for the inability of Congress to act decisively on farm legislation in 1959. (He went on to say one exception was "the National Grange, which is one of the most respected organizations on Capitol Hill. While the Grange has a program of its own, its leaders have shown statesmanship in their willingness to negotiate.") As early as 1954 Newsom had said, "It is a rather pathetic picture that those of us honestly seeking to serve the cause of rural families and agricultural producers in this Nation, should be so divided as we have sometimes found ourselves. If our recipe for reconciliation needs improvement, let us improve it. If there is a better one, let us find it."

Perhaps the congressmen and the general public were unable to see the major differences which divided the general farm organizations on policy issues. The groups did cooperate whenever the issues allowed agreement but, unfortunately, those common issues were less plentiful during the 1950s than they had been in previous years. Close identification of the American Farm Bureau Federation with the Republican Party and of the National Farmers Union with the Democratic Party also added to the disharmony. These groups had not had the benefit of a Bachelder scandal to teach the lesson of non-partisanship. Fundamentally, however, disagreements between the farm groups could be traced to the vast differences which existed between various segments of the declining farm population. For example, policies which helped grain farmers would work against poultry and dairy farmers while policies to promote conservation by planting grass might ultimately encourage increases in cattle herds and depress prices for cattlemen. General farm organizations representing a multifarious base of members found it difficult to arrive at specific policies to benefit all their members.

While Newsom could boast in 1952 that 22 senators and 57 congressmen belonged to the Grange, the influence rural America had in the nation's capital was declining. A large number of those senators and representatives would attend the annual congressional dinner put on by Potomac Grange at National Grange headquarters, but the fact was that each year fewer of these lawmakers were required by their constituents to be heavily involved in farm-related legislation. Farmers were increasingly assuming minority status in America and, at the same time, they were reacting more defensively because agriculture was being seen as the villain responsible for higher food prices. The media made much of the revelation that Commodity Credit Corporation (CCC) holdings had reached $6 billion in agricultural products in 1953 and Newsom termed this a tremendous public relations challenge for farmers. The non-farm public needed to be given a balanced presentation of the facts.

Secretary Benson, who later became a vocal spokesman for the John Birch Society and a top leader in the Mormon Church, has been viewed as a principal contributor to the weakened voice of agriculture in Congress and to the divisions which plagued the farm groups. His belief in the declining role for government in agriculture and the insistence upon lowering price supports and loosening acreage restrictions caused much vocal disagreement and, ultimately, his policies failed the farmers. The result was opening up debate on farm legislation more and more to consumer groups.

Legislative victories remain plentiful

Despite the growing difficulties in forming lobbying coalitions, the Grange under Newsom's guidance continued its aggressive representation in Congress for its rural members. Farm credit had long been a pet project for the Grange and the fraternity had for years enlisted the cooperative efforts of other farm groups. Meeting usually twice each year, the joint farm credit committee often was joined by representatives of the 12 districts of the Farm Credit

Presidents for decades have sought advice from Grange leaders. Above, President Dwight D. Eisenhower discusses farm legislation with Herschel Newsom and members of the National Grange executive committee and staff. From the left are Fred Bailey, National Grange consultant; Lloyd Halvorson, staff economist; Edward F. Holter, national lecturer; Roy Battles, Newsom's executive assistant; L. Roy Hawes and Ray Teagarden, executive committee members; Eisenhower; Harry Caldwell, executive committeeman; Newsom; Henry Carstensen, executive committee chair; and True Morse, under secretary of agriculture.

System. In 1953 Grange Legislative Representative Dr. J.T. Sanders, who had succeeded Fred Bailey in 1945, reported to delegates in Burlington, Vermont, that the newly enacted Farm Credit Act of 1953 fulfilled several of the Grange's longtime dreams. Under the act the Farm Credit Administration became an independent agency of the executive branch of the government, ruled by a 13-member Federal Farm Credit Board. Additional farm credit legislation in 1959 would bring the system to what Newsom called a "state of at least temporary perfection."

Establishment in 1953 of the National Agricultural Advisory Commission represented "another major Grange victory," Sanders said. This type of input to the secretary of agriculture had been championed by A.S. Goss and it was made part of the Republican Party platform in 1952. With the election of Eisenhower an executive order was signed creating the body. But in 1954 Newsom hinted that problems with the new group were surfacing. These advisers had always been viewed by the Grange, he said, as a forum for "reconciling differences in fundamental approach or of emphasis between various general agricultural organizations and between the various commodity groups and associations." Output from the commission would be valuable to the secretary of agriculture in making final decisions on farm matters. Apparently, the commission was operating in a cloud of "secrecy" and "more open discussion" was called for. The commission continued to struggle with its advisory function and, in 1961, President John F. Kennedy appointed Harry Caldwell, master of the North Carolina State Grange, as its chairman.

In 1953 a Grange resolution made a simple request for issuing an Internal Revenue Service pamphlet specifically designed to assist farmers in preparing their income tax returns. When approached by the Grange, IRS spokesmen acknowledged the idea had merit and later involved Grange representatives in the planning process for the new publication. The first guide was made available in 1955 and it has remained as a standard IRS publication since.

The years 1954 through 1956 were especially important to the Grange because of several vital pieces of agricultural legislation. In 1952 the National Grange executive committee voted to join the Cooperative for American Relief Everywhere, commonly known by the acronym CARE. A representative of the National Grange, usually the national master, was given a seat on CARE's board of directors and cooperative projects were developed over many years. This connection enhanced Grange leader understanding of food needs by hungry people around the world, nourishing the humanitarian seed which was planted by Goss when he urged support for the Food and Agriculture Organization in the U.N. and the Marshall Plan. One of the first Grange projects with CARE was a unique canning jar collection effort which resulted in thousands of jars being sent to farm women in Greece and Turkey so they could preserve food for winter months.

Prior to 1954, limited amounts of government-held surplus agricultural commodities were made available for distribution overseas by CARE and other relief groups, but the tremendous surpluses which had accumulated made further action imperative. That year the Agricultural Trade Development and Assistance Act, later abbreviated as PL 480 (Public Law 480), would revolutionize and expand America's food aid program. The law had the support of the Grange and CARE and eventually the food distribution activities promoted by PL 480 and other bills were collectively known as the Food for Peace policy. Years later, agricultural economists would point out that free food distribution and agricultural technical assistance not only boosted nutrition for people in Third World countries, but the resulting improvements would enabled those countries to become major paying customers of U.S. agricultural products. Besides being a humanitarian move, food aid programs were, therefore, international trade development tools. Newsom would note, following passage of the Food for Peace Act of 1966, that food had become "an instrument of the United States foreign policy" and that the nation was "embarking upon a program of utilizing our food production capacity as a positive instrument for peace and freedom," a posture which was definitely juxtaposed to the previous policy Newsom characterized as "surplus disposal." As a devout Quaker, dedicated to peace, Newsom welcomed that shift of thinking. His dedication to food aid earned him seats on the U.S. Food for Peace Council and the American Freedom from Hunger Foundation.

Another piece of legislation in 1954, for which the Grange took sole credit, resulted in increasing federal appropriations for vocational education by $5 million.

When Congress began debating farm legislation in 1956, they were greeted with President Eisenhower's soil bank plan as a potential solution to unacceptable CCC holdings. The plan, which was finally adopted, would pay farmers for taking land out of production. It was hoped this move would reduce production and raise prices. Only basic crops were included—cotton, wheat, tobacco, corn, rice and peanuts—and no other crop could be grown on the retired acreage. The Grange supported the concept of the soil bank program but pointed out the fallacy of thinking this course of action would do anything to help the most pressing problem, "development of expanded markets." Republican Grange member Senator Aiken commented, during Eisenhower's reelection campaign, that the opposite party was making some political points with the farm problems and, especially, with their attacks on

Secretary Benson. However, the senator had to admit that the administration's policies were not working either.

Throughout the remainder of the 1950s surpluses continued to multiply in spite of federal programs. With the mounting surpluses came consumer outrage about the cost of the ineffective farm programs. Farmers everywhere tried to tell their side of the story but the media focused instead upon the "scandal" of commodities being stored at government expense in every conceivable place. Farmers had "been subsidizing the consumer," retorted Minnesota Governor Orville L. Freeman in 1960, soon to be named secretary of agriculture by President Kennedy. Freeman, testifying before a congressional committee, complained that he was "very weary...hearing about how farmers were subsidized."

Grange / Farm Bureau disagree on Extension Service

Another battle which had engaged the Grange for years was resolved by a long-awaited pronouncement by Secretary Benson in 1954. The Smith-Lever Act of 1914 officially established the Extension Service as an outreach effort of the land grant colleges. The Grange had supported this plan for many years prior to its enactment, even though it brought to an end the Grange role, envisioned by Kelley, of providing education to rural families about the latest discoveries in agriculture and home economics. Ironically, the newly emerging county Farm Bureau units assumed that role and they became intimately involved with the new Extension Service. In some states laws were passed that required existence of a Farm Bureau unit in a county before an extension agent could be assigned there. Washington, D.C., extension officials openly stated their preference to disseminate their information through existing Farm Bureau organizations rather than working with other farm organizations or by reaching individual farmers.

Following formation of the American Farm Bureau Federation in 1919 at the call of New York State Federation President Silas L. Strivings (later master of the New York State Grange), it became evident that the organization had goals in addition to its educational pursuits and some Grange leaders raised objections to the marriage of a public agency with a private association. This relationship was not universal, however, but it did exist in about 15 states. In New York, for example, statutes specified the Farm

Bureau as the county extension organization and its officers were empowered to receive government money and appoint the extension personnel. Some bureau funds were used in operation of the extension programs.

Grange disapproval, beginning with congressional hearings in 1920, continued for over 30 years. Delegates in 1937 and 1938 passed strong resolutions attacking "favoritism of the Extension Service to a particular farm organization." In 1947, delegates at the Columbus session called for federal legislation separating extension from the Farm Bureau and Goss expressed the hope that "ways will be found for making a complete divorcement of the Extension Service from private control. The Service should be completely supported by public funds and should be available to all farmers alike." He cautioned that when any branch of our public education was under "private domination," then the public was "flirting with danger."

Goss thought he could negotiate the separation, however, and had engineered the carefully worded resolution himself. At that time, the separation issue was about the only area of shared opinion between the Grange and the Farmers Union. The Brannan Plan was being hotly debated and because of that, Goss felt a friendly alliance with the Farm Bureau was valuable and should not be upset by the Extension Service matter. The resolution threatening congressional action was his ace in the negotiation process. Goss also realized his own membership was split on the issue with his overseer, Henry Sherwood of New York, being one of the chief opponents to the separation policy. Sherwood's state had the largest Grange membership of any state at that time and its members, many of whom belonged to both the Grange and the bureau, felt the strong tie between extension and the Farm Bureau was working well. Negotiation meetings held at National Grange headquarters with Farm Bureau representatives proved fruitless and a bill was finally introduced into Congress. When Goss testified in favor of the bill at a congressional hearing, he was asked by a New York representative if he was speaking without the support of his largest state organization. When Goss admitted that was the case, the strength of his arguments fell apart. The bill never cleared the committee and the death of Goss put a practical end to the debate. In some states Grange and Farmers Union coalitions worked together on the issue with the two organizations publishing a joint 17-page pamphlet entitled *Free Our Extension*

Service in Minnesota.

Shortly after appointment of Ezra Taft Benson as secretary of agriculture, Newsom and other Grange leaders began to notice that Benson was consulting only with Farm Bureau officials regarding agriculture policy issues. Newsom used his position on the Study Committee on Federal Aid to Agriculture of the Commission of Intergovernmental Relations to prompt an investigation into the alliance between the USDA and the Farm Bureau, especially at the Extension Service level. The official response was that there was no favoritism. Newsom wrote to Benson in August 1954 asking him personally to state the department's policy "relative to contributions of private organizations, including the Farm Bureau, to county and state units of the Extension Service." When he received no definite reply, he wrote Benson again in November, prior to the annual National Grange session. He said the Grange had intended to avoid an "out and out slugfest with the Department of Agriculture and the Farm Bureau," but reports detailing discrimination on the part of extension personnel against non-bureau members made action necessary.

On November 24, 1954, Secretary Benson, a former extension agent himself, released a policy statement which put an end to the squabble. His policy, Benson said, stated that "it is not proper for employees of the Department of Agriculture to accept compensation from general or specialized organizations, that their services must be available to all persons requesting assistance or advice, and that the promotion of or the solicitation of membership for any...farm organization to secure the services of the Department's employees are not proper and not...permitted." The policy affected local extension agents as well as all employees of the USDA. While Benson said employees could individually hold membership in farm organizations, they could not act as an organizer for those groups or hold any office.

Grange continues transportation, shipping battles

The early years of the Newsom administration also were characterized by intense activity on legislation not directly farm related. Congressional action in 1954 authorized beginning stages of the St. Lawrence Seaway and Power Project, culminated over 20 years of vigorous Grange lobbying. It had long been felt that opening a navigation channel up the St. Lawrence River to the Great Lakes would enhance shipping options for Midwestern agricultural commodities. Public development of hydroelectric power potential on the river also seemed like a good idea. Halvorson's 1954 report called the move by Congress "a tremendous victory" but he cautioned that the organization would need to watch progress of the project carefully since the initial appropriation was merely start-up funding. Construction continued until the project was opened in 1959.

A new project, the Interstate Highway System, would occupy the Grange even more than the St. Lawrence Seaway. The highway network would grow into the world's largest public works project and, some suggest, become the most significant factor responsible for changing American social patterns since the invention of the automobile. As early as 1954 Newsom was publicly discussing President Eisenhower's proposal to expand the network of highways across the nation. Ostensibly, the president proposed the project as a matter of national defense; large highways were necessary to move troops and military equipment, the former general said. Trying to keep rural needs foremost, however, the Grange transportation committee noted in its 1954 report that of the 3,313,000 miles of roads and streets in the U.S., nearly 72 percent were county and local roads. Acknowledging that great improvements had been made, the committee pointed out, "there are still too many missing links between farms and improved roads, especially during muddy seasons. Our goal must be an all-weather road to every farm worth farming." Their report endorsed an expansion of highway building, nonetheless, because such a program would help the entire economy. "For fifteen years," the report said, "our economy has been geared to production for war. We hope we are now entering a period in which we can concentrate our efforts on production for peace. An expanded highway construction program would help take up any slack in employment resulting in the shift from a wartime to a peacetime economy."

Construction on the 41,000 mile Interstate Highway System began July 1, 1956. That year the Highway Trust Fund was instituted, collecting tax revenue (gas and auto excise taxes) from motorists and using that money to fund the construction on a pay-as-you-go basis. This feature pleased the Grange but Newsom warned that efforts were escalating to divert dedicated highway funds on state and federal levels to non-highway uses. When President Eisenhower proposed raising gasoline taxes to pay for increased costs of the system, Newsom recoiled in 1959 by saying that while the Grange had been an early supporter of the interstate system, farmers paid a disproportionately larger share of those taxes because of their heavy dependence upon fuel. The tax was increased by one cent per gallon for a limited time and Newsom reported that, in spite of the defeat, the Grange had won acceptance in Congress for some other important highway funding measures. The continuing saga of Interstate Highway funding would keep Legislative Representative Fred Bailey, who had returned to the National Grange, busy until his death in 1964 when those duties were taken over by Harry L. Graham.

Other transportation legislation capturing the attention of the Grange was the National Traffic and Motor Vehicle Safety Act of 1966. Grange support for this bill was so noticeable that President Lyndon B. Johnson had Newsom present for the bill signing ceremony. Major provisions of the act were the creation of national safety standards for motor vehicles and conducting of safety research. The Grange now had a unique opportunity, Newsom said, to provide leadership on the state level "to see that the best possible state [safety] programs are established."

Sputnik sparks member interest in education

Renewed Grange efforts for education were stimulated by the Soviet launching of Sputnik in 1957. The entire nation was taken aback by this demonstration of scientific accomplishment and educators everywhere began telling Americans that it was imperative to improve our schools, especially the science and mathematics classrooms. Two years before Sputnik, Newsom had been invited to be a participant at the White House Conference on Education. But with millions of Americans gazing at the night skies to see the Russian satellite flashing overhead with no U.S. competition, National Lecturer Edward Holter responded by calling attention to "an increase in the importance of science." His report stated, "It takes no extraordinary intelligence to calculate that the United States will need to place more and ever-increasing reliance on its scientific manpower and womanpower in the decades ahead. Our survival as a nation will demand it. The preservation of personal freedom and human dignity in the world makes it imperative."

Holter continued by saying it was disappointing that "this country has not been doing an adequate job of fostering and developing the scientific capabilities of its youth," partly because of an "anti-intellectual attitude" common with the American people. "The National Grange should concern itself with this national malady," the report urged, "which has perverted the once-honored American characteristic of exalting individuality and individual attainment, and now threatens to substitute in their place mediocrity and a devotion to mass conformity."

The answer was, Holter said, a renewed emphasis upon education and, perhaps, establishment of a "United States Science Academy" open to men and women, similar to military academies at West Point and Annapolis. Delegates responded to Holter's admonitions by calling for all schools and institutions of higher education to improve their instruction of science. A second recommendation followed up on the suggestion for an Academy of Science, an idea which never became a reality.

The old concerns about "objectionable" publications continued to be brought up from time to time and a new Grange worry was voiced in 1954 about the "secularization" of the educational system, a delayed response to the 1948 U.S. Supreme Court decision regarding the unconstitutionality of teaching religion courses in Champaign, Illinois, schools.

Grange worries about the changing texture of American thought and culture were being expressed concurrently with the spread of widespread fears of communist conspiracies. The undisputed leader of the anti-communist craze was Wisconsin Republican Senator Joseph McCarthy who, in 1950, publicly charged that the U.S. State Department had been infiltrated by communists. Later he led a series of highly publicized hearings in which he and other committee members attempted to identify alleged communist operatives within government, the entertainment industry, labor unions and other causes. In the process, the public became hysterical and lives and careers of those accused were often ruined.

Goss had warned about the dangers of the aggressive communist dictatorship in the USSR and, in 1952, the Grange went on record supporting the communist exposure program of the House Un-American Activities Committee. The resolution said the Grange had "deep conviction" that it was an "outrage against common decency to allow a single communist to draw a salary from the Government which he is pledged to do all in his power to destroy."

In 1956 another resolution supported removal from schools of those engaged in "subversive teaching," teachers "who may be disloyal to American principles, American government, and the American way of life." By 1962 some of the hysteria had calmed down and Newsom attempted to bring reason into the arena by quoting Henry Ford II: "A lot of people call everything we do 'creeping socialism.' They call Social Security that; they call pensions that. I don't really know what creeping socialism is. If the critics will define the term I will tell them whether I think this is creeping socialism. We have to keep up with the times. Every time we do something new, people cry that it is communism or socialism." That was a statement to which old-timers in the Grange could easily relate; their early efforts to establish cooperatives and their insistence upon government regulation of business had also been branded as subversive.

When the Supreme Court made its famous decision in 1963 banning the use of prayer and Bible reading in public schools, Grange members dissented and called for a Constitutional amendment which would permit the practices. There was fear expressed by Grange people that references to God would be erased from the Pledge of Allegiance and from coins. The Supreme Court decision was viewed as "hostility toward religion" and, conversely, the Grange's position was portrayed as an expression of our "democratic way of life."

Grange interest in health issues, which reached a zenith during the Goss administration, continued throughout the Newsom era. The scourge of polio, the disease which had crippled President Franklin D. Roosevelt before the eyes of all Americans, kept everyone in a perpetual state of anxiety. Grange people had been active raising money for research, primarily through the March of Dimes organization (then known as the National Foundation for Infantile Paralysis) founded by FDR. And in 1953, on the eve of the discovery of the Salk vaccine, Colorado women collected funds for a polio respirator to be given to the Colorado Polio Foundation. A meeting conducted in 1955 by the Department of Health, Education and Welfare was held with the purpose of designing a distribution system for the new vaccine. A National Grange representative was invited to attend the session, offering the input that dosages be distributed on the basis of the number of people needing vaccination, not the number of patients each doctor reported, because many rural families had no regular physician.

Internal issues become predominant

Grange interests placed the organization in the mid-stream of public opinion and the national master was doing everything possible to let Americans know the Grange's role. By 1953 it was apparent the organization had some internal problems which were crying for attention, and delegates called for a special study committee of nine individuals—dubbed the "Committee of Nine"—to come up with some answers. The next year, in releasing the report, Newsom exhorted the delegates to build an effective "sales force" to strengthen the organization. The committee reported the National Grange had been operating since 1948 with an average deficit of about $25,000 per year and the organization had borrowed against its Washington, D.C., property to make up the shortfall. In order to maintain the current level of services to a declining base of members, the committee recommended a dues increase, which was approved. Other portions of the report spoke of needs within specific departments of the Grange.

The persistent problem of national communications occupied the Committee of Nine. The *National Grange Monthly* continued to lose money and subscribers, and the committee recommended that a study be done which would explore ways to get the publication into every Grange home. Expanded circulation would hopefully attract more advertising income. The next year delegates were furnished with the study, calling for the publication to be subsidized by affiliated cooperatives and insurance companies. These funds, combined with advertising revenue and some subsidy from the National Grange, would allow issues to go into approximately 425,000 Grange homes beginning in 1956. Delays came, however, and it was in November 1957 that Newsom confidently announced the magazine would be arriving in each Grange family mailbox by the end of the year. Unfortunately, mechanics of compiling the mailing lists and other production problems combined with unanticipated shortfalls of contributions dashed the hopes of 100 percent circulation, creating a large financial burden for the National Grange. By 1961 delegates were asking for alternatives to the expensive magazine and the circulation was back down to about 50,000. In his master's address the next year Newsom announced the publication was dead.

Four years later, in two sentences of his master's address, Newsom revealed that the publication would be back again in early

1967. Ray Taylor, former managing editor of the *Washington World*, was in charge of the plan and the publication, mailed to each home, would be glossy, in full color and thoroughly contemporary in appearance—just in time for the centennial of the National Grange. The magazine's rebirth was short-lived, however, and it was eventually suspended again because of funding problems. In its place came newsletters with limited circulation to officers in subordinate and state Granges. The financial burdens created by the magazine throughout the 1950s and 1960s would dog the organization into the Scott administration.

National headquarters threatened

The publication problem seemed almost trivial compared to government actions aimed at taking over the National Grange building at 744 Jackson Place. In 1950 a building in the same block, directly across Pennsylvania Avenue from the White House, came up for sale and a bill was introduced in Congress which, if passed, would permit the government to buy that parcel and the entire block. Some fancy lobbying by Grange representatives saw the bill trimmed so only the building listed for sale could be bought. The affair was not over, however, and in January 1957 condemnation proceedings were filed against the National Grange building. A deposit of $360,000 was made by the government with the District Court as presumed payment for the property and the government assumed ownership. Value of the property was much greater with Newsom calling the figure "preposterous." The Grange resisted and, after a long period of litigation and negotiation, a property exchange around the corner was arranged. The exchange solution was not reached without tremendous pressure from Grange members across the country. Newsom issued appeals for members to contact their congressmen and the tireless support of Washington's Senator Warren G. Magnuson and Senator Styles Bridges of New Hampshire resolved the dispute to the satisfaction of the National Grange. Another principal player in the drama was Grange legal counsel Joe Parker. The Grange received the office site and the $360,000 for a new building. Plans were drawn and approved, but when the General Services Administration later added a requirement that the building be faced in expensive sandstone, Senator Magnuson—as chair of the Senate Appropriations Committee—

After only a few years in their first headquarters building, a move was made necessary because of government property needs in the neighborhood. This new building, dedicated in 1960 by President Eisenhower, still serves the National Grange.

responded by attaching an additional $700,000 to the federal budget request.

Construction on the new 11-story structure, located at 1616 H. Street N.W., was completed in the spring of 1960. More than 1,500 people attended the ceremonies where President Eisenhower and Secretary of Agriculture Benson dedicated the structure on June 29. A heavy mortgage was necessary, but rental income from nine floors of tenants provided much of what was needed for debt service. In 1967 National Home Economics Chairman Alta Peck led Grange women in a special fundraising project which netted $25,000 for the building fund. Retirement of the debt would take several more years and some serious innovation, however.

Efforts to bolster sagging membership were noticeable in every part of the fraternity. When Newsom became national master, he inherited a delicate problem of Grange-church relationships which had been festering since the early days of the fraternity. Conservative Lutherans who belonged to the Missouri Synod of that church were being discouraged from joining the Grange because, they were told by their clergy, the Grange ritual made the organization appear to be a religious denomination. While Missouri Synod leaders were highly complimentary of the moral teaching and con-

The Speech That Ike Forgot

When the new National Grange building was completed in 1960, leaders were thrilled that President Eisenhower agreed to speak at the dedication ceremony June 29. When the day arrived, everything was ready for the president.

Eisenhower had asked Secretary of Agriculture Ezra Taft Benson to write the dedication speech but, reportedly, the president was not entirely pleased with Benson's efforts. National Master Herschel Newsom was then requested to draft a short address which the president could deliver. Eisenhower was happy with Newsom's creation.

On June 29 the dignitaries gathered at their appointed spots and the ceremonies began. President Eisenhower and Secretary Benson were sitting together, next to National Lecturer William Brake. Just before the president was introduced, Ike reached into his pocket for the copy of the speech drafted by Newsom—the speech he had to give in just a few moments. Brake saw Eisen-

duct of the Grange, the organization's attempts to incorporate some non-denominational religious instruction into its affairs made it unsuitable for Lutherans.

A.S. Goss had entered negotiations with the denomination just prior to his death and the executive committee voted October 27, 1950, that Newsom be empowered to continue the meetings. Newsom, accompanied by C. Jerome Davis, his field assistant and later high priest of Demeter, met at least twice in Chicago with church leaders and Newsom felt that substantial progress was being made which would result in the church's endorsement of Grange membership. Unfortunately, the chair of the church committee died before the matter was resolved and resumption of conferences never occurred. However, Newsom did issue a ruling which he hoped would cover disagreements evangelical Christians would have with the fraternity's ritual. The 1951 official pronouncement, which expressed the Grange's philosophy that nothing in the order should be construed as coming between the member and his or her adopted religious faith, says that "The Ritual of the Grange is dedicated to the dignity of the individual and of rural life. Its high moral tone, its effort to build a 'better and higher manhood and womanhood among ourselves' and to promote participation in and atten-

---

hower fumble in his pocket and then whisper to Benson, "I left the speech at home. What in the hell should I do?" Benson, somewhat ruffled, turned to the president and said, "I don't care what you do, but get up there and dedicate this building for Herschel!" The president carried the situation well, in spite of not having a prepared script to work from, and the National Grange headquarters building was appropriately dedicated.

Another hitch occurred shortly thereafter. Youth Director Wib Justi was the Grange liaison with the U.S. Secret Service that day as well as official building tour coordinator. Members of the National Grange Youth Team served as guides. "One of the two new elevators stuck," Justi recalled, "and we had an hour and a half emergency with California youth representative Dick Dopkins and his group aboard." Although the building was air conditioned, the elevator was not and the Dopkins party sweltered in the elevator until their rescue could be effected.

---

dance of the church of one's choice shall not be interpreted to take precedence over or conflict with the freedom of conscience or religious conviction of any member of the Order."

Membership woes prompt self-examination

Grange leaders were perplexed by the decline they were experiencing. The organization had an enviable track record, a list of accomplishments unequaled by most groups. The grass-roots nature of the Grange made it almost one-of-a-kind in America and, surely, the emphasis upon family in an age when the nuclear family was disintegrating made its services to Americans even more important. When James C. Farmer, past national lecturer, was honored for his years of service at the 1961 session, he said that "Granges have infinitely more to offer than any other organization in this world, where members receive in one entity the benefits of Juvenile Granges, youth groups, home economics activities, community service, national legislative and cooperative services. In fact, the Grange embodies the ultimate in service and citizenship." Although most members probably agreed, potential members did not seem to get the message. Newsom had said the Grange is "America's greatest force for community improvements" and its service program should produce new initiates if the existing members would promote and "sell" membership.

There were some encouraging signs, though, including the organization in 1961 of the Florida State Grange with 21 subordinates and one Pomona and the existence of several Granges in Alaska and in the Philippines. When rookie National Lecturer William Brake made his first report in 1962, he advocated a "searching analysis of the total Grange structure" to determine if changes should be made which might better "meet the changing conditions" of a new era. A few years later the master of the New Hampshire State Grange would challenge the delegates by saying "none of us will ever again find an easy path in Grange work.... We belong to a family fraternity faced with the greatest challenge ever given to man. No longer are we permitted to turn our heads, looking to the past, and say 'look what the Grange did for America.' We are caught up in a revolutionary era such as the world has never witnessed before. The fact that the reports of masters in session after session show a struggle to maintain the status quo ought to be enough to awaken this delegate body to the needs for change which is long overdue." That same session the New Jersey state master would admit that in his state the Grange no longer was an agricultural organization because they were rapidly losing their agriculture base.

Delegates to the 1963 Portland, Oregon, session were greeted with a 55-page report from the National Grange Special Study Committee on Grange Structure and Program. Subsequently referred to as the Eastman Report, after Robert Eastman, the man who coordinated the research, the work was under the direction of a committee headed by A. Lars Nelson, master of the Washington State Grange, national overseer and a Newsom rival. To prepare for the report, the committee polled Grange leaders nationwide and investigated similar organizations. Population shifts, competition for time and attention from television and other activities, death of aging members, loss of member services and shortages of juvenile Granges were cited by the research report as some easily discernable causes of the membership decline which had taken 19 percent of the Grange in the decade leading up to 1962. There were Granges, though, which were growing, and the report attempted to analyze what was responsible for that development. They found service to the community to be the biggest drawing card for new members, followed by a good social program, willingness of members to enlist new members, a hard working master and other officers, and good publicity. The need for a respectable national publication also came out in the survey. In looking at similar organizations, the Grange dues and degree fees were found to be a bargain; dues were only one-fifth of the comparable groups and initiation fees were one-seventh of the other fraternities. The Grange was clearly trying to do too much with a limited resource base.

The message of the report was that members must fit the Grange and its programs, "its manner of organization, its methods of operation into today's and tomorrow's context—or die." The next year freshman Rhode Island State Master Woodrow Tucker would begin his personal campaign for a "secondary program" for use by the Grange in "those areas where agriculture is no longer the dominating field of endeavor." The organization needed an "alternative approach to reach the non-farm resident." Tucker would go on to be a member of the National Grange executive committee and high priest of Demeter.

Grange programs were in a state of flux with leaders trying fresh strategies in order to stimulate added participation. Newsom's assistant, Roy Battles, initiated a regular newsletter to deputies in the field with the purpose of generating enthusiasm and more fruitful work. National Lecturer Brake was especially cognizant of the key role played by his army of lecturers and he worked to bring in new ideas to make Grange meetings more interesting. He acknowledged, in 1964, the implementation of an art contest by his predecessor and said it showed "that many of us do not understand nor fully appreciate art." He attempted to bridge that knowledge gap by recommending subordinate lecturers put on an art enjoyment series. Materials, including slides, were available for their use and his recommendation was that the local units use a "study club" approach. Unwittingly, he was calling back the successful model developed by the Chautauqua Literary and Scientific Circle nearly 90 years before.

Farm leaders anger JFK and LBJ

Shortly before his inauguration in 1961, President-elect John F. Kennedy issued personal invitations for a strategy conference to Herschel Newsom, National Grange master, and eight other leaders of prominent farm groups. Other guests were to be Jim Patton, president of the Farmers Union; AFBF President Charles Schuman; National Farmers Organization president Oren Lee Staley; and leaders of the National Council of Farmer Cooperatives, the National Milk Producers Federation, National Association of Wheat Growers, the National Feed Grains Council and the Cotton Producers Association.

Newsom recalled that "the telegram [from Kennedy] was very clear to the effect that the nine of us were being invited and no more." When Newsom arrived alone in New York for the meeting, he found six of the nine had brought along staff members or association officers.

President-elect Kennedy was angered by the actions of the farm leaders and criticized them for bringing extra people. He went on, Newsom reported, to "make it clear that personal invitations in the future should be interpreted as just that."

Newsom also recalled that at the meeting Vice President-elect

Grangers join Peace Corps

One of the most dramatic areas of Grange involvement came after inauguration of the Peace Corps by President Kennedy in 1961. Over one-third of the Peace Corps volunteers were destined to serve as agricultural advisors in small villages around the globe and the Grange was seen as an important ally in recruiting qualified applicants from rural America. Early on, there were a number of Grange young people who responded and enlisted for a two-year hitch with the Peace Corps, the first one being James Gregory of Longmont, Colorado, who was assigned to a small village in Colombia. He wrote Wib Justi and Grange members in general that his assignment took "understanding, patience, and hard work. We will give these for two years and maybe more. We all hope that you are with us and will back us up in any way possible. We can't do it alone, but with help we can try." Justi advised Grange members everywhere to support the Peace Corps "in word and in deed, for it deserves a chance to prove itself as a positive

---

Johnson "went into quite an exhortation on the necessity of our reaching agreement across-the-board if we expect anything to be done agriculturally speaking." Kennedy, however, "gave us a much more encouraging statement," Newsom noted, by saying he "hoped everyone of us would accept our responsibility for broadening our areas of agreement and that, where need be, we would make reasonable compromise with each other." Kennedy added that he would not expect farm leaders to compromise their principles in order to reach consensus.

Kennedy opened the door for dialogue with his office on agriculture matters. His administration did not want to "start from scratch in resolving disagreements" but they would expect farm groups to at least give the background of their disagreements and reasons for believing as they did so the administration "may then be more speedily in position to make our own judgements."

Newsom told his own leadership following the meeting that "frankly and bluntly" he was "thoroughly convinced that failure to get unanimous agreement among ourselves will *not* be used as an excuse, so far as the president-elect is concerned, for doing nothing about the problems."

United States effort to practice international brotherhood."

Justi's leadership was recognized by his appointment as U.S. administrator for the introduction of the Peace Corps to Guatemala. Upon his recommendation, the National Grange agreed to sponsor the program in Guatemala from 1963 to 1965 and Justi assisted with the volunteer training program at New Mexico State University. Granges raised funds for extra materials to help ensure success of the Guatemala project.

An unfortunate announcement by the Sears Roebuck Foundation on the eve of the National Grange centennial radically changed one of the Grange's most positive functions, the community service contest. After 20 years of sponsorship with an ending annual budget of nearly $150,000, the foundation terminated its relationship. In an effort to be more than just a farm organization, the Grange had used the contest as one vehicle for transforming its image to that of a rural community service group. Without the highly visible contest and its substantial prizes, that public relations strategy would be much more difficult. The value of the program was obvious, however, and National Lecturer Brake continued sending out information about community service including the report forms which had been used in the past. In his 1971 report he quotes a letter received from a subordinate officer supporting reestablishment of the contest. "We hear all of the talk about how to get youth members and how to hold them," Brake's correspondent wrote, "but not once was community service mentioned. Our Grange has never been more active, nor had more interest shown, than when we had the National Grange Community Service Competition. We had more participation from the youth, young marrieds (and everybody) during those years than before or since." Brake recommended the Grange reestablish a contest. Delegates agreed and, although the value of prizes was greatly reduced, the contest started again. Participation by subordinate Grange members continued at an impressive level and the nationwide effort continues to be one of the organization's premier events.

Grange centennial celebrated

The centennial of the Grange, in spite of organizational difficulties, would be held in typical Newsom style and grandeur. The festivities, several years in planning, would center around the 1967 session in Syracuse, New York. Caravans brought approximately 1,500 members to the Washington, D.C., headquarters prior to the convention and over 500—including senators and congressmen—attended a special banquet November 10. Grange people were given VIP seats for the Veteran's Day ceremony at Arlington National Cemetery the next day and on the third day the caravan journeyed to Gettysburg, Pennsylvania, to witness the unveiling of the plaque honoring William Saunders, the first national master and designer of the Gettysburg National Cemetery. Pennsylvania Governor Raymond P. Shafer, a Grange member, addressed the crowd of 1,200.

On November 13, New York Governor Nelson Rockefeller, accompanied by his wife, welcomed Grange members to the state, describing the fraternity as "a lively century old organization"

In honor of the Grange centennial, the U.S. Postal Service issued this commemorative stamp. Secretary of Agriculture Freeman and Herschel Newsom were among those participating in the ceremony where the stamp was officially released.

which should turn its attention to solving contemporary urban problems. While doing that, though, the Grange should continue its efforts to create economic prosperity on America's farms. "This is a must," Rockefeller said, "if all Americans are to continue to enjoy the world's highest standard of living." The governor and his wife were given a standing ovation. Entertainment that day was provided by the West Point Cadet Glee Club.

Over 5,000 Grange members were present November 18 to hear and see President Lyndon B. Johnson speak to them through a closed-circuit television hook-up. He extended congratulations to the Grange on its anniversary and then continued the theme introduced by Governor Rockefeller the day before—the economic prosperity of American agriculture. His address closed with an admonition for the Grange to continue its "forward look" in seeking the programs which would keep the country as a "land of opportunity" and abundance. Johnson's Secretary of Agriculture Orville L. Freeman spoke in person, telling the Grange audience that without federal agriculture programs, farmers' incomes would drop by one-third and the "family farm" would disappear entirely.

The farm programs Freeman spoke about at the National Grange centennial session were becoming an even greater challenge for farm groups. In 1964, in order to attract the votes of Northern urban Democrats, sponsors of a bill to benefit wheat and cotton growers agreed to support the first permanent food stamp legislation. This was typical of the increasing number of trade-offs necessary to enact farm legislation. The food stamp bill had support of the Grange and the Farmers Union but was opposed by the AFBF. The bureau's objection, that inclusion of food stamp expense in the USDA budget would swell the department's appropriations and make subsequent gains for agriculture more difficult to secure, was later seen to have some merit.

This coalition-building in Congress was becoming even more crucial for rural citizens because of two 1964 Supreme Court decisions dictating that congressional districts and state legislative districts be apportioned by population rather than geographic areas. Farm groups were surprised by the decisions because they had long felt that at least one house of state legislatures would be based on geography and land area, creating a time-honored check-and-balance system. The change presented an immediate challenge to farm organizations; the Farmers Union supported the Supreme Court decision while the AFBF and the Grange criticized it. The *Kansas Farmer* noted that the "fading importance of rural America is brought sharply into focus in the recent U.S. Supreme Court ruling." Their editor went on to prophecy "it is going to take thoughtful legislators and sound legislation to protect farms and ranches on both the state and national level in this country." The National Grange found an ally in Senator Everett Dirksen, a speaker at their national session held in Topeka, Kansas, in 1965. Dirksen led a fight for a constitutional amendment allowing states to apportion one house in their legislature on the basis of territory rather than population. The move gained little actual support and eventually backfired because it opened farm groups to the criticism that they were trying to circumvent and change the decisions of the U.S. Supreme Court. "I personally have no desire at all to reverse the Supreme Court of the United States, on this or any other issue," Newsom assured delegates at the Topeka gathering. Resolutions favoring the constitutional amendment were passed at each national session between 1964 and 1967.

The apparent fragmentation of the nation into exclusive rural and urban groups, illustrated by the effects of the reapportionment decision and the move to open farm legislation to urban interests, tended to crystalize Newsom's approach to his mission in the latter years of his administration. Borrowing some terminology used by Grange policy makers in the 1920s, Newsom pointed out that American agriculture was the victim of a "dual economic system." Only for brief periods following World War II and the Korean conflict did farmers enjoy a balanced "parity ratio between prices and income for agricultural producers and agricultural workers in comparison to nonagricultural industry and nonagricultural labor...." Bringing the return for agricultural crops and labor in line with returns enjoyed by those engaged in other types of American industry—and maintaining that balance—would equalize this dual economic system and bring equity to American farmers. Prior efforts had only adjusted the imbalance; what was needed now, Newsom said, was equalization—equality for rural Americans.

Newsom accepts new role

In his last master's address, delivered in Peoria, Illinois, in 1968, Newsom noted "The Grange is, indeed, worthy of our best efforts, to make it a vehicle through which we, as individuals, in organized effort, can cope effectively with the fragmenting influences in our society." The Grange structure and all its programs were designed to enlist the involvement of everyone. Newsom quoted his friend Dwight D. Eisenhower when he said, "Every citizen must become involved, for on the current scene, apathy is scarcely less than a crime." As a retiring national master, Herschel D. Newsom was leaving the Grange with fewer members but with an expanded vision of its role in a new America. Perhaps the mission of the organization should be to preserve opportunities for involvement, opportunities which would lead to better individuals and improved communities. The result of organized effort on the part of rural Grange members must bring the country closer together, economically and socially. "We can serve America well," Newsom told his admirers at Peoria, "by bringing rural and agricultural Americans effectively into the total American social and economic life-stream."

Newsom would continue to do his part to improve conditions for the nation's agricultural industry by serving on the U.S. Tariff Commission. That work would be cut short by his untimely death July 2, 1970, less than two years after leaving the National Grange, and Grange legal counsel Joe Parker would be named to take his place. Newsom, like Goss, had gained many friends both inside and outside the Grange. His commanding presence had been useful in building the image of the organization he led; National Lecturer Bill Brake would later reflect that "Herschel added dignity to the organization. When he walked into the room, you knew a leader had arrived." But the natural consequences of declining revenues placed the National Grange in an unsure position. Herschel Newsom's successor, John W. Scott of Pennsylvania, would accept the challenge of restoring balance to the National Grange finances in order to continue its programs to extend equality to rural America.

12

Pressing for Rural Development

1968-1979

JOHN W. SCOTT'S ARRIVAL at National Grange headquarters as the new national master signaled a major transition within the organization. In retrospect, the 1968 convention in Peoria, Illinois, represents one of those points in the evolution of the Grange when the national organization took a dramatic turn in response to both internal and external pressures. Similar moves had been made during the 1870s due to near collapse of the infant organization's fragile structure, and after the 1911 departure of Nahum Bachelder as national master. Scott faced a new set of challenges, however, and reflection on the Grange's early history would provide little guidance.

Upon the resignation of Herschel Newsom at the 1968 session, delegates advanced Scott, their national secretary, to the master's office. He had been master of the influential Pennsylvania State Grange since 1962, was named national gatekeeper the following year and rose to the secretary's chair in 1965, replacing Harry Caton of Ohio who had served in the job since 1928. Scott had been a full-time dairy farmer in western Pennsylvania before his Grange career.

Twenty years later, as Scott reflected upon his entrance into the national master's post, he approached it from a positive perspective. His first comment was that he had inherited five outstanding staff people from Herschel Newsom: Robert Frederick, who had been hired as legislative representative in 1968; Judy Taylor Massabny, director of public relations (daughter of Ray Taylor, former editor of *The Grange,* successor to the *National Grange Monthly*); Ed Hadlock, youth director; Mamie Barbour, an office staff person who had worked for the National Grange since the early Goss days; and Lorena Stigers, another longtime office employee.

Scott then recalled the challenges which required his immediate, undivided attention: over a quarter of a million dollars in debts with banks refusing to extend additional credit; a continuing decline in members nationwide; near total absence of methods or funds to communicate with the membership; looming threats to terminate member benefits such as insurance plans; and a new administration in the White House with the election of Richard Nixon. It had been 90 years since a national master had to face such intimidating circumstances.

The pull-out of the Sears Roebuck Foundation from the Grange Community Service Contest was evidence enough that national demographics had changed significantly and that those population shifts were affecting the Grange. Sears had previously relied heavily upon patronage from rural people and contest sponsorship was good for business; when it became apparent that urban customers

John W. Scott (1917-)

were responsible for a majority of Sears' sales, courting the rural dollar was much less important. Shrinking Grange membership figures with, in some areas, declining involvement, were reflective of the changing population and deminished vitality of rural America. From the high point of 858,105 members in 1952, numbers had fallen to 539,163 when Scott was elected. Many Grange states had fewer than 1,000 members with major strength located in the Northeast, in Kansas and Ohio, and on the West Coast. Major losses were occurring in Ohio with smaller drops being recorded in New York and Pennsylvania, all strong Grange states. Out West, Washington was growing while Oregon and California figures fluctuated little. When Scott took office, Ohio still had the most members, but it would be overtaken just four years later by Washington, the state which continues to have the largest number of dues-payers. In 1977, seven of the 10 states gaining membership were located in the West. Overall, national figures would continue their plunge, resting at 427,114 when Scott retired from national office in 1979. Despite the gloominess caused by these trends, Grange leaders found encouragement in the 1975 *Wall Street Journal* report that the Grange was second to only one other national organization in the length of time new members remained on the rolls (an average of 13.5 years). Scott's wife Dorothy worked without salary as membership director throughout much of her husband's term of national office.

Declining membership and resistance to trimming services had caused the largest part of the National Grange's financial woes, resulting in the overwhelming short-term debt load. Scott entered office with an immediate cash-flow problem and his simple but effective strategy was to reduce the debt and cut expenses. He traveled to state Grange executive committee meetings, explained the situation and converted bank-held notes to ones held by the state Granges. This provided greater flexibility and extended repayment schedules; drastic slashing of expenses allowed quick repayment of the notes. Nonetheless, another period of tight finances occurred in 1975 and, in a 1978 report, a Potomac Grange study committee ominously stated, "...it seems...National Grange financing is so limited and unrealistic that effective long-term planning and actions are nearly impossible." That year the National Grange had to borrow $100,000 to finance its convention.

Harry Caton

Services shrink

There was abundant speculation about the fundamental causes of the membership loss. Harry Caton, in a letter read to delegates at the 1969 Daytona Beach, Florida, convention, cited a drop in member services with money-saving features as his reason. That definitely was the case in many areas, as some Grange-founded companies traditionally serving only members had opened their services to non-members as well. That was the root of member loss in Ohio. Also, in an era of fierce competition, Grange insurance companies increasingly found it difficult to offer rates which were much better than those quoted by rival firms. Blue Cross health plans, that added membership years before, were no longer the drawing card they had been and they ceased to be available in many states. Cooperatives formed by the Grange also served anyone regardless of their Grange membership. The economic motivation for joining, which had been there since Kelley originally began promoting the Grange, had largely been lost.

Fortunately, there was a powerful base of members who

remained true to their fraternity in spite of the disappearance of some benefits. These people were determined to keep their Grange afloat. Toward the end of Scott's administration, National Lecturer Bill Brake, while noting that he had presented 944 workshops nationwide, said he was always impressed with the enthusiasm that greeted him at each new Grange. However, he went on, "we must find some way to transfer this enthusiasm into membership gains, which I think is our number one internal problem."

Many responses to this "number one internal problem" were developed during the Scott administration, each with its measure of success. *The National Grange Newsletter* was initiated as an attempt to restore communication links which were broken with the demise of the *National Grange Monthly.* Then, in 1975, the National Grange resumed an abandoned program of producing and distributing tapes of interviews, discussions and commentary to those radio stations agreeing to broadcast them. Known as "The Grange Point of View," the programs were prepared by a Washington state member and radio station owner, Adrian DeVries. The informative programs continue to reach a wide audience in the 1990s, still with the familiar voice of DeVries. Judy Massabny began training Grange volunteers in the art of media contact with the goal of enhancing coverage of Grange activities by local newspapers and electronic media. Most state Granges had regular publications and information pertinent to National Grange activities was being sent to them for inclusion in their papers. Although during the Newsom years public information was a function to which much funding was allocated, budget constraints now required the job to be done with less resources.

Replacing declining member services with new ones proved to be difficult. One attempt was made to satisfy members' economic needs by inaugurating, in 1970, a national mail-order pharmacy which offered prescriptions at reduced cost. The plan generated moderate enthusiasm and a host of problems. Grange leaders everywhere doubled their efforts to maintain cordial relationships with the various Grange insurance companies; the link between them and the Grange was still mutually beneficial and any further deterioration of member services had to be forestalled.

A number of proposals to modernize the fraternity and implement new programs were greeted with openness. In an effort to restart the highly successful community service contest, the National Grange co-sponsored, in 1971, the community more beautiful program with the Keep America Beautiful organization. The promotion focused on community clean-up, recycling programs and education about ecology issues. Participation prompted national leaders the following year to bring back the old community service contest as an in-house program. The scope of the program was scaled back, shown by 1972 contest budget of $7,500 compared with the $144,000 spent by Sears during the last year of their sponsorship. Members had come to identify their Grange with community service and the new contest, even with the slashed budget, was easy to sell. Additionally, the Grange women greatly expanded their efforts during this time to involve members in a broad range of charity work. The projects to raise funds for CARE continued and an ongoing program to collect used eyeglasses gained robust support. Hundreds of thousands of glasses have been shipped overseas where they are matched with needy people having the same vision correction requirements.

A bicentennial boost

In 1975 a unique opportunity was presented to the National Grange by the National Endowment for the Humanities. The Grange was already engrossed in plans to recognize the nation's bicentennial and the National Endowment proposed that, nationwide, local Granges sponsor rural discussion groups on topics which would help make the bicentennial celebration more meaningful. A series of nine guidebooks were developed by a panel of experts at the University of Michigan and costs of production were covered by the Endowment.

Some cosmetic changes within the Grange were attempted during these years, with the objective of streamlining the work and modernizing its appearance. The old booster night programs were renamed "Community Night." In 1964 the juvenile Granges had been renamed "junior" Granges and, in 1972, the junior Grange superintendent post was renamed director of junior Grange activities at all levels in the Grange. The old home economics committee was known as the women's activities committee after 1967 and in 1972 the name changed again to the committee on women's activities. The 1973 decision to promote the organization as the "Suburban Rural Family Organization" rather than the "Rural Family Farm Organization" highlights the subtle shift of self-image which was occurring. Because of changing demographics and lifestyles, the Grange needed to move from the farm to the sprawling suburbs.

A much more dramatic expression of internal change was evident at the 1974 convention in Sacramento, California. A report tells that at the host state banquet, prior to opening the convention, tables were decorated with bunches of grapes and wine bottles used as candle holders, "representing the various brands of wines bottled in California." Following the talent contest several days later, 500 Grange youth and others assembled for "The '49er Hoe-Down" dance complete with Wild West "dance hall girls, gold miners, orientals and ranch hands." Root beer was on tap at the bar. Although still "dry," behavior, attitudes and lifestyles of the

Women's Activities Director Jenny Grobusky proudly passed the earnings from her department's cookbook fund-raiser to National Master Scott in 1976. The department's work helped retire the mortgage on the national headquarters building.

members had moderated somewhat from the days of the Grange-WCTU alliance which promoted its own brand of "social purity" and helped bring about Prohibition.

Self-examination was in vogue the next year for the women's activities department. The International Women's Year had been declared and Grange women took up the cause by adopting the theme, "Behold...Your Image." In her national director's report, Jenny Grobusky noted, "Farm and rural women are the same as our town and city cousins—they want the same things as any other woman—they are educated and knowledgeable. The flower-hatted, dimwitted, over-corseted matron type of club woman is no longer true. I meet women who are tremendously active in their communities. The questions they ask are alert and intelligent. They are concerned about business, government subsidies, travel, art and many things. Women are more sophisticated, and the media is beginning to notice."

Service to hearing impaired

Grange women had long been considered the driving force in many subordinate Granges. Because of their growing sophistication and community-minded spirit, rural women in the Grange were tackling new challenges in the 1970s. One of these would become a permanent fixture within the Grange and bring the organization a great deal of publicity and good will. In 1971 the women set up a national health project targeted to assist the hearing impaired. Alta Peck, director of women's activities, headed up the effort which began by collecting funds. A flash of insight the next year resulted in a collection and recycling project for used hearing aid batteries which, over the years, has generated much funding for the deaf activities program. Community education and awareness about the needs of the hearing impaired became a driving force within the project, and in 1975 the women financed production of a television public service announcement, "I Hear Your Hand," which received widespread use. Sign language flash cards for junior Granges were made and Grange youth were involved. At the 1975 convention a choir of young people performed "musical" selections by signing, under the direction of Dan Pokorny, chaplain at Gallaudet University, Washington, D.C. Gallaudet is the only accredited university in the nation exclusively serving

For many years Grange women were instrumental in assisting people in Third World countries through CARE. This village in the Philippines posed in 1961 for a group "thank you" photo when badly needed hand tools were received from CARE and farm women in America.

those with hearing disabilities.

The signing choir was a prelude to the release in 1976 of the world's first sign language song book, *Lift Up Your Hands.* Grange women enlisted the help and support of the youth department and its current director, Bill Steel, for this complex project and the novelty and usefulness of the resulting publication earned recognition for the Grange as one of the most important groups working to help the hearing impaired. A second volume of songs for signing was published in 1980. A popular youth competition, the "Sign a Song" contest, has enlisted heavy participation since its inception in 1979. Leadership of the deaf activities has been largely under the direction of Beulah Winter, Michigan, since her appointment as director in 1982.

A U.S. Bicentennial women's project inspired by Judy Massabny would be responsible for retiring the debt on the national headquarters. Unveiled at the 1975 convention, a colorful National Grange bicentennial cookbook became an immediate best seller. A marketing plan was adopted which allowed women in subordinate Granges to make money selling the book and each copy sold also made a profit for the National Grange. Orders began flooding in and by the following May a total of 150,000 copies had been printed.

At the headquarters mortgage burning ceremony March 25, 1977, it was announced that sale of 175,000 cookbooks had brought in the $300,000 which retired the debt. Jenny Grobusky, whose women raised the money, joined Scott, James Ingwersen, chair of the national executive committee, and a representative of the life insurance company which had held the mortgage, in the burning ceremony. Remarks were made by Russell Stauffer, national treasurer, Blanche Newsom, widow of Herschel Newsom, and Maynard Dolloff, past master of the Maine State Grange and an official in the U.S. Department of Agriculture. Patrons nationwide felt a sense of relief and encouragement; the $65,000 which had been dedicated annually to mortgage payments could now be diverted to struggling Grange programs.

No time to stitch

The contest format had been popular with Grange women for years and Scott complimented Jenny Grobusky's troops in 1975 when they were able to garner a net gain of 5,000 more entries in the sewing contest. Underwriting of contest expenses and prizes was provided by national companies which made products used by contest entrants but, although there still was much interest by Grange women, these companies were wavering in their support. As Scott was praising the renewed interest, Grobusky noted four companies had dropped out. The role of women in America was changing, and with more two-career and single parent households, women would find less time for traditional domestic skills emphasized by the contests. This would be especially true in rural America where farm wives found it necessary to commute to jobs in town in order to keep the family financially solvent. It would be another decade before declining participation would force reduction in the contests. The sewing contest lasted until 1988.

One contest, though, would grow in importance. Originating in 1976, the annual stuffed toy contest became immediately popular for two reasons: Making the creative toys was fun and, more important, the toys were all donated after judging to childrens' wards in hospitals, where they were given to recuperating young patients. Grange women, men, youth and children all became captivated by this project and, by the early 1990s, over 30,000 toys each year were bringing cheer to hospitalized children.

The most prominent move to modernize the fraternity occurred near the mid-point of Scott's administration. Delegates in 1974 had instructed the national master to bring a draft of a "new and modern" *Declaration of Purposes* to the Columbus, Ohio, session the next year. High Priest of Demeter C. Jerome Davis, National Lecturer William Brake and John Burgess of Virginia, an executive committee member, prepared the draft. While some of the language contained in the 1874 *Declaration* survived, the historic document was radically shortened and some key concepts were either dropped or restated to suit contemporary conditions. The changing composition of the membership was recognized, and instead of acknowledging unity "by the strong and faithful tie of Agriculture," patrons were now brought together by the "tie of an agricultural fraternity." "[A]ll of good moral character," not farmers exclusively, were welcomed to join. This had been the practice for generations, but now the *Declaration of Purposes* made it official.

Gone from the new *Declaration* was Kelley's original selling tool, cooperation "to reduce our expenses, both individual and corporate." The stinging denouncement of credit, "the mortgage system, the fashion system and every other system tending to prodigality and bankruptcy" was scrubbed from the new document, too. And the initial rallying call of the Grange, its unified statement concerning transportation which caused the organization's name to become synonymous with reform of American business legislation, is also missing from the new *Declaration.* That chapter had been closed. (A full discussion of the *Declaration of Purposes* appears in Chapter 15.)

A changing world presence

Although there was a conscious attempt to broaden the Grange's base of membership to include many non-farmers, the fraternity remained an important spokesman for the agricultural industry in Washington, D.C., and many state capitals as well. There was a slight shift, however, in the Grange's presence on the international scene.

Since the early days of the Grange, farmers had realized international trade of agricultural commodities was important to America's farmers. Goss had taken the lead in heightening the visibility of the National Grange overseas and Newsom, who become known as an expert on international agriculture, continued that trend. The primary vehicle for this exposure was the International Federation of Agricultural Producers (IFAP). Goss had been a prime mover during the early days of the IFAP and he served as third vice president of the group which involved farmer representatives from all continents. Newsom had been named to the organization's executive committee at its 1960 meeting in India and he then rose to be vice president and eventually president. However, serious National Grange financial problems in 1968 forced some drastic steps and IFAP membership dues were pulled from the budget.

Delegates at the National Grange session in 1968 verbalized their strong support of the IFAP and pledged to reinstate membership as soon as it was feasible. The executive committee authorized rejoining the following year and Robert Frederick was the organization's representative at the IFAP meeting in Tokyo. Scott told delegates at the national session in 1969 that federation participation was extremely costly and "deserves a critical evaluation in terms of its worth." He read his listeners well when he acknowledged benefits of international involvement were "somewhat intangible," but there was always the hope that it might bring a long-term benefit to American farmers. Speaking to his largely non-farm audience, he quickly added, "We must always remember that an economic gain for American farmers is in reality an economic gain for all Americans." Scott was aware that Newsom had been criticized in some Grange circles for being "too interested" in the international agriculture scene.

Delegates heard from Frederick in 1971 that North American IFAP meetings he attended with Scott in Ottawa had been "not only a waste of time but also a waste of finances." The IFAP general conference was held later that year in Paris, and again, Frederick and Scott attended. The meeting was dominated by discussion of the emerging European Economic Community (EEC) and the recent international monetary crisis; Frederick summarized the conference as "disappointing." By 1973 the EEC was said to have overshadowed the conferences and National Grange membership was permanently withdrawn. Nine years later, then National Master Edward Andersen attended the 25th IFAP conference in London and reported he observed no improvements in the organization. His recommendation to the National Grange was to remain unaffiliated.

Nationally, the Grange kept a visible presence in behalf of agriculture. Scott became national master just two weeks after the election of Richard M. Nixon as president. During the campaign neither Nixon nor his principal opponent, Hubert H. Humphery, talked much about agricultural concerns. Despite their longstanding insistence that government should get out of farming, the Republicans agreed with the Democrats that it would take government action to preserve suitable prices for commodities. By 1973, Nixon was returning to hackneyed rhetoric by calling farm programs "old fashioned Federal intrusions...." During the last half of the 1960s farm prices had climbed somewhat, due primarily to expanded exports. Then, in 1972, Soviet farmers had an unusually poor harvest, prompting them to quietly purchase U.S. wheat and feed grains. This stimulated a tremendous boost in international agricultural trade and Nixon's new but controversial Secretary of Agriculture Earl Butz pleaded with farmers to take advantage of the trading climate by planting "fencerow to fencerow." The reverberations of that statement would be heard for over a decade. Many farmers took Butz at his word and, feeling there was little chance to fail, expanded their operations with heavy reliance upon credit. The agricultural downturn several years later, dubbed the "Farm Crisis," drove thousands of family farmers off their land because of their inability to pay off those loans.

The welcome peace in Viet Nam was dulled by run-away inflation at home. Wage and price controls were implemented and, in 1973, President Nixon was being pressured by consumer groups to roll back prices and place price controls on raw agricultural products. Scott and Frederick continued to reiterate before the Cost of Living Council the Grange's position that food prices were not high in relation to the overall economy and that food was not the largest contributor to inflation. Commodity prices should not be regulated at the farm, they argued, expressing a view also held by Secretary Butz. Even though Americans, contrasted with people around the globe, spent a smaller portion of their income to buy food, inflationary prices resulted in a revolt. Housewives, who had picketed stores in 1969 and 1970 protesting meat prices, renewed their complaints, resulting in beef being placed under price controls in 1973. Consumers again boycotted beef in an attempt to drive prices down while ranchers responded by sending fewer cattle to market. Eventually, cows were sent to slaughter in enormous numbers and it was this action which forced prices below the cost of production. Price controls had been shown to be ineffective and obviously harmful to producers.

Organized labor also championed consumer protests against food prices. In 1974 members of the International Longshoreman's Association refused to load U.S. grain on Soviet ships until they learned how the commodity sales would affect domestic food prices. The president responded by calling for an investigation into the effects of foreign agricultural trade on inflation. Power over farm programs had shifted almost entirely from the agricultural community to the consumers, as evidenced by the later embargoes implemented by the administration of President Gerald Ford.

Price controls had minimal effect and, with the advent of Watergate and resignation of President Nixon, the Ford administration retreated and initiated a series of national discussions about the problem. Scott represented the Grange at a food and agriculture conference in Chicago in 1974 and, two weeks later, participated in the Economic Summit Conference chaired by the president. The resulting plan adopted by the Ford administration became known as "WIN," Whip Inflation Now. At the national session that November, delegates and guests attending the rural America luncheon heard assurances from Clayton Yeutter, assistant secretary for international affairs and commodity programs at USDA, that most of the farm problems were only "temporary." Yeutter would become special trade representative under President Ronald Reagan, secretary of agriculture and, during the George Bush administration, he was named chair of the Republican Party.

United we stand

The challenges were obvious when Scott assumed office. American farmers had become more politically astute but their minority status accentuated the need for organized action. In February 1969 Scott took the lead in rebuilding the bonds of cooperation between farm groups which had been absent from the Washington scene for years. His motivation was the Agricultural Stabilization Act of 1969 and present at Scott's meeting were representatives from the Grange, American Farm Bureau Federation, National Farmers Union, the National Farmers Organization, the Mid-Continent Farmers Association and many commodity organizations. The only "united front" coming from this meeting was a stand on the office of the special trade representative. Scott and Frederick felt this was a good start, with Frederick later reporting that the united front concept was a goal the Grange had nurtured off and on since 1889. The unity of agriculture groups, he said, "is so vitally needed if we are to influence the urban congressman and his constituents to be in support of farm legislation that is so important to the preservation and economic growth of our family farm structure...."

The federation of farm groups, called the National Farm Coalition, met in July in conjunction with the Washington gathering of the National Grange agriculture committee. Scott served as chairman. A subcommittee consisting of Frederick and representatives from the Farmers Union, NFO, Milk Producers and Wheat Growers continued to meet regularly, drafting legislation which eventually was introduced in Congress as the Agricultural Stabilization Act of 1969. Frederick pointed out the bill itself was not the important occurrence; the unified approach was. "The important fact is that this is the first time since the '30s that a true farm bloc or farm coalition has united behind one piece of legislation," Frederick emphasized. The "unity" of 22 groups was less than complete, due to the obvious absence of the Farm Bureau, by then the largest general farm organization. In 1971 the coalition dissolved but by 1973 the cooperation returned, resulting in passage of a new farm bill in the House by an impressive margin. The coalition acknowledged their success was assured in large part by active support of their cause by the AFL-CIO and consumer lobbyists.

Attempts by the Grange to keep the coalition alive were persistent, but differences in policy between the various groups made agreement difficult. One later appearance during the Scott years occurred in 1979 when the farm groups united to propose the National Agriculture Bargaining Act. A Grange report confidently stated, "Legislative history was made when the leaders of the Farmer's Union, Farm Bureau, National Council of Farmer Cooperatives and the Grange appeared before a committee of Congress unified in their support for the bill." The coalition lived on through the Edward Andersen years with Andersen serving as chairman. However, the differences in farm policy which had started to tug at the unity broke out into party politics in the late 1980s, with the last effort toward accord between the farm groups occurring in 1985. The Grange could not accept the political polarization taking place and eventually withdrew its participation. The coalition came to a quiet end in 1992.

All agriculture groups were wary of attempts to create the Environmental Protection Agency in 1970. The fear was that the new agency would promote legislation to ban the use of agricultural chemicals which had become essential for farming. The Grange, one of the first agriculture organizations to issue friendly endorsement of sound and realistic environmental legislation, reiterated its position on the necessity of agricultural chemicals. But it was obvious there was a rational need for "responsible regulations" to ensure the safety of farmers, the environment and the food supply. Frederick summarized the Grange's concern by stating, "If we let emotionalism run away in writing the rules of the game, it will not only be the American farmer that suffers, but ultimately it will be the consumer." Scott, at the 1972 session, admitted agriculture's worst fears had not materialized because the EPA had "acted in a very responsible manner" during its first year of existence. He went on to press subordinate Granges to promote environmental consciousness and responsibility through community service projects.

By 1977, Grange delegates were calling for the authority of the EPA to be restricted. The arrival of the EPA signaled yet another expansion of the forces holding ultimate control over the future of America's farmers and another group of lobbyists were born which the Grange and other farm organizations would have to include in any coalitions.

Desperate farmers contemplate strikes

Plummeting farm prices in the late 1970s resulted in a new set of conditions for agriculture and a different voice was heard in rural America, the American Agriculture Movement (AAM). During the summer of 1977, AAM leaders, situated mostly in the Midwest, began advancing the concept of a farm strike as an answer to plunging prices. On September 22, AAM sympathizers, numbering 2,000, cornered the new Secretary of Agriculture (and Potomac Grange member) Robert Bergland at a speech he was scheduled to make in Pueblo, Colorado. He shared with the crowd his doubts about the effectiveness of a strike and urged them to wait for the benefits of the recently passed Food and Agriculture

Act of 1977. Convinced that public action was the only solution, the AAM farmers began a series of demonstrations that fall known as "tractorcades," events where hundreds of sign-carrying tractors would gather in processions. The largest tractorcade occurred in December when between 5,000 and 8,000 tractors drove through Georgia. Several days later hundreds of the units circled the White House and Washington Monument. The strike was set for December 14 but when the date arrived, no effects were noted.

The Grange became involved in the national fall-out created by the AAM. In July the executive committee had a personal meeting at the White House with its new resident, Georgia peanut farmer Jimmy Carter, where they discussed wheat, feed grains, the plight of family farmers, and Western reclamation law revisions. When the strike talk began, Scott urged President Carter to call a meeting of farm leaders to discuss the economic situation. "To be silent on the strike movement only invites more criticism," Scott told the president, "and gives more credence to the strike leaders' statements that the President and the government don't care about farmers and that we must take things into our own hands."

The Grange then presented testimony to the Senate and House Agriculture Committees and at field hearings in Kansas City. When the Governor's Conference set up a meeting in Omaha to allow representatives of major farm organizations to meet with Secretary Bergland, the National Grange was represented and made its recommendations known. At the request of the president, Scott joined five other farm leaders to make specific suggestions for White House action and, as the report given to delegates the following year notes, the organization "had a major impact on the administrative changes made in implementing the farm programs provided for in the Food and Agriculture Act of 1977."

The Grange also was a participant in several small farm conferences jointly sponsored around the country by USDA and the Community Services Administration. These conferences were designed to provide practical assistance and advice to farmers grossing less than $40,000. After all the dust cleared, Congress passed an emergency farm bill in May 1978 which provided some relief.

In November 1978, in his annual master's address, Scott praised Bergland for his unswerving support of family-based agriculture. "Many times his voice was the only voice being raised in support of programs beneficial to farms within the higher circles of government," Scott said. "He not only took on the Office of Management and Budget, Council of Economic Advisors, State Department and some members of Congress of his own political persuasion, but, at times, a vocal segment of the agriculture sector. In the end, he had the support of President Carter and the agriculture leadership in the House, and received the necessary support from organized agriculture to bring about needed improvements in the 1977 Act."

Later, in the same speech, Scott attempted to explain the changing structure of America's farms and the impact made by federal programs. It was apparent, he said, that farm units were getting larger and that federal farm programs had unwittingly "encouraged larger and larger farms." Aside from economic impacts, the changes in farm structure had a negative influence upon "the socio-economic infrastructure associated with the family farm. As farm families leave rural America, it affects schools, churches, medical services and weakens the moral fiber we have associated with rural living." The Jeffersonian attitude that American moral character is rooted in its family farms was still alive, as was the idea that everyone would benefit by supporting the traditional farming structure. "Yes, I am nostalgic about family farms, and rural America," Scott went on. "The question we must answer and the public must answer is: Is the family farm and the socio-economic infrastructure associated with family farm living worth saving? I think it is. And I call once more for a change in federal farm support programs, tax and credit policies that will assist family agriculture, not hasten its death."

Size of family farms was a central issue which proved difficult to resolve. The Grange had supported the 160-acre limitation written into the Reclamation Act at the turn of the century and the arbitrary acreage figure needed Grange defense several times since. In 1975 the Grange supported the 160-acre limitation for a dispute in California's San Joaquin Valley; water from tax-supported projects should be made available to family farms, those which were 160 acres or less.

The next year Washington voters passed that state Grange's Initiative 59, the Family Farm Water Act. The initiative, which regulated irrigation water rights, was seen as a strong statement against the intrusion of corporate, conglomerate interests into agriculture, a condition present in California for generations. In the Washington act, the definition of "family farms" included acreage holdings of up to 2,000 acres of irrigated agricultural land per person in the family. Clearly, the concept of what constituted a family farm was changing rapidly.

In 1977 Scott urged delegates to reexamine their 160-acre limitation policy because Secretary of Interior Cecil Andrus was proposing a major overhaul of the 1902 Reclamation Act. As guidance, Scott asked Grange leaders to consider how much acreage was necessary to maintain an "economic unit." The type of farm and crops grown could very well affect the size of an economic unit. The final outcome, Scott suggested, might have a dramatic impact upon rural communities with some farmers feeling efforts to change the regulations were part of an "agrarian reform movement that seeks basic change in our market enterprise system and the principle of private property rights." A year of research and debate resulted in a resolution of compromise on the 160-acre rule. A series of conditions were outlined which, the Grange leaders felt, would ensure water would flow to the largest number of small-sized family-owned farms. The fear that America's countryside would be taken over by huge corporations and wealthy investors from foreign nations was real. Control of the water, long seen by the Grange as a public resource, was one possible way of averting the move to large-scale corporate, tax-loss agriculture. Everyone in America had a stake in this battle, the Grange said.

Rural renewal

The decay of rural America was of intense concern to Scott and his personal campaign to bring the needed relief brought some dramatic results. During the early years of his administration he envisioned "A Twentieth Century Granger Movement" which would spearhead planned rural development. The Rural Development Act of 1972 had consumed the majority of Grange staff time during the 92nd Congress and, as a result, many of its provisions were Grange-inspired. The thrust of the bill, and the new "Granger Movement," was encouraging "collective efforts by rural people" who were "willing to become involved" on a local level "in making plans and developing their communities through a systematic and realistic approach." This had been the Grange mission for over 100 years and it was felt the new legislation would help the Grange mobilize its membership to make lasting contributions. Funding provided by the act could be used by communities under 10,000 in population to improve housing, provide public sewer and water systems and attract new industry.

Scott saw rural development achieving movement status and he challenged Granges to provide the necessary leadership. "I hope the Grange will be the organization that calls the meetings to discuss how the Rural Development Act can help their community," Scott urged. "So far, the surface of rural development has only been scratched. There is a desperate need for grass-roots leadership that will reshape our rural environment." Many Granges responded by redirecting their community service to this task. An impressive outcome of this push was dedication in 1975 of the 92-unit Ukiah (California) Autumn Leaves Retirement Hotel, sponsored by the California State Grange. This project parallels Grange Acres, a 275-unit senior citizen housing project sponsored by Capital Grange in Haslett, Michigan, and Pomona Villa, 40 retirement units backed by the Pierce County Pomona Grange and located near Sumner, Washington. An additional Grange retirement and

The Ukiah Autumn Leaves retirement facility in Ukiah, California, is one of several housing projects built and managed by the Grange. (California State Grange photo)

nursing care facility exists in Belleville, Illinois. Rural housing, especially for seniors, was seen as a critical need, and Grange-inspired projects made significant contributions to these communities.

Part of the massive job of rehabilitating rural America involved correcting some negative conditions which adversely impacted citizens, hampering their chances for economic development. There were new Grange causes in this area, such as working to overcome pollution caused by feed lots and arguing for regulations to limit cable television's impact on the free, major network TV being received in rural areas. But the organization found its traditional role of fighting for improved transportation, roads and highways was perhaps the most valuable contribution that could be made for revitalizing America's countryside. One hundred years after the enactment of the Granger Laws, the railroads returned as a major area of Grange concern.

Transportation keeps rural America moving

The world's largest railroad, Penn Central, went into bankruptcy in June 1970, one of the factors prompting Congress to inaugurate Amtrak. Penn Central's problems were indicative of many rail corporations and spinning off the unprofitable passenger business was only part of the solution. Freight rates had been edging upward for some time and the National Grange was prominent in protesting these increases before the Interstate Commerce Commission. Another bone of contention with the railroads concerned the perennial shortage of boxcars, a condition which seriously hampered farmers' efforts to get their commodities to market. At the root of this problem was mismanagement by the railroads, allowing empty cars to sit idle in parts of the country when they were desperately needed elsewhere. National Grange protests helped push through ICC regulations that alleviated this condition. The Grange also endorsed legislation to create the National Freight Car Corporation, a quasi-governmental structure to build and lease a large pool of freight cars.

Construction of the Interstate Highway System was well underway during the Scott administration but the debate was still hot about the Highway Trust Fund. Urban interests, joined in 1972 by Secretary of Transportation Volpe and the railroads, wanted to raid the fund for badly needed revenue for mass transit projects. Scott called the congressional struggle on this issue "one of the biggest contests" of the session. He complained that some rural congressmen voted on the wrong side and the complex congressional maneuvering occupied a major portion of Scott's master's address that November at the Hartford, Connecticut, session. He noted that fund money would not be used for mass transit but, because the issue was still unresolved, the next congressional session would make the final decision. Scott proudly stated that Grange efforts since 1928 had resulted in constitutional amendments in 28 states "dedicating highway user revenues to highway purposes only." The national fund should be similarly structured. He also reiterated the fact that the Grange was the only general farm organization supporting the 1956 act which launched the interstate highway construction.

In 1973 Congress passed the Federal Highway Act, legislation Scott termed "the most significant piece of highway legislation since establishment of the Highway Trust Fund in 1956." The reality of money diversion for urban mass transit remained and Scott urged delegates to look earnestly at the transportation needs of the cities. They responded by endorsing a Federal Urban Transportation Trust Fund, financed by sources other than the Highway Trust Fund. They also indicated strong support of legislation and funding to remove road hazards and promote other highway safety programs.

By 1974 Scott was expressing alarm that inflation and other factors were delaying completion of the Interstate Highway System. With another 6,000 miles to go, he said the job would not be done by the year 2007 at existing funding levels. Additional money must be appropriated, a need which was met, in part, by the Federal Aid Highway Act of 1976 and the Surface Transportation Act of 1978. Although pleased with this legislation, Scott still expressed Grange concerns that about a third of America's local roads remained unpaved.

The tenuous railroad situation in the Northeast also moved closer to successful resolution with passage in 1976 of the Railroad Revitalization and Regulatory Reform Act. An outstanding feature of this bill was establishment of the Consolidated Railroad Corporation (CONRAIL) which would take over operations of Penn Central and five other bankrupt lines. "Let us hope that this plan will be successful," Scott said. "Otherwise, we may be threatened with nationalization of our railroad system," a prospect feared by Grange members in the 1970s but championed by some of their distant patrons a hundred years before.

Energy becomes a major concern

Closely related to the Grange's concern for transportation was its support for a national and world-wide energy policy. Gasoline shortages had already plagued rural residents and it was apparent that a systematized approach to the world's supply and demand for fuel must be developed. Delegates at the 1975 Columbus, Ohio, session called for such a policy, but the next year Scott said he was doubtful permanent solutions would be forthcoming. Even the soon-to-be-completed Alaskan pipeline would offer no more than temporary relief, primarily for the West Coast; the rest of the nation would remain dependent upon petroleum imports. Off-shore and on-shore domestic exploration and development of oil reserves must be expanded, Scott said, and the use of alcohol made from farm products was encouraged as a potential new source of domestic fuel. The energy package eventually passed by Congress contained some Grange provisions but, on the whole, it was viewed as only a start in the right direction. Much remained to be done, Grange leaders admitted.

Grange members have a rich tradition of speaking out on controversial issues and during the Scott years there were several of those which sparked spirited discussion. In 1970 Congress passed the Family Planning Services and Population Research Act, providing funds for services and research in family planning. It had not been many years since dissemination of birth control information and devices was made legal in all states and the Grange enthusiastically endorsed the need "of having family planning and population control information readily available to all those who need or desire it." In 1973 the delegates entered the growing abortion controversy, expressing a belief that legalizing abortion, "except in the case of rape, incest, or a doctor's recommendation concerning the well-being of the mother and/or child," should be opposed. After the landmark U.S. Supreme Court decision on abortion the next year, delegates softened their policy by calling for "educational efforts which would emphasize the necessity for licensed hospitals and medical doctors when abortions are necessary." In 1981 delegates came out strongly in support of a woman's freedom of choice for abortion and opposed any attempt to limit that freedom by amendment of the U.S. Constitution.

Tackling tough issues

A vigorous stance for separation of church and state continued to be molded in the Scott administration. In 1971 delegates voiced strong opposition to the use of any tax revenue for non-public schools run by sectarian groups. The delegates went on to state that "profit-making branches of church organizations" should be expected to pay taxes on income and real estate other than churches, parsonages and schools. This was followed in 1976 by suspicions that some religious organizations were soliciting funds and not using them for religious programs or services to the public. Grange members felt the answer was legislation to require public disclosure of the assets, net worth and disposition of funds of any religious organization which makes a concerted effort to solicit funds from the general public in more than one state. Voluntary prayer in schools was all right, the Grange felt, and the Bible could be taught as a book of literary merit in high school English classes.

Other hot issues tackled by the Grange during this era included opposition to busing of school children in order to achieve racial balance in the classroom and a call for welfare reform by providing work experience and job training for all recipients of aid.

One social issue which captured Scott's attention resulted in a new policy for the National Grange. The national master had been appointed by President Nixon as a member of the President's Employ the Handicapped Committee and later he rose to be chairman of the group's rural areas sub-committee. Scott noted that the Grange had no policy specifically encouraging employers to hire disabled workers and, at his urging, the delegates responded with a whole-hearted endorsement.

Scott also had served on the USDA's Commission on Agricultural Credit, as a member of the White House Conference on Aging and the President's Productivity Commission. Recognition was given for his contributions to the International Farm Youth Exchange and by New Holland Machine Company for his service to agriculture.

John Scott, unlike his imposing predecessor, was a quiet, unassuming leader. Observers told how he would sometimes slip unnoticed into a room of patrons and work his way around the crowd, unobtrusively enjoying conversation with the people he met. Often those people would have no idea they were talking with the national master. He was well liked, respected and effective in gaining cooperation. His tenure with the National Grange was impaired by recurring, serious health problems and some thorny, internal difficulties which were time consuming. After declining to run again for national office, Scott returned to Pennsylvania where he was employed by the state department of agriculture until retirement in 1991.

The last national session where Scott presided as master was held in 1979 on his home turf, Lancaster, Pennsylvania. He had led the organization well in spite of the serious handicaps of declining membership and almost daily cash flow problems. But he was frustrated most by the lack of "common direction" within the Grange; he felt a solution would be the adoption of a list of national goals. These were drafted, distributed to all Grange states, revised and released to delegates at Lancaster. Heading the list was the desire "to become the largest and most effective farm and community service organization" in America. To do that, delegates felt the successful Grange community service contest had to be upgraded "to the status of a major program." This would enhance the development of the Grange's image, making it appear "more progressive and dynamic."

The bottom line, though, was encouraging growth in membership. The key to growth would be "to develop innovative programs and services that provide necessary incentives for growth in membership and development of individual members and prospective Grange leaders." Such a thrust would not only help the Grange organization move into the '80s, but the pool of leaders within the Grange could be an effective force in working to enhance the quality of life in rural America.

Although many of the problems facing Scott as he assumed the national master's post still remained, adoption of the goal statement helped solidify the organization and move it progressively forward. Elected to take Scott's place was Edward Andersen, a livestock farmer from Waterloo, Nebraska, a man who was no stranger to the challenges which would require his immediate attention.

13

Defining and Preserving Family Agriculture

1979-1987

EDWARD ANDERSEN was a product of the Grange. After Army service during World War II, he began a career as a dairy farmer and joined the Grange in 1950. In 1956, Ed and his wife Darlene were named Nebraska's Young Couple of the Year. Remaining active in their subordinate Grange, he eventually was elected master of the state Grange in 1970 and overseer of the National Grange the following year. As overseer, he was a member of the national executive committee during the majority of the Scott years.

When Andersen became the 18th national master there was renewed talk about rationing gasoline, prompted by increasing tension in the Middle East. Ayatollah Khomeini had assumed control in Iran and U.S. embassy employees in Teheran were being held hostage. The Soviets invaded Afghanistan a month following the election and American reaction from that hostility eventually would have far-reaching impact upon American farmers. National and international conflicts were convincing evidence that the work of the National Grange was far from over.

Delegates at the Lancaster session, where Andersen received his master's sash, spoke out loudly about energy-related questions. They authorized a telegram to President Carter stating his "diplomatic firmness in dealing with international political blackmail reflects the attitude of a mature, peaceful people." The Grange's old pacifism was flowing into the open again. "The times call for quiet diplomacy, uncluttered by acts of revenge [which are] founded on injured pride and fed by emotionalism," the telegram continued. The statement closed with a strong endorsement of the president's decision to cut off purchases of Iranian oil in protest over the hostage crisis.

Scott had spent much time cultivating Grange interest in energy issues and the recurrent turmoil in the oil-rich Middle East vindicated his persistence. At Lancaster, delegates expanded their energy policy by endorsing the use of oil-saving nuclear energy, provided that precautions be taken to ensure safety. They also approved the ambitious Northern Tier Pipeline plan as an option for moving Alaskan oil from tanker terminals in Washington state to the Midwest. The pipeline idea never materialized and accidents in the '80s decelerated the nation's experiment with nuclear energy production.

Farmers: A tool of international diplomacy

American farmers had long complained that their economic livelihood had often been used as a tool of international diplomacy. President Ford had, in 1975, restricted grain sales to the Soviet Union because it was thought by the administration (under pressure from consumer and labor groups) that the Soviet grain trade might contribute to domestic inflation. The agricultural sector was infuriated, and when farmer Jimmy Carter was stumping for a chance in the White House he criticized Ford for the unwise move, promising never to approve any embargo on agricultural exports.

During the Carter years exports gradually grew, exerting an upward push on farm prices. The Soviets, because of poor harvests in 1979, were scheduled to buy a large amount of American commodities in 1980 but the Afghan invasion triggered Carter's promise-breaking announcement that sales to Russia beyond those already negotiated would be disallowed. The Grange immediately publicized its support of the embargo, believing that steps would be taken to protect farm prices. The Grange was involved in several discussions with Secretary of Agriculture Bergland and Andersen later noted that all of the Grange's recommended protective actions were eventually adopted. "I believe," Andersen said 10 months after Carter's order, "the embargo has very little, if any effect on our grain prices." Many farmers disagreed. In 1981 Andersen conceded the embargo allowed the Soviets to search out other suppliers for agricultural commodities; American farmers lost much of their preferred standing in the international marketplace.

The embargo, overwhelming influence of consumer activists on farm legislation, and President Carter's appointment of Carol Tucker Foreman as assistant secretary of agriculture were focal points for farmer frustration. Foreman's role as administrator of USDA's food and nutrition services gave her responsibility over the majority of the agency's budget. Her consumer-group, non-farm background came up in her Senate confirmation hearing and many in agriculture felt scorned by the choice. It was increasingly obvious that farmers had minimal control over agricultural policy; the role once performed by the Farm Bloc was now taken over by consumers, labor unions, the president, Office of Management and Budget, the nation's disadvantaged, and non-farmer bureaucrats such as Foreman. The Grange's job was becoming increasingly difficult because of these shifts in power, requiring a much more sophisticated approach. The National Farm Coalition, held together primarily through the efforts of the National Grange, continued to seek unity of farm organizations when approaching Congress.

In July 1980, Andersen met with President Carter at the White House. Andersen had requested the meeting and he used it as an occasion to relate farmer discontent for their weakening influence on the "decision making process" which had dramatic impact on their way of life. Andersen said the president "seemed unaware of this problem" and promised to do something about it.

Endangered lifestyle

The real problem was the transformation of agriculture in America from easily identifiable family units of production to industrialized farms, both family-owned and those under corporate ownership. The process had been underway for decades, but it was only now becoming obvious to many policymakers. Family farming was one of the last remnants of American working people owning and controlling the means of production and, as the Grange had been warning for several generations, that way of life was disappearing. There were fewer people engaged in agriculture, there were fewer farms, there was less political power and decreased understanding on the part of non-rural citizens. By the end of the

1980s, four percent of the nation's farms would produce over half of our food. The cultural institution known as the family farm was crippled and dying but, as Andersen tried to tell the president, forces beyond the farmer's control were exacerbating the situation.

In 1980 National Grange delegates met in America's heartland, Cedar Rapids, Iowa. The policy statement issued by the session's agriculture committee attempted to articulate the Grange's role in a rapidly disintegrating environment. "We must make the public aware of the importance of both large and small family farms," their statement read, "and the role that each play in providing food, fiber and shelter to a growing world economy." But the family-based agriculture issue for most Americans was never strictly markets and economy, so the statement ended by reiterating the cultural elements which made the family farm worth preserving: "...we must preserve those rural values that stem from family agriculture, values that feed the moral fiber of a great nation." Agricultural observers could now see the possibility of a future without family farms. As the primary champion for family-based agriculture, the Grange was seeing its role as the group to redefine

Edward Andersen (1926-)

the family farm and fight for its preservation.

Out of the Cedar Rapids session came a call for action. Delegates expressed again the opinion that farm industrialization and concentration of ownership were partly the result of federal farm programs and tax regulations. Although they were not specific about what new policies would best solve the problem, delegates did back "legislation that truly provides economic and tax incentives for family farms without escalating advantages for larger farms." A potential solution, at least to the tendency for farms to go into corporate ownership, would be to encourage young people to enter the profession. There was a shortage of rental farms and the combined obstacles of high start-up costs and low profits barred most would-be farmers from actualizing their dreams. Delegates were convinced something could be done in Washington, D.C., to make it more practical for young farm families to get started.

Andersen read his first master's address at Cedar Rapids. In the recently concluded presidential race it was painfully obvious to all farmers that both candidates avoided talking about agriculture; the winner, Ronald Reagan, even admitted the familiar term "parity prices" was a puzzle to him. Andersen's address was worded to set the tone for Grange encounters with a new administration and he restated the organization's strengths which would help it meet the challenges ahead. "The National Grange is in a strong position to work with all national leaders regardless of political affiliation," Andersen said. "Our position is enhanced by our grass roots traditions, our non-partisan actions and our belief that what benefits agriculture benefits the nation."

Fighting a hands-off government

By the time the 1981 convention was convened in Spokane, Washington, the Reagan administration was rolling with its inflation-curbing actions, but delegates telegramed the president from the session that they were still "vitally concerned with the economic crisis of depression proportions in agriculture." Producers were facing "the lowest income...since the 1930s," delegates said, and despite a bumper crop, "the blessing of abundance will do little to relieve the severe cash squeeze which is forcing many farmers to liquidate their holdings." Finally, the president was told the Grange strongly believed "no economic

In order to help combat the shrinking visibility of American farmers, Ed and Darlene Andersen show off banners on the National Grange headquarters building in downtown Washington, D.C.

recovery program can be successful if it's being led by a depression in agriculture." U.S. Representative Thomas S. Foley, a seventh degree member from Spokane and vice-chair of the House Agriculture Committee, spoke to his fellow Grange members about farm conditions at their rural America luncheon. Foley would advance in Congress to become Speaker of the House, gaining the distinction of being the Grange member with the highest position in government since the retirement of President Truman.

Earlier in 1981 the National Grange had launched another effort to help combat a growing threat to farmland preservation—encroachment by urban development. Nearly 40 members from 14 states converged in Chicago for the National Agricultural Lands Conference, sponsored in part by the Grange. Topics considered included conversion of agricultural land to non-farm uses and means for reserving land for farming. Grange Assistant Legislative Director Jim Miller presented a seminar on taxation issues and their impact upon farmland conversion. There was some legislative activity that year on policies to discourage conversion and supportive Grange testimony was offered. When the resulting language appeared in December as part of the 1981 Farm Bill, the Reagan administration announced its opposition. Nonetheless, the Grange was successful in gathering sufficient congressional backing to make the administration retreat. In 1983 Bob Frederick noted the administration retained "a deep and entrenched hostility to farmland protection policies in general."

The adverse economic conditions in rural America deepened and newscasts were filled with images of farm foreclosure sales and families devastated by losing their homes and livelihoods. The term "Farm Crisis" was on everyone's lips and public sympathy for farmers was intensifying. Along with the expressions of concern were worries about the escalating costs of farm program benefits. The taxpayer cost for commodity price supports jumped from $4 billion in fiscal year 1981 to nearly $19 billion in 1983. But the bankruptcies continued, small town banks were seen with boarded-up windows and protests were becoming commonplace again. Unemployment in rural communities was climbing, hundreds of small town hospitals were closing and poverty was claiming more victims each year. Resulting social problems included suicide rates for farmers that were 60 percent higher than for other groups. Dr. Kenneth Robbins, assistant professor of psychiatry at the University of Wisconsin, later stated this was "profoundly disturbing because there is no profession where an occupational hazard ought to be suicide."

In February 1984 Andersen testified before the House Agriculture Committee, calling for a "new direction in farm legislation that would reflect the changing structure of U.S. agriculture." The committee was discussing the pending farm bill destined to replace the 1981 act. Andersen's vision for a new direction included policies and payments to "aid the size farm that is family-owned and operated" by directing money toward those who need it rather than rewarding production volume across the board. He also brought up the Grange's concern that tax-loss farming was strangling the industry. Tax-loss farming was described as a wealthy investor or corporation maintaining a large farming operation as a tax shelter for income earned elsewhere. Andersen directed the congressmen to the president's economic report to Congress which acknowledged that more funds to the Treasury were lost through farm-related tax shelters than the Treasury earned by taxing all farm profits. For every dollar a farmer paid in legitimate income tax, Andersen said, some non-farm investor was using a farm tax shelter to hide more than a dollar of income earned in some other business. "We have failed to target our farm program benefits to family agriculture, and we also have failed to target our tax policies to those whom we intended to benefit."

Andersen's comments were well received and requests for printed copies were greater than for any previous testimony by a Grange leader. State Grange spokesmen also provided similar input for Congress during field hearings on the legislation throughout 1984.

The Reagan-inspired Economic Recovery Act of 1981, while it accommodated most Grange-sponsored tax reform views, was poorly timed, Andersen said, because it inspired crippling increases in interest rates and was enacted prior to balancing the federal budget. Further, it did nothing to discourage the tax-loss farming which was distorting prices and encouraging further concentration in farm ownership. Andersen also saw problems in the act's provisions concerning investment tax credit, capital gains tax and the "fast-track" depreciation schedule. In 1985 the administration unveiled its major tax reform proposal and the National Grange again listed dozens of points which, if enacted, would work to agriculture's disadvantage. The resulting overhaul of the nation's tax structure was signed October 22, 1986. As it emerged in final form, Frederick assessed its impact upon agriculture as "positive."

A notable achievement in 1984 was passage of bankruptcy reform legislation, a topic which occupied the Grange for several years. Throughout the Farm Crisis, news reports had featured the plight of struggling farmers whose stored grain was confiscated when grain elevator companies filed for bankruptcy. There were incidents where farmers were arrested for attempting to move their own grain from the elevators and the Grange had pressed for a solution which would recognize the farmers' rights to their own commodities. The Bankruptcy Reform Act granted farmers priority status in making claims and set reasonable time limits for reclaiming their grain. In 1986, with strong Grange support, a new provision specifically designed for family farmers was added to the federal bankruptcy code.

Despite tinkering with tax laws and bankruptcy codes, American farmers were still hurting in the mid-'80s. Led by popular singer Willie Nelson, 38 renowned entertainers in 1985, during the height of the Farm Crisis, presented in Champaign, Illinois, the first of several benefit concerts. Named the "Farm Aid

Grangers drawn to overseas projects

Examples abound of Grange folks coming to the aid of their friends or neighbors. When people are down on their luck, Grangers try to bring about a solution.

This yearning to help, for some members, has motivated them to set aside personal ambitions and dedicate years of their lives in caring service to others. Sometimes those decisions have carried the Grangers overseas.

Fred Midgley and Carrie Bancroft both joined the Grange when they were very young and it was in their Massachusetts Grange hall where they met. Fred and Carrie later married, bought a farm in Worcester and raised six children. The family remained active in the Grange, rarely missing a meeting. Fred eventually served as subordinate master.

Another Grange member, Senator Arthur Capper of Kansas, was involved with an international assistance organization based in New York City, Near East Relief (now the Near East Foundation). He and other Grange leaders searched nationwide for a suitable couple to tackle agricultural education for 2,000 children housed in the Near East Relief orphanage on the island of Syra in the Aegean Sea, off the coast of Greece. Dr. A.W. Gilbert, Massachusetts Commissioner of Agriculture, recommended the Midgleys and, even though they were then in their late fifties, they cheerfully accepted the challenge.

On September 16, 1926, the Midgleys left Providence, Rhode Island, with five pounds of seed and promises of livestock donations. The *Boston Globe* quoted Frank W. Ober, head of Near East Relief's agriculture committee, as saying, "Instead of sending over shiploads of food, we are sending a trunkful of seed and Mr. Midgley with his head full of sense and his life full of experience." Midgley was expected to share his years of successful market gardening experience with his young charges so they could eventually sustain themselves through agriculture.

Concert," the event was used as both a means of informing the public about conditions in rural America and as a fund-raiser for assistance to farm families displaced from their homes. The National Grange was represented at the concert by Russell Stauffer,

---

During the two years at Syra, Fred imparted the latest in farming and gardening techniques to the students. The cattle and poultry finally arrived and animal agriculture skills were also learned. Mrs. Midgley taught homemaking and piano.

Fred and Carrie Midgley in Greece

Senator Capper was present at the dock when the steamer Eureka prepared to disembark with the purebred bull and 15 other cattle for Midgley's orphanage farm. He arranged for a blessing of the animals by a Greek Orthodox clergyman and the ceremony received publicity in the newspapers. When the Midgleys returned home after two years, Capper praised their dedication and good work at a subsequent National Grange convention.

Sixty years later, and a continent away from the Midgleys' Massachusetts, a couple in Washington state followed a longstanding Grange tradition by volunteering to serve as Peace Corps volunteers in Paraguay. Jim Bauermeister and his wife Louise Dix, both in their thirties and active Grange members for years, decided they had better act on their dreams before children or responsibilities

(continued on next page)

master of the Illinois State Grange and national overseer.

Andersen issued a lengthy statement offering the Grange's "strong support" of Nelson's efforts. "The Grange believes that the human values that are learned by persons engaged in a commercial family farm enterprise have been overshadowed by economic

---

of a home or farm mortgage prevented it.

The National Grange had coordinated Peace Corps activities in Guatemala during the early 1960s and many members had joined the international program. Like the Midgleys, Peace Corpsmen and women were dedicated to teaching people skills to improve their way of life.

Bauermeister and Dix had no institutional setting to greet them. They lived and labored in the dusty, poor village of San Carlos. "Domestic animals—cattle, horses, burros, dogs, pigs, ducks and chickens," Bauermeister later wrote, "wandered freely about, as did scores of barefoot, raggedy children. The birthrate of the area was, as noted in one government report, 'at or near the limits of human reproductive capacity.' Every blade of grass in town was grazed as short as a Marine's first haircut. The ribs of the horses and cattle could be counted beneath their taut skins. The bellies of the pigs were distended with parasites."

The couple was expected to help the locals diversify their agricultural crop base in order to create a more steady cash flow for the small farmers. Complications, such as an untimely drought, the lack of irrigation and long distances to markets unfortunately made the project less than successful.

Reflecting on their frustrating two years in South America, Jim wrote that "our impact on San Carlos was minimal. We touched a few lives perhaps, left behind a few ideas. We left with a feeling that there wasn't much sacrifice on our part. By getting to know these people and this part of the world it was we who came out ahead."

Regardless of the outcome, the Grange practice has been to seek out ways to help, whether it be in the local community or on a different continent.

Many other Grangers have recently served in the Peace Corps, including former Wisconsin State Master Phil Holmes and his wife Jean. They were stationed in Peru in the 1980s.

forces that are beyond a farmer's control or comprehension," Andersen said. "It is very easy to forget that behind the abundance of food and fiber that blesses our country, there stands an American farm family, a family who financially and socially sustains agriculture's infrastructure that encompasses a whole segment of our country called 'rural America'." The survival of those farm families was the focus of the concert, Andersen said. "The money raised by our unselfish and dedicated country-western entertainers on behalf of American farmers is secondary to the attention that will be focused on the social and economic depression that engulfs the providers of our nation's abundance."

Andersen expressed deep commitment to helping American farmers cope with the diverse challenges they were facing in the 1980s. In 1986 he was offered a seat on the board for the Family Farm Defense Fund, a public interest law firm established primarily to litigate precedent-setting cases on behalf of family farmers and ranchers. Operating capital for the defense fund came from the Farm Aid Concert and another country music benefit held earlier in 1985 in Omaha. Andersen's involvement in the Family Farm Defense Fund continued and he was elected chairman in 1987. Other farm organizations represented on the board included the National Farmers Union, the National Farmers Organization, and Women Involved in Farm Economics (WIFE).

A major concern, with roots back to the 1870s, was the accelerated pace of ownership concentration and corporate control of agricultural production and processing. Alarm had been expressed during the Newsom administration about vertical integration in the poultry industry and in 1984 delegates called for a federal investigation into the matter. In 1986 a peculiar set of circumstances caught Grange eyes in the state of Georgia. An Irish-owned corporation revealed plans to build a 20,000 cow dairy at a time when the U.S. was drowning in a surplus of milk. Aside from the milk glut, Andersen learned a major portion of the funding for this unnecessary dairy was coming from tax-free, state-sponsored industrial development bonds. Andersen wondered how U.S. taxpayers would feel about "aiding in the construction of a 20,000 dairy cow enterprise that will be in competition with family-owned and operated dairy farms, when at the same time we are paying for a reduction in domestic production of milk."

State Grange officials were urging Andersen to do something about the Georgia situation but, as Andersen told them, National

Grange policy about industrial development bonds was unclear. A modified resolution was mailed to delegates with the result that the Grange posture was firmly set. A Grange-sponsored amendment was slipped into the Omnibus Trade Bill to prevent the Irish firm from enjoying the benefits of dairy program prices if they used industrial development bonds. The project backers quickly withdrew their bond financing, redesigned and refinanced their operation.

Public alarm about the use of tobacco, including warnings from the National Grange itself, provided fuel to the campaigns of health activists who felt federal agriculture programs should not benefit tobacco farmers. Tobacco farmers, fearful of attacks if their program was included in a general farm bill, opted to have the tobacco measures included in another bill. Unfortunately, their substitute bill failed to pass and the North Carolina State Grange (which represented many tobacco farmers) engineered a solution with the assistance of their state's controversial senator, Jesse Helms. A compromise was negotiated in Congress and it passed in 1985 by being incorporated into a small deficit-reduction bill containing additional provisions for Medicare reimbursements.

A natural consequence of the Farm Crisis was substantial stress on the Farm Credit System (FCS). Much of the blame for farm problems in the '80s could be traced to unwise use of credit in the prosperity of the previous decade. When land values and commodity prices dropped, farmers defaulted on their loans, creating compounding problems for the FCS. The Farmers Home Administration had suffered as well, and commercial lenders were closing their doors in rural areas. One of the first acts of business at the November 1987 Syracuse, New York, convention was to send a telegram to President Reagan and key leaders in both the House and Senate calling for immediate legislation "to assist the farmer-owned Farm Credit System," the nation's largest source for farm credit. Grange leaders were especially concerned because the stock market crash in October created an uneasy feeling that the overall economy was teetering in a dangerous way. The National Grange had been involved in farm credit issues since the inception of the FCS, but during the Farm Crisis the organization's presence was especially felt. The administration had been launching attacks and the FCS needed all the friends it could muster. One month following the Syracuse session Congress passed the Agricultural Credit Act of 1987, incorporating numerous Grange-authored measures to ensure continued health of the FCS.

Attempts to pass protectionist trade legislation provided a new battlefield for the Grange during the Andersen administration. Foreign trade of American agricultural products was highly beneficial to the balance of trade, the Grange said, and attempts to restrict U.S. imports from any trading partners could provoke retaliatory refusals to buy farm commodities. Congressional attempts in 1985 to pass a textile import quota were seen as threats to farmers marketing products to China, Korea and Taiwan. The Grange spearheaded a coalition of 20 agricultural organizations to fight the textile bill, resulting in what Frederick characterized as "one of the most contentious trade issues in recent years." The bill did pass, was vetoed by President Reagan, and the coalition prevailed in the House by blocking an effort to override the veto. During his term, Andersen was appointed to the Agriculture Trade and Export Policy Commission by then House Majority Leader Thomas Foley. Many of the commission recommendations have been incorporated in U.S. trade policy.

While the Grange and the White House cooperated in opposing protectionist trade legislation, there were times when unity was not the prevailing trend. When President Reagan announced in his January 1982 State of the Union address that he intended to eliminate the national vocational education program, Grange leaders were shocked. Various attempts to turn vocational education entirely over to the states were seen as signals for states to drop their leadership in this area. Such a move would be the deathblow of vocational education. In response to the threat, both the California and Washington State Granges lobbied similar bills through their legislatures in 1983, each mandating a vocational education unit in their state's office of public instruction.

A moving problem

Transportation, a perennial topic, occupied Grange workers at the same time they were fighting to preserve family farming. Efficient, low-cost transportation had always been seen as one of the economic cornerstones for America's family farms and the Grange under Andersen's leadership continued the organization's commitment. When he assumed authority from Scott, railroad deregulation and the status of CONRAIL were hot topics. The railroads and the Carter administration had been pressuring Congress to deregulate the industry, but the Grange naturally pulled away from those proposals. Although recognizing reform was necessary, total deregulation was viewed as several steps backward. Deregulation in the trucking industry was viewed somewhat differently, due to the fact that the entire industry had never been totally regulated like the railroads. Nonetheless, complete deregulation was again out of the question; there had to be some controls on both rail and truck transportation because of their importance to the entire economy. The Grange opinion was the prevailing one and Andersen proudly announced in his first master's address that the Motor Carrier Act of 1980 had been signed. That same year Congress finished work on regulation reform for the nation's railroads. Contained in that act were Grange-supported amendments granting agricultural shippers greater protection from rate increases and rail line abandonment.

The government's attempts to get out of the railroad business by selling off its interests in Conrail drew Grange involvement. When the federal government accepted a bid by Norfolk Southern Corporation to purchase CONRAIL, the National Grange and 18 state Granges joined forces as the first agricultural groups opposing the deal. The sale would create the largest railroad company in the nation, essentially eliminating rail competition from a large portion of the East and South. Rail jobs would be lost and the government would not recoup its CONRAIL investment due to tax advantages Norfolk Southern would receive. Grange agitation was largely responsible for the merger legislation dying in the House Energy and Commerce Committee and, in its place, a victorious bill to sell Conrail to the public through a stock offering was drafted. The popularity of the stock on Wall Street validated the Grange's legislative victory and showed that investors agreed CONRAIL should be an independent competitor in the rail industry.

Complications with federal highway funding surfaced concurrently with the CONRAIL sale. The Federal Aid Highway Program went out of existence the end of September 1986 and, by the first of January, 44 states had run out of federal primary highway funds, half the states had no interstate or secondary road money and 16 states had to stop bridge repairs. The Grange legislative staff worked hard to help effect compromises and eventually an $87.5 billion bill was passed. President Reagan vetoed the package but the Grange and others urged the House to attempt an override. The override was successful, causing Frederick to comment, "Rural America's investment in a strong transportation infrastructure was protected and maintained."

Andersen recognized the inevitable fact that the structure of American agriculture was changing. Although the nation could never retreat to the "good old days" with its smaller farms and less complex problems, there was a role the Grange could play in promoting preservation of our family farms. The Grange needed to insist that change was directed so as to have minimal negative impact upon the rural population which still constituted the bulk of its membership. The Grange's image had been that of an organization which took carefully measured steps and its policies were based in a wealth of research. The clear-cut attitude of the Grange had been expressed by Andersen in his letter appearing in the March 29, 1985, issue of the *New York Times*. After responding to statements made in a recent editorial entitled "Setting Agriculture Free," Andersen went on to quote government statistics which supported the Grange's opposition to the Reagan plan to "dismantle the farm subsidy system."

The Grange must evolve

Changes which were transforming American rural life were also making themselves felt within the Grange during Andersen's administration. The membership decline which had begun years before showed no sign of abating, the average age of members continued to rise, finances to maintain member services and lobbying were always in short supply and many leaders viewed with alarm the resistance to modernization which was expressed by rank-and-file members in many states. "We...have a commitment to build our organization into a stronger, larger, and more vital fraternity capable of serving the best interests of our members," Andersen said in 1982. "We are in a changing world, a changing nation, a changing economic atmosphere, a fast-changing technological revolution in agriculture and industry, and a changing population age. Our organization must be prepared to meet these realities in the 1980s and the 1990s." It seemed prudent for the organization to learn if there were inhibiting structures in place within the fraternity which might be causing some of its problems. If so, these could be corrected.

But Andersen's efforts to encourage self-examination were unappreciated by some. Two months after making the statement above, Andersen expressed in the *National Grange Newsletter* his personal dismay about the response he had received from some members. He acknowledged that many members "expressed some degree of shock when I spoke about needing to update, modernize and revitalize many of our Grange methods and traditions." Others were concerned when Andersen said the Grange should be "a progressive organization." What he meant by the word "progressive," he said, was a willingness "to use new ideas, new findings and new opportunities" and did not imply any particular political stance. "We must be willing to take another look at how or why we do things as we do in the Grange," Andersen wrote on. "Let's be willing to recognize tradition for what it is and continue to use or follow it only if it does not hinder us or if we cannot improve on it. Our Grange cannot afford to be bogged down with excess baggage. If we are going to meet and beat the competition for people's time, we must change."

One innovation Andersen supported was instituting a new category of membership for interested individuals or businesses to support the organization without the commitment of full participation in meetings, degree work and social events. Such a membership category would allow participants to take advantage of some Grange-sponsored benefits such as insurance. The organization had flirted with such a concept in its early years but the scandals resulting from Kelley's non-farm subordinates in Boston and New York City made the membership nervous about involvement by business people or those who were simply interested in member services. A resolution endorsing "supportive memberships" for businesses was killed at the 1981 national session. Four years later "associate" memberships were approved, allowing individuals to belong, purchase Grange insurance and enjoy other member benefits without the degree work or the right to attend meetings. A concession was made to states resisting this move by making implementation of associate membership status a prerogative of each state Grange or council. Since 1985 several states have chosen to expand their resources by permitting associate members, resulting in increased members and income. Lifetime memberships, obtained by paying a set sum based upon the applicant's age, also have been viewed as a positive member-retaining feature by the states which have initiated this program.

Early in Andersen's leadership he saw the necessity of having a full-time membership director at the national level. Dorothy Scott had been doing that job voluntarily when her husband was national master, but, in 1981, Andersen opted to make it a staff position. He hired the young Harry Massey, a 12-year member from North Carolina. Massey was supported in his efforts by a volunteer advisory committee made up of leaders from across the country. One of the first orders of business for Massey and his committee was motivating state and subordinate Granges to name individuals who would become personally committed to reversing the decline of dues payers in their Grange. The national network was established and, after some years of hard work, there were some successes. Although the decline has not yet been reversed, it has slowed considerably, and in the 1990s it is again realistic to look toward the possibility of growth.

Other innovations receiving Andersen's attention helped to move the fraternity into the 1980s. He promoted a complete redrafting of the *National Grange Digest,* the organization's rules and regulations, bringing them more in line with contemporary laws and patterns of organizational operation. Another long overdue project was a new edition of the Grange songbook. The completely revised book was a difficult undertaking but the outcome was a much more useful tool for local Granges. His curiosity about the corporate status of the National Grange revealed that the incorporation had been allowed to lapse decades before and it required an act of the Kentucky Legislature to correct the oversight. He was also cognizant that the National Grange was a large organization which should be run no differently than a business. An efficiency study was conducted, resulting in office practices being updated and computer technology employed to boost efficiency. Finally, Andersen felt the future of the organization rested, in part, upon its public image. That image was molded by national media and he was supportive of Judy Massabny's successful efforts to get the Grange story woven into as many media reports as possible.

In August 1986 National Grange staff, department directors and executive committee members met in Moline, Illinois, for an intensive long-range planning workshop. After reviewing the goals set in 1979, they heard from Andersen the facts about the organization's current status. In addition to a steady drop of members, there were two less state Granges since 1979 and some other state units were in a seriously weakened condition. Several state Granges were functioning without full-time masters, deputies, organizers or legislative representatives. Some were not conducting leadership conferences and many were existing without the benefits of a viable membership program, an information director, youth or junior Grange programs.

For the next two days the group tackled the problems and their final report, "The Grange: Outlook and Future Priorities," was presented to delegates at the Madison, Wisconsin, session in November. The activities of the subordinate Granges were seen as the key to either success or failure of the entire organization. The National Grange, however, could not directly affect much at that level because its function was primarily to strengthen the state Granges. The best way for the national organization to help would be provision of effective leadership training to "strengthen the weak units and encourage Grange leaders as they are building their units. If the membership loss is to be stopped, we must concentrate on a program that bears directly on what happens in the subordinate Granges." The innovative Leadership-Membership program of later years owes its genesis to this proposal.

Consensus was reached by the long-range planners in several other areas as well. The slogan, "The Grange is a family-oriented, rural community service organization with a special emphasis on agriculture," was seen as appropriate as was the continuing role of the organization as a legislative voice for its members. The changing diversity of the membership did bring about the recommendation that national legislative priorities be reexamined on an annual basis. The competitive nature of many national and state Grange contests was viewed as counterproductive and should be deemphasized, the report urged; educational and informational programming should appear in their place. Additionally, the usefulness of the Pomona Granges was questioned and further study about their future was called for.

The final item of consensus in "The Grange: Outlook and Future Priorities" concerned the national youth program. Institutionalized by A.S. Goss, the youth department was coordinated by a paid staff person for many years. Following the departure of Bill Steel in 1982, the position was filled by a volunteer youth director. There was some concern that the youth were, in some areas, setting up a parallel system within the Grange and they should become more focused upon the activities involving all members at the subordinate level. "The National Grange Youth/Young Adults Department," the report concluded, "should provide learning opportunities for young Grangers and should assist them in becoming full participating members."

The previous year, at the 1985 national session, New York State Master Bert Morse had presented a lengthy report on his study committee's two year investigation into the youth program. Questionnaires had been utilized in addition to interviews, discussion groups and program analysis exercises. Among other recommendations, the committee suggested different activities be developed to match the interest levels of members aged 14-20 and 21-35. Various existing programs, such as the youth ambassador and young couple contests, Grange interstate youth exchanges, public speaking and sign-a-song contests, were worthy of retention. A new project called "Youth in Government" was suggested as an opportunity to involve young adults interested in this field. The current part-time volunteer director for youth was seen as sufficient for current needs. Morse concluded his account by quoting from the first report of the national committee on youth in 1947: "This Committee believes our youth to be our greatest asset. If the Grange is to interest and hold youth in its membership, we must activate a program for them."

Such a program was in place and, in most instances, Morse's group felt it was functioning well. An attempt to broaden the appeal of the Grange youth program had begun in 1981 with activation of an educational series intended to teach young people the basics of career planning, financial management, will and estate planning, and home buying. Called "Meeting Tomorrow Today," the open meeting series also was seen as an opportunity to engage the interest of potential young members. This effort was endorsed by Morse's team.

The junior Grange program was encountering slightly different circumstances. In 1981, Director of Junior Grange Activities Patty Carncross of Michigan reported that, although many new junior units had been organized recently, others went dormant and overall junior membership was declining. She was frustrated because subordinates were allowing this trend; in her view the junior Grange was "one of our best membership building tools." The program was seen as a good one. "All the children of rural America would benefit from the junior Grange experience. These children are the future of our heartland; they are the future of the way of life we have sought to preserve. It is a heritage that may die without our assistance. It is up to us as Patrons of Husbandry to exercise our 'support and influence' in developing the junior Grange organization and junior Grange members." Such an effort "will have a lasting affect on the subordinate Grange of the future." Carncross retired the following year, being replaced by Mary Beth Heberer of Illinois.

Many junior units were remaining active, and attempts were being made to integrate their activities with those of other departments. Like their counterparts in the youth department, juniors were becoming involved with the Grange interest in helping the disabled. Young members nationwide raised funds to place specially trained "hearing ear" dogs in homes of hearing impaired people. Community service projects were still popular for junior Granges with the annual announcement of national winners being as suspenseful as it was for the larger contest for adult subordinate members.

Community service expands

More than most other national programs, community service continued to capture adult member interest. The annual contests continued, despite a one year suspension due to lack of prize money in 1980. By 1984 National Lecturer Kermit Richardson of Vermont was announcing an all-time high of 1,279 entries had been recorded in the contest that year.

Grange community service and efforts to help the less fortunate were not confined to a specific contest. In 1984 national delegates sent a telegram to President Reagan from their session requesting that he release more surplus grain to help with devastating famine in Ethiopia and Mozambique. "America has a moral duty to share our bounty with those in need," the telegram said. When North Carolina farmers experienced the worst drought on record in the summer 1986, they were facing threats of livestock starvation on top of difficult economic conditions. Grange activists across the nation became concerned and organized a massive "hay lift" to assist the struggling farmers. Truck loads and railroad carloads of donated hay were shipped to the livestock farmers, prompting a letter of thanks from North Carolina Governor James C. Martin which was read at the national convention that year at Madison,

Wisconsin.

The guiding force behind much of the Grange's outreach work in the community continued to be its women members. In addition to supporting and, in many cases, spearheading the official community service projects at the local level, the women remained dedicated to raising funds for CARE.

Over the years the women had taken special interest in the Kelley Farm, and that interest did not wane after the property was transferred to the Minnesota Historical Society. National Director of Women's Activities Mary Buffington reported in 1983 that funds had been raised to purchase a pair of draft horses for the farm and that her slide program about the historic site was popular with Grange people across the country. She noted the women also remained active with collection of used eyeglasses.

One of the most miraculous achievements of the department continued to be the stuffed toy contest. Buffington conceded the popularity of this event was inherent in the fact that all the toys were "given away to make others happy." Beginning in 1985, 10 percent of all toys were donated to Ronald McDonald Houses for

Jeanne Davies

use by families of hospitalized children with the remainder being distributed to hospitals for the same purpose. In 1987 the total annual number of toys entered in the contest and later given away rose to nearly 33,000.

Buffington, from Pennsylvania, would go on to become the National Grange's first woman lecturer in 1987. She was following the lead of two other prominent Grange women. Joanne Passmore, Delaware, was elected secretary at the 1985 Eugene, Oregon, session and at the next convention the status of women in the national organization would rise to new heights with the election of Colorado State Grange Master Jeanne Davies as a member of the executive committee. After 119 years the National Grange finally had its first female as a member of the fraternity's most important and powerful ruling body.

Acting on the need for leadership training on the local level and the desire to expose members in each Grange state to new ideas from their National Grange, Andersen and department directors conceived an arduous series of workshops in 1987. Beginning on the East Coast in March, the meetings would progress through the South in April, return to the Middle Atlantic states in May, move on to the Mountain States in June, cover the Midwest in July and August and then to the Pacific Coast states in late August. Held in Grange halls, the training sessions were led by Andersen with assistance from National Lecturer Robert Barrow, Membership Director Harry Massey, Legislative Director Robert Frederick and his staff. Numerous meetings were held in 31 states in an effort to boost participation and enthusiasm in Grange programs. Thousands of Grange members turned out for the sessions, many of them visiting with a national officer for the first time. Andersen suffered a serious health problem at the end of the tour and had to return home from Oregon, missing the last few scheduled sessions.

The theme for the meetings was "Communication and Motivation." Presenters evaluated the conferences positively, as did those in the audience. Feedback from the local members indicated they were now more comfortable with some changes in direction within their organization and were eager to receive training relative to transforming their subordinate Grange into a more meaningful community role. Many expressed the realization that there was a drastic need for development of leadership skills within the rank-and-file membership.

In his last master's address, delivered in November 1987 at

Syracuse, New York, Andersen said the Grange "must find and develop new and innovative services and programs that will catch the attention of our Grange leaders and cause them to get excited about the opportunity to serve their members and communities." He then proceeded to summarize the major recommendations of the "Outlook and Future Priorities" report. In his quiet but direct, Midwestern fashion, Andersen stated his belief that "we spend (waste) too much time creating a problem for ourselves by trying to identify (or create a term for) what the Grange is." He continued by saying the Grange at each level could be whatever the members wished it to be, the only limitations being Grange law, the members' desires and their willingness to work. "'What the Grange is' will constantly change as our society changes," Andersen continued, "and the Grange members need change."

During the Syracuse session Andersen spent three days in the hospital and, as announced in August, he declined to seek renomination. Following the election of National Lecturer Robert Barrow to the master's office, the Andersens retired in Omaha, later returning to a new home on the family farm in Waterloo, Nebraska.

Andersen had brought to the organization a new awareness of the transformations which were occurring both within the Grange and in American agriculture. He helped mold a desire for solving problems in the organization and across rural America by sharpening leadership skills of those within the Grange—people who could then go on to effect necessary change. The mechanisms for providing that training would soon emerge.

14

Leadership for Tomorrow

1987-

TWO DAYS AFTER National Master Robert E. Barrow delivered his first master's address—at the 1988 Redding, California, session—delegates and guests were given some sobering details about the nation's heartland. "Rural America Ain't What She Used to Be" was the title for an address given by Jim Barron of Washington State University's Department of Agricultural and Resource Economics. Barron revealed that most rural communities could no longer exist if they depended totally upon their agricultural income. New means of survival must be studied by coalitions of agriculturists and other interests. But now, when rural areas needed it the most, their pool of leaders, quality schools and up-to-date means of communication were sadly missing, Barron said. The Grange could fill the void by providing training opportunities for citizens who wanted to lead their communities back to health.

National Master Andersen had seen these needs and the unique role the Grange could fill in rural communities around the nation. The focal point of his last year on the job was the nationwide road trip to every Grange state. The tour was an attempt to motivate Grange leaders to unleash again the powerful force for change which they had at their disposal: the subordinate Grange.

When Andersen chose not to stand for reelection, delegates paid respect to the direction he had charted by choosing a successor with an uncompromising aspiration to see the Grange return to prominence as the leadership school for rural America. Although Bob Barrow's background was far different from any of his predecessors, his dedication to the Grange movement was unquestioned.

Barrow was a former bank vice president from Swansea, Massachusetts, just a few freeway minutes from Providence, Rhode Island. He had never been a farmer, but since high school days he had been an active member in the "farmers' fraternity." Holding most offices in Swansea Grange and the Pomona Grange, he culminated a succession of Massachusetts State Grange offices by serving four years as its master. While in the top state post he was delegate to national sessions, where his business ability landed him the national secretary's job in 1983. Shifting to the lecturer's office in 1985, he served in that capacity until being elected national master at the 1987 Syracuse session. Aside from Grange activities, Barrow studied voice and was a featured professional soloist for several large churches. He and his wife Dolores raised two daughters.

Barrow's small town background was typical of what was happening across rural America. The 1990 census would disclose some of the trends Barron had spoken of: many rural areas were now gaining population but the number of those involved in farming was still shrinking. Commuters were moving urban sprawl into

Robert E. Barrow
(1930-)

the countryside and small towns; farm families were being crowded even more into minority status within their own communities. In the decade of the 1980s, farmers and their families dwindled from 2.7 percent of the total population to only 1.9 percent (down from 39.3 percent at the turn of the century). The total number of farms also dropped significantly and the average acreage of the remaining farms grew even more.

In some parts of the nation conditions were tragically different. Small communities with no urban center nearby, particularly in the Plains states, were drying up because unfavorable economic conditions, caused partly by the changing structure of agriculture. People were leaving boarded-up buildings behind as they moved on to greener pastures. Family agriculture and the small communities that depended upon it seemed doomed as never before.

Promoting change through leadership

The Grange's strength as an organization had initially been its connection with families engaged in agriculture. They viewed their fraternity as a vehicle for self-improvement and community enrichment. As demographics changed in rural areas, needs also shifted and, especially since World War II, the Grange on a national level was attempting to adapt. In 1987, National Grange Executive Committee Chairman Jack Silvers, from Washington state, spoke openly to national delegates about the seriousness of the membership decline which had been plaguing the organization since the mid-1950s. He proposed three solutions: a strong legislative program focusing on issues with broad-based appeal; streamlining of National Grange services and coordination of organizational efforts; and, most important, implementation of leadership training.

The message was clear and, following the convention, work began in earnest. In the spring of 1988 national officers and department directors met at the Washington, D.C., office to participate in special training conducted by community resource development specialists from the University of Maryland and the USDA's Economic Research Service. Harry Massey, director of membership development, coordinated the effort. The group would become known as the National Leadership Team and the process they developed was labeled the Leadership-Membership Program. National staff was present at the training and department directors attending were the Grange's first woman national lecturer, Mary Buffington (elected to succeed Barrow); Betty Jane Gardner, director of women's activities; and Bernard and Helen Shoemaker, youth directors.

Barrow opened the training session by recalling, "The Grange nationwide has an excellent reputation for hands-on leadership. I believe we can build on that reputation by addressing concerns of the community. But because of the many new trends developing across the country, the Grange needs to take advantage of all available resources," such as modern training techniques used regularly in business and government. "As each local Grange becomes energized with a new enthusiasm, new life will be added to the Grange."

The Leadership-Membership model which evolved from the training session was to approach state Granges with a proposal. If the state would commit some motivated and qualified volunteers, the national team would conduct an intensive training session for them. The process would be repeated by the state teams in subordinate Granges. The overall goal was to provide local people with usable skills in group leadership, communication, community service, issue identification and program development. State teams would guide local members to identify their own organizational and community needs, target other resources and develop concrete plans to achieve their goals. It was a bold step but absolutely necessary, national leaders felt.

With the Leadership-Membership process finally in place, Barrow set the stage by paraphrasing Andersen's statements concerning the need to change. Change shouldn't be feared or resisted, Barrow said. "What is to be feared is our inability to adapt." By 1989 membership had fluctuated so there were only nine states with over 10,000 members each, while 16 states had less than 1,000 members each. Some of these were not returning enough dues to the National Grange to cover their portion of national convention expenses.

Within one year of its initiation, the Leadership-Membership plan had been presented to 17 state Granges, many of them making a commitment to its success. Teams were tailoring the program to meet the needs of members in their own state and there was optimism that improvement would be imminent. Members in Michigan even employed telemarketing practices, calling 10,000 prospective members as a follow-up to mass mailings. Further successes were being reported by states which had adopted the associate member classification. It appeared that the keys had finally been found to slow the decline in membership and eventually start the organization on an upward climb again.

Throughout the fraternity, members began seeing themselves as spark plugs for positive change. Leadership development emerged as the preeminent goal in many Granges. By 1990, the National Grange citizenship and public affairs committee was reporting, "Every rural community is entitled to a viable economy, wholesome family living space, a sense of community pride and adequate funding from state and national levels of government. The National Grange must support all efforts to develop rural leadership. Rural people need the Grange's help in solving difficult problems for which there are no standard answers. These problems include a breakdown of the family structure, social ills that are caused by drugs, incurable diseases such as AIDS, affordable health care for people of all ages, an aging rural population, and the deterioration of the infrastructure of schools, churches, businesses, and transportation in rural communities."

Streamlining services

Another component of the renewal plan involved streamlining and modernizing the Grange. When President Reagan wrote delegates at the Redding session, "No organization has contributed more to our rural heritage than the National Grange," longtime members pointed out that the organization's ceremonies and ritual should be given a large part of the credit. The new ritual study committee concurred. "Our ritual is something which sets us apart as an organization," their report stated. "It is a vital part of the Grange and has helped to sustain us." The committee, however, did not have the same permanence as the ritual they were examining. Their suggestions for minor changes at the 1988 and 1989 conventions were largely ignored and a resolution to dissolve the group was passed.

Part of the streamlining effort involved provision of added member services, and those plans advanced more successfully than ritual reform. Some of the greatest historic periods of Grange growth occurred when the promise of economic gain attracted potential members. Insurance programs, available only to members, were still in force in many states and the North Carolina State Grange continued to offer Blue Cross/Blue Shield medical insurance. Cooperative buying clubs were still popular as were Grange credit unions. The few Grange retirement housing projects were always full and, in 1988, the California State Grange announced its second such development, joining large projects already in place in Michigan and Washington states. By 1990 the consensus was that a national program offering discounts for members would be appealing.

Working with a national marketing firm, National Grange Director of Information Judy Massabny put together a package of travel discounts, reduced price outlets for eye wear, hearing aids and prescriptions, and pre-paid legal services. Called "The Grange Advantage," the plan was to offer the program to each Grange household in America. The marketing firm would take care of the mailings if the National Grange would supply the lists of members.

That was the hitch. Even in the days of *The National Grange Monthly,* the National Grange had no listing of all members because the magazine was not universally distributed. Theoretically, state Granges should have lists for their own publications, but in some cases they did not. Furthermore, although some larger state Granges had computerized, others kept records in a more primitive fashion. Preparing for the mailings was a gigantic task for the national office but it was generally agreed that the potential benefits for members outweighed the drawbacks to staff. Having a centralized database of members was a tremendous advantage for future promotions and...maybe, someday...fulfillment of a dream as old as the Grange itself—a publication distributed to all member households. Response to the Grange Advantage mailings was encouraging and a large number of Grange families signed up for the program.

Closely related to Grange Advantage was promotion of a VISA credit card for members. Although there were some logistical problems to overcome, the card was eventually offered and some members responded enthusiastically. A third membership benefit, having appeal to younger families with high school children, was a service providing tailored portfolios of data about choices of colleges, scholarship leads and information beneficial to parents. This service was offered to Grange families at a discount, making difficult choices easier and less expensive.

The goal of these benefit programs was to provide members and potential members with tangible economic benefits. It had been observed for generations that a significant percentage of Grange members, both active and inactive ones, were originally attracted to the organization by the availability of competitive insurance. Other general farm organizations had similar insurance programs. The challenge was to expand the variety of benefits which would make Grange membership an even better bargain. Dues income and dividends paid by benefit sponsors would better equip the Grange to tend to its other activities.

Perhaps more than anything else, the National Grange had always been a legislative action organization. In 1987 it was suggested that a national legislative project might captivate a broad spectrum of the membership, much like struggles for Rural Free Delivery had done 100 years before. Taking demographic changes of the membership into account, it was obvious that the arcane maneuverings of farm legislation held little appeal for most people affiliated with the Grange. Certain consumer issues might attract some, but an old Grange standby, transportation, was finally selected for the targeted approach.

A push for rebuilding

In 1986 and early 1987 the nation had seen its roads and bridges receive little maintenance attention because of a congressional impasse that kept dedicated Highway Trust Fund user fees from being dispersed. When legislation finally reached President Reagan's desk, he promptly vetoed it. The Grange successfully used its congressional influence to encourage a veto override and repairs resumed. The Federal-Aid Highway Program would be in place until the end of September 1991.

The debates on this legislation made the deterioration of America's roads and bridges a matter of public concern. People were horrified by television news stories showing school children leaving their bus, following it on foot at a safe distance as it crossed a bridge too unsafe for the combined weight of the bus and its passengers. They heard other stories of bridges in all parts of the country falling into the rivers below. And they were too familiar with potholes and crumbling asphalt in their own neighborhoods.

Grange leaders suspected Americans, particularly rural and

suburban ones, had more experience with crumbling roads than they wanted. The disintegration of the nation's roads and bridges was an issue which affected everyone and an organized campaign to do something about it was chosen as the Grange's legislative focus. Speaking in September 1988 before 500 leaders assembled for the National Highway Users Congress, Barrow called for a new national program to link rural roads to our national highway network. Sufficient funds must be channeled toward improving the local transportation infrastructure, he said. The Grange initially became involved in transportation issues to "get farmers out of the mud." But now, Barrow announced, with rural roads and bridges rapidly decaying, "we're back in the mud again."

In 1991 the Interstate Highway System was scheduled for completion. It was thought that part of the $3 billion annual allotment for interstate highways could be diverted to local roads and bridges. Advance organized Grange action could make a difference.

Materials were prepared and sent to Grange leaders at each level, encouraging them to adopt the Local Roads and Bridges legislative project. Subordinate members learned that nationwide one out of every four miles of county roads were judged by highway engineers to be less than "barely adequate." Rural residents using those poor roads were, on the average, paying $9.16 more per capita to the federal Highway Trust Fund. Although 70 percent of the nation's roads were under local government control, those governmental units received little or no federal funds.

Part of the Local Roads and Bridges project was educational. The hope was that subordinate Grange members would use the materials to promote community-wide discussion and local action. On the national level, the Grange became a major player in a 20-organization Rural Road Coalition comprised of farm, commodity and rural interest organizations. Also participating were the National Association of Towns and Townships and the National Association of Counties. The coalition worked for legislative authority to divert some federal money to local use through the Intermodal Surface Transportation Infrastructure Act of 1991. A suitable bill passed the Senate in June 1991 and in October the House version passed. After emerging from a conference committee, the final bill passed in the last hours of the session, just prior to Christmas recess 1991. Grange Legislative Representative Jeff Kramer's activity on the Hill was largely responsible for inclusion of the Grange language. Measures in the legislation ensured an improved transportation system for rural America over the six-year life of the act. Grange activists around the country could congratulate themselves; their agitation had paid off and was at least partly responsible for the legislative victory.

Farming remains a Grange focus

There were continuing legislative battles across the whole field of traditional Grange involvement. Barrow had just started on his new job in June 1988 when he had the opportunity to visit at the White House with Vice President Bush concerning the Grange's 14-point drought relief program. Portions of the country were being besieged with persistent shortfalls in precipitation, conditions which were creating havoc with all portions of the agricultural industry. The vice president was heading the administration's drought relief task force and Barrow's comments were well

National Master Barrow was successful in promoting the Grange concept of targeting farm benefits during a conference with then Vice President George Bush in 1988.

received. Within a few days of the visit, several of Barrow's proposals were adopted by the USDA under authority already granted by law. Within a few weeks, the department also implemented additional parts of the plan but additional points required congressional action. By mid-July agriculture committees in both houses had passed drought relief legislation and on August 11 President Reagan held a Rose Garden signing ceremony to finalize the resulting $3.9 billion bill. National Grange staff and visiting members from Maryland attended the ceremony.

Perhaps the most surprising part of the drought relief bill was the fact that a longstanding Grange proposal for a means test was included. Grange lobbyists and other advocates for family farms had long noted that government farm programs often perpetuated the status quo, allowing the rich to get richer, the poor to get poorer while those in between were squeezed. As Barrow said in his 1988 master's address, "We have built an agricultural production machine that has consumed farmers. We have seen, or are seeing, the demise of moderate-sized commercial farms." The drought relief package was a refreshing change from regular farm programs where even the largest corporate-type farms were eligible to receive some direct government farm subsidy payments. The drought legislation said livestock producers with gross incomes of $2.5 million or more or crop farmers with gross incomes of $2 million or more were ineligible for benefits. At last, the Grange's counsel to target farm program benefits to small- and medium-size family farms had surfaced in this legislation.

Unfortunately, the Grange idea of targeting benefits was not as successful in the 1990 farm bill. President Bush's new Secretary of Agriculture, Clayton Yeutter, sent a telegram to delegates assembled for their 1989 national session in Greensboro, North Carolina, praising them because they had "always supported reasonable, sensible policy positions" and had always done so with "great integrity." Although the Grange-supported 1985 farm bill had improved conditions for farmers, its replacement, delegates felt, could help family agriculture even more if the targeting of benefits concept was incorporated.

Despite improved conditions on America's farms, Barrow noted in 1990 that there were still a million farmers "teetering on the edge" of solvency. He pointed at the "increasing concentration of the United States' agricultural sector" and the fact that it "poses a threat to the continued viability of the small- and medium-size family farmers and the rural communities they support." The largest operations, Barrow said, were singled out in the president's budget report to Congress as receiving more than their share of federal payments. Furthermore, the Executive Branch's own Office of Management and Budget estimated that almost $1 billion a year could be saved by making those farmers with gross sales over $500,000 a year ineligible to receive farm commodity program benefits.

As the congressional farm bill debate heated up, Grange legislative representatives were on hand to point out these inequities. Democratic Senator Harry Reid of Nevada mustered 29 other colleagues to propose a means test amendment on the Senate bill and Democrat Senator Thomas Daschle of South Dakota attempted to introduce a measure which would satisfy Grange proposals for targeting benefits to smaller farms. In the House, Representative Silvio Conte, a Republican from Massachusetts, secured hearty Grange support for his unsuccessful effort to reform farm program payment limitation laws through an amendment to the 1990 farm bill. His plan would have attributed all farm program payments to "natural persons," rather than corporations, trusts, estates or partnerships. The Grange stood alone in this battle; other farm organizations in the loosely formed farm coalition did not support the plan. In fact, other farm groups unexpectedly alligned themselves with the environmental groups who together, Barrow admitted, "expressed a convoluted belief that if the large farmers were ineligible to participate in the program, the environmental organizations' objectives would suffer." Their thinking was that large farms, without the restraints built into the farm bill, would abandon their compliance with sodbuster, swampbuster, conservation and cross compliance provisions. Barrow warned afterward that the "environmental groups' effort may backfire because, as farm program changes are made due to budget restraints, the amount of the direct payments to producers will decrease."

Missing the chance to implement targeted benefits wasn't the Grange's only disappointment with the 1990 farm bill. The national economy was in a slump, the federal deficit escalating, and pressure—some of it from the Grange—was on Congress to trim spending. The final farm package made "the deepest spending cuts in the farm support programs since their beginning in 1933," Barrow said. National Grange Legislative Director Bob Frederick, back on the Hill following open heart surgery, commented that the "total budget for the 1990 Farm Bill makes up only one percent of the total United States' budget but is being cut by 10 percent, which is a greater reduction than most of the other segments of the budget." Once again, agriculture was being called upon to subsidize other portions of the population.

The debate about targeting benefits was far from over, Grange leaders warned. "Society as a whole will benefit in the long-term," Frederick said, "if government programs help to maintain the family farm and help to prevent the continued movement of the land and other production inputs from the hands of the many into the hands of the few." Interestingly, President Bush had stated in 1990 that it was "hard to justify" siphoning limited farm program resources "to large, wealthy farmers." With that support, perhaps the Grange agenda dating from 1978 could still see the light of day.

A sustainable position

Barrow's testimony before the House Agriculture Committee on the farm bill highlighted another Grange position which had been adopted long before it was popular. For years there had been agitation from consumer and environmental groups about the perceived lack of wisdom in pursuing large scale agriculture with its heavy reliance upon larger and larger machinery and massive applications of agricultural chemicals. Critics of this view could easily justify the present system because it boosted production to the point that fear of food and fiber shortages was nonexistent in America. Barrow called on congressmen to increase their support for the USDA's Office of Small Scale Agriculture, thinking that it would assist not only the nation's most needy farmers but also reap benefits for medium-sized farm operations. Barrow went on to champion increased research for "Low Input/Sustainable Agriculture," a program exploring the more cost-efficient and environmentally benign agricultural practices largely ignored by the largest operations. New crop production practices resulting in effective reductions of chemicals was a dream that could revolutionize American agriculture. Those who accused farmers of being bullheaded about abandoning agricultural chemicals simply did not know the full story. But the switch to new technologies would not be possible without exhaustive research, much of it government supported.

Grange leaders had long held the position that the farmer was the first environmentalist. It was to the family farmer's best interest, and to his heirs, that conservation be practiced, and activities posing a potential threat to the fragile environment be avoided. The Grange had been an early supporter of conservation moves on the part of government and, in his 1989 master's address, Barrow proudly pointed to the statistics which revealed 30 million acres of highly erodible land had been enrolled in the Conservation Reserve. Most all of the land identified as at risk for erosion was under the plan and the conversion of wetlands and fragile land to production had slowed dramatically. On these points the Grange and environmental lobbyists shared a sense of accomplishment.

The 1980s was the decade when the organized environmental movement gained its niche in American political action. While the Grange and environmental groups agreed on many elements, there were others where no compromise could be reached. One of the first clashes between the Grange and environmental groups occurred in 1988 when the Grange spoke openly in support of oil exploration in Alaska's Arctic National Wildlife Refuge. Since the U.S. was importing over 40 percent of its oil, it was felt full usage of domestic production would be economically advantageous. Oil exploration should also resume offshore, the Grange informed Congress, and, in all cases, measures should be taken to protect the environment. The search for oil must be matched by the search for alternative fuels which could eventually replace petroleum as our primary energy source, the Grange said.

Other disputes with the environmental lobby surfaced when the National Grange, in conjunction with the Oregon State Grange, opposed addition of 1,700 miles of that state's waterways—some of it in private ownership—to the Wild and Scenic Rivers System. On the heels of this confrontation came the American Heritage Trust Act which the Grange labeled as a government-funded land grab. The Grange quickly mobilized opposition to the act that was supported by a broad base of environmental and conservation groups, with the result that the bill's sponsor, Arizona's Representative Morris Udall, soon withdrew it.

At about the same time, animal rights activists gained a national audience and began pressing for legislation characterized by the Grange as severely limiting to American animal agriculture. Efforts to take animal management decisions out of the hands of farmers were successfully opposed in 1988 by state Granges in

Massachusetts, California and New York. The battle continues on state and national levels.

In 1990 another animal, the spotted owl, became the subject of a bitter fight between environmental groups and private timber interests. Owl activists, concerned about the alleged negative impact of logging on the endangered species, became increasingly successful in blocking timber harvesting in the Pacific Northwest. State Granges and others in the region became alarmed about the negative impact on timber-related jobs. Debates, court challenges and hard feelings continued, prompting Washington State Master Robert Clark to comment at the 1990 national convention that many resolutions from the West focused on the environment and related economic issues. "As a rural-based fraternity," Clark said, "we find that we must concentrate on maintaining a common sense balance between those who would advocate no growth and those who want unlimited growth. The farmers are caught squarely in the middle and their very independent nature can be their undoing."

The Grange's "reasonable, sensible policy positions" mentioned by Yeutter were engineered to keep it in the mainstream of sensitive issues. Since the days of its first master, the national organization had sought that balanced approach whenever possible. At times, though, it was impossible to stay in the middle as the peacemaker. Emotionally charged environmental concerns erupted into wars where occupying the middle ground posed the most danger and, many times, proved to be the least effective position.

Barrow tried to mend some fences with the environmental groups—and many of these shared members with the Grange—by emphasizing conservation of resources at the 1990 convention in Wichita, Kansas. "As Grange members," he spoke, "we are well aware of the importance of good stewardship of our natural resources. The Grange was preaching about the benefits of soil and water conservation when Theodore Roosevelt was President. Many of the founding members of the modern environmental movement, such as Gifford Pinchot, were both active farmers and active Grangers. Today, the Grange remains committed to the practical and reasoned protection of our nation's natural resources.... If we are then to be good stewards, we must realize that our legacy is far greater than the physical environment. If we preserve our natural resources in a pristine condition but leave our children ignorant

National Master Barrow and Director of Deaf Activities Beulah Winter present a $10,000 check to King Jordan (center), president of Gallaudet University in Washington, D.C. The money will fund an endowment at the university which provides higher education opportunities to the hearing impaired. The money came from Granges nationwide.

and fearful, or living in poverty for want of meaningful employment, or without the right to exercise the basic human liberties, then we will have failed as stewards." It is doubtful this appeal impressed the environmental lobby.

Renewed focus on health issues

Rural jobs, in regions dominated by agriculture and forestry, were only part of the problem. As National Master Scott had articulated more than a decade before, America needed and deserved more rural development attention from government. With the Grange doing its part to provide the leadership, the entire rural infrastructure needed increased attention. Improved highways and roads were a primary target but other needs were there as well. Hearkening back to the days of Goss and Newsom, the Grange again raised its voice about health issues.

While outlining advances in medicine which were diminishing the effects of cancer, heart disease and others, Barrow told delegates at the 1988 session that there were new challenges. Rural Americans were "now faced with new issues—Acquired Immune Deficiency [Syndrome] (AIDS), health needs of teen pregnancies, and health care for the homeless." Most important, he said, were health problems associated with AIDS and drug abuse. "The effects of these two issues alone are tearing at the fabric of American families because they are not limited to economic status, race, color or creed and, in many cases, their impact crosses the patterns of different lifestyles. It's important to remember that rural America is not immune to either of these problems."

The Grange, Barrow continued, would increase its efforts in support of research on health problems. But, he instructed, "the biggest contribution the Grange can make is in your local communities. Open up your Granges and your Grange halls for public forums on illegal drug use and AIDS. Through our Junior, Youth and Young Married programs, opportunities are available for service to communities on these issues.... What an opportunity for community service!"

The old problem of inadequate health resources for rural residents still existed in many areas, Barrow admitted. He pointed at recent enabling legislation establishing the National Advisory Committee on Rural Health, the Office of Rural Health and the Rural Health Research Centers Program. No money had yet been appropriated for these functions, but the Grange was doing everything possible to see these efforts become operational.

Funding was a perpetual problem for rural hospitals and clinics. Barrow pointed out that Medicare paid rural facilities less than urban centers for the same medical procedures and that was, in part, squeezing small town hospitals out of business. In his 1989 master's address, he singled out Grange action in Washington state which was responsible for setting up local tax-supported hospital districts. He said voters were enthusiastically supporting this concept, much as they rallied around Grange-sponsored public utility districts in that state during the 1930s. "Rural economies are under financial stress, limiting the ability of the local communities to support their hospitals," Barrow said. "I urge both state and local Granges to investigate the Washington State Grange's experience to see if such a plan is applicable to their localities."

Education in rural regions also was suffering. In 1990 the National Grange joined with other groups in a rural education coalition called Organizations Concerned About Rural Education. The Grange's hope, Barrow summarized, was to stimulate members to "create comprehensive 'real life' programs in rural communities that address...local needs. By playing an active role in this vibrant and innovative coalition, we can help to bring rural America out of its economic doldrums into a state of economic strength and security." Barrow added that the future depended upon our schools because "rural education is directly linked with rural development."

Hospitals and schools, like other services and businesses, depend upon the economic health of the community for their own vitality. As Grange Legislative Representative Leroy Watson, testified before the House Agriculture Subcommittee on Conservation, Credit and Rural Development, rural residents continued to be poorer than urban citizens. They experience more unemployment and tend to have a less formal education. They are more likely to live in substandard housing and lack adequate access to information services, communication systems, financial services, health care facilities, transportation systems and other benefits taken for granted by their urban cousins. Watson proceeded to outline a 13-point Grange program for rural development including proposals to touch all aspects of the problem.

The subcommittee chair, Representative Glenn English of Oklahoma, had made an unusual request of each organization presenting testimony. As part of their presentation, speakers were to outline existing organizational efforts targeted to improving the quality of life for rural citizens. Watson was proud to enumerate the many accomplishments of the Grange, including activities of the Grange's new Local Roads and Bridges program, a Grange-sponsored health insurance program, health maintenance organizations (HMOs), retirement homes, credit unions, insurance companies, discount product purchase programs, supply cooperatives, marketing services, investment services, computer information services, newspapers and newsletters, bed and breakfasts and travel services. Granges award over $100,000 annually in scholarships and low interest loans to rural students each year, Watson said, and $35,000 is spent in coordinating national programs for Grange youth. A $10,000 Grange endowment had been presented to Gallaudet University, thousands of copies of the National Grange's hearing-impaired educational packets are regularly distributed to rural schools and, finally, the National Grange had initiated a new leadership, volunteer educational effort called the Grange Leadership-Membership Program. Grange investments in rural communities, Watson noted, included Grange halls, ball fields, fire and ambulance stations, county fairgrounds, summer camps and office/retail space. He had made his point: The Grange was not satisfied by asking only for government action...Grange members had for generations tried to be part of the solution for rural America's problems.

As Watson had hinted, the heart of the Grange was still its subordinate Grange. Membership losses meant there were fewer of them now, but many of those that survived were, through the efforts of the Leadership-Membership Program, beginning to experience new vitality. Watson could have cited many examples. He could have mentioned Volunteer Grange in Knoxville, Tennessee. Their state has few Granges, but this group of members placed again in the top four Granges nationwide in the Community Service Program (this time for coordinating a large planting project in a local park). Grange officials couldn't remember the number of times this subordinate had been a national finalist. Another Grange out West was trying to meet the needs of widows by offering day-long seminars from experts in grief therapy, financial planning and career training. Watson also could have shown the new poster being distributed by the Grange deaf activities department, another first for the organization. The poster pictures the Pledge of Allegiance in sign language. Another point of pride was the successful Grange safety petition to ban exact replica toy guns. And he would have felt comfortable mentioning Grange lobbying efforts—all inspired by grass-roots resolutions—to promote farmland preservation, support measures to reduce global warming and increase the availability of biodegradable plastics. Grange people could be proud of the progress they had made.

The pillars of grass-roots Grange activity were still supporting the organization on the eve of its 125th anniversary. Organized self-help at the local, state and national level, effective legislative action, and strengthening the community by offering individuals the opportunity to serve and grow remained central to the success of the organization in all parts of the country. The agenda continues to change and evolve, but the fundamental tenets outlined in the

Declaration of Purposes still provide the solid base for successive generations of rural members.

15

Brothers and Sisters

> America! America!
> God shed His grace on thee
> And crown thy good
> With brotherhood
> From sea to shining sea!
> —Katherine Lee Bates
> *America The Beautiful*

BROTHERHOOD is an elusive human bond which everyone endorses, few can adequately define, and fewer still actively pursue. The term describes the highest form of linkage, aside from marriage, between unrelated individuals, and qualities invariably associated with it—liberty, equality, honor and obligation—constitute the foundation of every society.

It is not accidental that the term brotherhood, referring as it does to a union of unrelated people, was borrowed from those expressions describing kinship relationships. Family ties are the strongest forces uniting individuals and of all bonds within the family, those between siblings are glorified most because of the implications of equality which are present. Paternal and maternal relationships are always tinged by the presence of power and authority; ideally, siblings share equally in the benefits of the family. In the Grange, the term brotherhood holds no sexist connotation; it describes an attitude of love and allegiance which is experienced by both men and women.

In America today, kinship is much less important than in older, more traditional, agrarian societies. In those settings, an individual was often defined by his family, and his reputation was assessed by how he fulfilled kinship roles and duties. Societal relationships outside the family in more primitive cultures were risky and threatening, so bonding rituals were devised to allow men to become "brothers," sharing the loyalty existing between blood kin. The Native American "blood brother" ceremony, popularized by Hollywood, and covenant rituals mentioned in the Old Testament are examples of efforts to build strong relationships outside the family unit. According to social theorist Wilson Carey McWilliams, these covenant rituals created "a community of interests and affections among those already presumed to share an identity of aims and essence."

Not unlike modern communalists, the earliest colonial settlers set up an experiment in brotherhood and from that emerged the unique American notion of community complete with its democratic political structure known as the town meeting. When the population expanded and society entered new phases of complexity, more elaborate political patterns were necessary. With them came a thriving fascination for organizations structuring the fraternal bond of brotherhood, uniting those with shared values or goals which they considered most important. In lodge halls, members called one another "brother" and later, in the Grange and other groups admitting women, "sister." Fraternities became increasingly popular, especially the Masons and Odd Fellows, which were, respectively, eighteenth and early nineteenth century English imports. Significant contributions to the new republic were made by members of these fraternities and most of the liberal ideals woven into the evolving government owe their origin to the lofty principles regularly illustrated in ritualistic dramas in early American lodge halls.

When the country entered its most pronounced cycle of change following the conclusion of the Civil War, men found they were unambiguously bound to a commercial chain which united them to the centers of industry and trade. Unfortunately, this bonding to commerce divided men from each other on the local level because of the relentless forces of competition. Farmers, who as a group were becoming dependent upon commerce for the first time, were especially vulnerable. McWilliams notes that in towns and, for Granges, in the countryside, lodges "sprang up across America in the townsman's [and farmer's] search for some safe retreat from his daily life of competition, insecurity and hostility." Fraternal involvement allowed these men to know "that in the gigantic and expanding nation he was not alone and insignificant, but one of a band of brothers with lodges about the land." Organizations unit-

The Golden Rule, "Do unto others as you would have them do unto you," is an underlying principle in fraternal orders. This representation of the Golden Rule was created in mosaic by longtime Grange member Norman Rockwell and is on display at the United Nations in New York City. Among Rockwell's other creations was a portrait of National Grange Master Herschel Newsom.

ing women had similar goals.

The trend to organize fraternal groups turned into a prosperous "business" and many people, perhaps even O.H. Kelley, hoped to make a comfortable living setting up and administering these groups. By the mid-1920s, when collective membership in fraternal orders apparently peaked, it was estimated there were 800 different fraternities (often called secret societies) operative in America, with a combined membership of 30 million.

Even in the heyday of American fraternal groups, there were problems. When sociologists Robert S. and Helen Merrill Lynd did research for their classic study of Muncie, Indiana, they noted the seeds of potential decline. "The great days of lodges as important leisure-time institutions in Middletown have vanished," they wrote in *Middletown: A Study in Modern American Culture.* "At present (1924), despite the heavy building programs of leading lodges, business men are 'too busy' to find the time for lodge meetings that they did formerly; the man who goes weekly to Rotary will confess that he gets around to the Masons 'only two or three times a year.' Working men admit, 'The lodge is a thing of the past to what it was eight or ten years ago. The movies and autos have killed it.' 'He belongs to a lodge but never goes,' said more than one of the working class wives interviewed." The Lynds returned to Muncie 10 years later and found conditions worse. "While the lodges still struggle on," they observed, "they appear for the most part to have even less vitality than in 1925."

If membership growth is any indicator of vitality, there is evidence that some fraternal orders, including the Patrons of Husbandry, kept their spirits high for some time beyond the 1920s. Certainly the Grange grew and prospered at an amazing pace, with the exception of a few years during the Depression, until the early 1950s. Membership in Masonic lodges peaked a few years later.

Today, a few fraternities are experiencing encouraging turnarounds of interest. Those with the greatest growth in the 1980s and 1990s, however, are lodges which feature the most social services for members—such as restaurants, bars, gyms and exercise programs—and are located close to the suburbs. Interest seems to be greater, too, in areas with high concentrations of retirees, people with time and willingness to get involved.

Research has shown this "active citizenship" factor, the drive some people have to socialize and get involved outside the home, tends to follow class and status in society. People in the lower strata tend to be more alone, alienated, insecure, and their diminished concept of self-worth means they are less likely to risk themselves by associating in formal groups. William Lloyd Warner found membership in associations of all kinds involved 72 percent of those classified as being in our upper class, falling to only 22 percent of the lower-lower class. Ironically, those who could profit most from groups are the least likely to join.

In looking at the overall decline in participation in fraternal orders, McWilliams observed that bonds beyond the family unit remain weak and easily subject to disruption. Competing, home-based attractions (such as television and the VCR) interfere, making involvement outside the home "less necessary as it has become more threatening." In America today, social and political events "become more akin to funerals, something entered into only by compulsion (and even the funeral, once, was a social 'event'). The roots of loyalty run thin, and partisan commitment with them." Even though our local communities are as fragile as they were in the latter part of the nineteenth century, the fraternal self-help option chosen by our forefathers now seems to be holding less attraction.

Leaders in fraternities speculate about causes. Some groups, long dead, clearly existed because of a special need and when that condition no longer remained, the fraternity disappeared. The Grange faced a crisis such as this in the 1870s, but internal modifications and a refocusing of its mission assured survival. In the 1990s there are numerous reasons given for America's waning interest in fraternal groups. Ready access to quality entertainment is one factor. Some organizations maintain large facilities in downtown areas of large cities, an inconvenient location for evening events. The rise in day-oriented service clubs such as Rotary and Lions has taken many potential members away and, some say, the role of fraternal orders as bastions of conservative middle-class American values seems a bit out of step with our changing social scene.

Members themselves sometimes point to fraternal trappings as elements which evoke little interest. Bemoaning a drastic decline in membership for the Knights of Pythias, their supreme chancellor said in 1940 that "the day for all our fancy signs, salutations, passwords, and similar matters has long since ceased to exist." These opinions also have been heard from some within the Grange. So far, no fraternity has devised suitable substitutions for these bonding rites which pre-date the brotherhoods by millennia.

Grange historian Charles M. Gardner was correct in maintaining that "fraternities proved their worth by practical ministry to their members—bringing financial aid in times of misfortune; hope and cheer to victims of accident and illness; and courage and confidence to households of sorrow...." Additionally, he saw they played "a mighty part in preserving and extending the spirit of genuine democracy" by gathering people in lodge or Grange to make plans together, "drilling together and in countless ways working together for the common good."

All activities of the fraternal group, especially its ritual, are designed, Gardner said, "...to bring out the finer side of life and to elevate the thoughts and practices of members." The Grange founders, many of them active Masons, aspired to create an organization and a ritual which elevated the best qualities of farm life, using the everyday experience of the farmer as a reminder "of man's actual partnership with the Almighty in producing the harvest of food—the first and noblest of all occupations, and the only one directly instituted by the Great Creator."

Conditions for the Grange are somewhat different than for other fraternal groups. The Grange fulfills a dual role as a fraternity and as a special interest group representing farmers and rural residents in the legislative process. Additionally, there are myriad activities, contests and programs to keep members of all ages committed. Community service, family involvement, social activities, self-enrichment opportunities and, of course, a voice in Washington, D.C., all combine to make the Patrons of Husbandry a vital influence in rural America. Unquestionably, the wide variety of activity within the Grange is largely responsible for its perseverance for 125 years and will probably safeguard its survival for generations to come.

Document solidifies Grange roles

Plowing new fraternal ground, as they were, the early leaders of the farmer's fraternity fortunately saw the need for a unifying set of principles—in addition to the ritual—to keep their fledgling order together. Their answer, the *Declaration of Purposes,* was adopted in 1874 and the document has largely fulfilled their dream.

The *Declaration,* as it now exists, consists of a preamble and seven sections. The entire document was shortened in 1975 with language modified to meet current conditions. The *Declaration* begins with the bond of brotherhood, uniting members in "an agricultural fraternity," permitting them to "labor for the good of our Order, our country, and mankind."

Remaining from the 1874 draft are the aims which appealed so intensely to the fraternity's first members. Accomplishment of these would ensure elevation of the "lowly" farm class to a plane of equality with the wealthy merchants and moguls of industry who looked down on the tillers of the soil. Working together in the Grange would allow members:

> To develop a better and higher manhood and womanhood among ourselves; to enhance the comforts and attractions of our homes; to strengthen our attachments to our pursuits; to foster mutual understanding and cooperation; to maintain inviolate our laws, and to emulate each other in labor, in order to hasten the good time coming.

The Grange prescription for ushering in the times of prosperity and a heightened social standing was as fundamental in 1874 as it is today:

> We propose meeting together, talking together, working together and, in general, acting together for our mutual protection and advancement. We shall constantly strive to secure harmony, good will, and brotherhood, and to make our Order perpetual. We shall earnestly endeavor to suppress personal, local, sectional, and national prejudices, all unhealthy rivalry and all selfish ambition. Faithful adherence to these principles will insure our mental, moral, social and material advancement.

Subsequent sections of the *Declaration of Purposes* outline the Grange's positions on commerce, education and political action. The statements on business activity are characteristic of the spirit of Grange brotherhood and the desire to achieve harmonious working relationships:

> For our business interests we desire to bring producer and consumer into the most direct and friendly relations possible, remembering that, "individual happiness depends upon general prosperity."
>
> We are opposed to such spirit and management of any corporation or enterprise which tends to oppress people. We long to see the antagonism between capital and labor removed by common consent, and by statesmanship worthy of an enlightened people.
>
> We are opposed to wages and salaries that exceed productive efficiency. We recommend that farmers buy wisely and produce efficiently to make their farms profitable; to make maximum use of the innovations of science and technology; to systematize their work and to calculate intelligently on probabilities.
>
> To all we recommend sound money management that we may avoid insolvency and bankruptcy.

There is no question that a primary motive of all those involved with organizing the Grange was advancement of education. Aside from the Granger Laws, there has been no greater accomplishment of the organization than that which resulted from decades of persistent pressure to improve the educational system at all levels. The *Declaration of Purposes* solidifies the Grange's commitment to quality education:

> We shall advance the cause of education by all just means within our power.
>
> Influenced by our strong belief in the institution of the family, we are convinced that education begins in the family circle.
>
> Discipline is an essential part of education. Self-discipline comes with maturity. Until such time as this level of competency is reached, families and schools have a responsibility for enforcing adequate discipline.
>
> We recognize the necessity of experimentation to develop new and better methods of education, but we caution against the widespread adoption of these innovative and experimental methods until they have been proven effective.
>
> We recognize that education is a continuing process. We encourage all to continue their education through adult education classes, by continued reading, observation and such other methods as may be available, including radio and television.
>
> We recognize the valuable contribution made to education by the printed word, especially in newspapers, periodicals and books, and will continue to advocate their widespread availability.

No fraternity has been more visible in the national and state capitols than the Grange. From its beginning, it was necessary to stress that the organization could not survive if it yielded to temptations to advance its cause by alignment with a political party. There have been instances, particularly in the Bachelder administration, when the National Grange drifted from its longstanding pledge to remain non-partisan. By and large, however, the organization on state and national levels has avoided entanglement with political interests. Of the three major general farm organizations active in lobbying, the Grange tends generally to support positions which place it about mid-point between the policies of the other two. Again, the Grange is the only major fraternal organization which makes legislative action one of its primary functions.

The founders of the Grange were cognizant of the need to remain non-partisan, and that view discouraged some radical early members who departed to form the ill-fated Farmers' Alliance. The wisdom of the moderate, non-alignment stance has been repeatedly validated and the Grange's policy, so clearly stated in the *Declara-*

tion, is proudly championed by those within and without the fraternity.

> We emphatically and sincerely assert the oft-repeated truth taught in our Constitutional law, that the Grange—National, State, Pomona or Subordinate—is not a partisan or party organization.
>
> The principles we teach underlie all true politics, all true statesmanship, and, if properly carried out, will tend to purify the whole political atmosphere of our country; for we seek the greatest good to the greatest number.
>
> We must always bear in mind that no one, by becoming a Patron of Husbandry, gives up that inalienable right and duty which belongs to every American citizen, to take a proper interest in the politics of one's country.
>
> On the contrary, it is right for every member to do all in his or her power, legitimately, to influence for good the action of any political party to which he or she belongs. It is reserved by every Patron, as the right of a free citizen to affiliate with any party that will best carry out his or her principles.
>
> We acknowledge the broad principle that difference of opinion is no crime, and hold that "progress toward truth is made by differences of opinion," while "the fault lies in bitterness of controversy."
>
> We desire a proper equality, equity, and fairness; protection for the weak; restraint upon the strong; in short, justly distributed burdens and justly distributed power. These are American ideals, the very essence of American independence, and to advocate the contrary is unworthy of the sons and daughters of our Republic.
>
> We cherish the belief that sectionalism is, and of right should be, dead and buried with the past. Our work is for the present and the future. In our agricultural fraternity we shall recognize no North, no South, no East, no West.

Cooperation is the Grange's tool for achieving the American dream of equality and elimination of corruption in government and business. The attitude of cooperation sets the tone for broad-based, grass-roots involvement by members in collaboration with those representing other like-minded interests. The Grange's preoccupation with coalition-building goes back to its belief that the organization represents much more than its own dues-paying membership. Grange policies, it is presumed, are indicative of the views of a wide swath of Americans and, because of that, the Grange has a moral obligation to work with as many other groups as possible in order to ensure success in its efforts.

> Our Fraternity, being agriculturally based, family oriented and dedicated to the pure principles of equality under Constitutional Law, ...appeal[s] to all good citizens for mutual cooperation and assistance toward reform that we may remove from our midst the last vestige of inequity and corruption. We believe that harmony, equitable compromise and earnest cooperation are essential to future success.

The *Declaration of Purposes* concludes with a long narration on the operation of fraternal brotherhood within the Grange.

> It shall be an abiding principle with us to relieve any of our oppressed and suffering members by any reasonable means at our command.
>
> We proclaim it among our purposes to continue our historical appreciation of the abilities and equality of women.
>
> Imploring the continued assistance of our Divine Master to guide us in our work, we pledge ourselves to faithful and harmonious labor for all future time; to advance by our united efforts, to the wisdom, justice, fraternity and political purity so earnestly sought by the wise and courageous men and women who founded our noble Order.

For generations the *Declaration of Purposes* has been respected as an historic statement of rural independence and strength because its first edition so clearly stated pioneer dreams and outlined the action necessary to realize them. Conditions changed over 100 years and new language was needed, but the dreams clearly remain. The *Declaration* still exists as an imposing statement of fraternal cooperation and, under its guidance, the activities of one of America's most unique fraternities continue to enrich the lives of countless Americans from coast to coast.

Afterword

AS MASTER OF THE NATIONAL GRANGE, I have deemed it an honor to serve the Order of Patrons of Husbandry.

The closing words in this history book were to be my predictions for the future of the Grange. When I complete my term as national master and return home to Massachusetts, I cannot predict or perceive what my future there will be. I faced a similar ambiguity when I first arrived in Washington, D.C., to serve in my present position. Predictions are fine, but they are uncertain and do not always hold true.

My prediction for this organization is that I truly believe there will always be a Grange. Perhaps it will not appear as we see it today, but there will be a Grange. As our history shows, this organization has served a distinctive purpose in America over the past 125 years, and that role is not over. All through my life in this fraternity, which at the moment numbers 45 years, I have tried to be positive and to maintain positive thoughts about the Grange. At this milestone in our history, I hope all of our members will do likewise.

Change will come—not the superficial change usually anticipated when that word is used, but change in the total organization of the Grange. Our direction, goals and purpose have to be open for constant reevaluation and adjustment as our society evolves.

Our Grange was built upon a strong foundation: the belief in Faith, Hope, Charity and Fidelity. With a conscious effort to preserve these principles of the order, we will never fail.

The future Grange, as I see it, is one where members are very closely tied together by a strong commitment to a national health program, an extensive community service program, and a powerful youth regeneration effort. Grange is a place to use our abilities, share our experiences, exert our influence, and stimulate action.

It is truly the expression of the American spirit, providing people with opportunities to serve their brothers and sisters and their community at large. The Grange future lies in the hands of those who "plan wisely...for the future."

When we first joined the Grange, we were told in the initiation ceremony that our road to progress would be long, uneven, and include rough places, leading us where we did not know. Our road has been long—125 years—and we have encountered many obstacles. The future years will be no different, and we cannot afford to take the path of least resistance. Our road for the future must be positive, straight and forward looking.

I ask you, all the members of the Order of Patrons of Husbandry, what are your predictions for the future of the Grange? Often heard among the comments from longtime Grangers as they reflect upon their membership, is, "I don't know what I would have done if it weren't for the Grange." Their membership has had a positive value in their lives and this tells me that we have been successful in the past.

Brothers and sisters, challenge yourself to answer truthfully the question, "What is the future of the Grange?" I believe you will come up with past National Youth Program Director Wib Justi's answer: "LET GRANGE BE GRANGE." Let's continue to mold this wonderful organization to serve our individual needs and those of our community. As long as we are doing that, the Grange will remain as a powerful force in the lives of individuals everywhere.

—Robert E. Barrow, Master
The National Grange

Appendix

National Grange Officers 1991-92
Robert E. Barrow, Master (MA)
Kermit W. Richardson, Overseer (VT)
Mary R. Buffington, Lecturer (PA)
Clyde G. Berry, Steward (ME)
Donald W. Johnson, Assistant Steward (ID)
Donna Wiles, Lady Assistant Steward (MD)
Wayne Johnson, Chaplain (OR)
John A. Valentine, Treasurer (IN)
Donna Obert, Secretary (WY)
Norman Tooker, Gatekeeper (NE)
Virginia Henderson, Ceres (MO)
Ruth Lampman, Pomona (TX)
Shirley Lawson, Flora (RI)

Executive Committee
Kermit W. Richardson, Chair (VT)
Jeanne Davies, Secretary (CO)
Jack Silvers (WA)
Lester Wallace (WI)
John U. Maple (NJ)
Robert E. Barrow (MA)

Assembly of Demeter
Woodrow W. Tucker, High Priest of Demeter (RI)
Forest Farris, Priest Archon (MT)
Fae Snyder, Priestess Annalist (PA)
C. Jerome Davis, High Priest Emeritus (IN)

Current State Masters
California: William "Bill" Booth

Colorado: Jeanne Davies
Connecticut: Duane K. Wetmore
Delaware: Jane T. Mitchell
Florida: Sharon K. McHenry
Idaho: Don W. Johnson
Illinois: Russell Stauffer
Indiana: John A. Valentine
Iowa: Charles Routier
Kansas: Paul Martin
Maine: Clyde G. Berry
Maryland: Maurice L. Wiles
Massachusetts: Floyd E. Murphy
Michigan: Roland G. Winter
Montana: Olof Billquist
Nebraska: Norman Tooker
New Hampshire: Paul W. Davis
New Jersey: John U. Maple
New York: William S. Benson Jr.
North Carolina: Robert H. Caldwell
Ohio: Howard Caldwell
Oklahoma: Larry Shafer
Oregon: Dale Morris
Pennsylvania: William H. Ringler
Rhode Island: John A. Lawson Jr.
South Carolina: Albert B. Tomlinson
Texas: Clifton J. Lampman
Vermont: Margaret G. Richardson
Washington: Robert J. Clark
West Virginia: Edgar Hall
Wisconsin: William Stinemates
Wyoming: Donna Obert

Current State Council Masters:
Alaska: Sig Restad
Arkansas: Leland W. Starkey
Minnesota: Patricia Cutting
Missouri: Dean Henderson
Tennessee: Marian Moore
Virginia: James E. Taylor

Bibliography

It has been noted by others that the early years of the Grange movement have been examined by many historians. The present volume is, so far, the only one to include events within the Grange after the late 1940s. Two recent books, Marti's *Women of the Grange* and *Knights of the Plow* by Woods, shed needed new light on early Grange history and they were invaluable tools in preparing this work. Gardner, of course, will remain the exhaustive source of information on the Grange until the mid-1940s.

Secondary sources were primarily used for the period covered by Gardner (origin of the Grange through 1947). Added insight for this time frame was gained by examining Grange archives at National Grange headquarters in Washington, D.C., and at Cornell University. Tom Woods shared some revealing documents during a visit to the Kelley Farm in Minnesota and George Spies supplied numerous photocopies of old records from his extensive collection of Grange memorabilia. Primary sources, principally the *Journal of Proceedings,* were used as the only source from the 1940s on. Valuable collateral information was gained through interviews of John Scott, William Brake, Robert Barrow, Bob Frederick, Judy Massabny, Leroy Watson, Harry Massey and Jack Silvers. Correspondence and telephone contacts were made with Edward Andersen, Roy Battles, Wib Justi, Charles F. Brannan and C. Jerome Davis. Some new information on the Grange connection with the Chautauqua movement was obtained while visiting the Chautauqua Institution.

Ander, Fritiof. "The Immigrant Church and the Patrons of Husbandry." *Agricultural History 8* (October 1934): 155-168.

Anthony, Susan B. and Ida Husted Harper, editors. *History of Woman Suffrage*. New York: Arno Press, 1969.

Atkeson, Thomas Clark. *Semi-Centennial History of the Patrons of Hus-*

bandry. New York: Orange Judd Co., 1916.
Albertson, Dean. *Roosevelt's Farmer: Claude R. Wickard in the New Deal.* New York: Columbia University Press, 1955.
Baker, Gladys L., Wayne D. Rasmussen, Vivian Wiser and Jane M. Porter. *Century of Service: The First 100 Years of the United States Department of Agriculture.* Washington, D.C.: U.S. Dept. of Agriculture, 1963.
Barns, William D. "Oliver Hudson Kelley and the Genesis of the Grange: A Reappraisal." *Agricultural History 41* (July 1967): 229-242.
Benson, Ezra Taft. *Freedom to Farm.* New York: Doubleday, 1960.
Berger, Samuel R. *Dollar Harvest: The Story of the Farm Bureau.* Lexington, Mass.: Heath Lexington Books, 1971.
Bertels, Sister Thomas More. *In Pursuit of Agri-Power.* Manitowoc, Wisconsin: Silver Lake College Press, 1988.
-----. *The National Grange: Progressives on the Land, 1900-1930.* Doctoral dissertation, Catholic University of America, 1962.
Billington, Ken. *People, Politics and Public Power.* Seattle: Washington Public Utility Districts Association, 1988.
Block, William J. *The Separation of the Farm Bureau and the Extension Service.* Urbana: The University of Illinois Press, 1960.
Blocker, Jack S. *Give to the Winds Thy Fears: The Women's Temperance Crusade, 1873-1874.* Westport, Conn.: Greenwood Press, 1985.
Bowers, Douglas E., Wayne D. Rasmussen, and Gladys L. Baker. *History of Agricultural Price-Support and Adjustment Programs, 1933-84.* Washington, D.C.: U.S. Dept. of Agriculture, 1984.
Browne, William P. *Private Interests, Public Policy, and American Agriculture.* Lawrence: University of Kansas Press, 1988.
Buck, Solon Justus. *The Granger Movement.* Lincoln: University of Nebraska Press, 1965.
Buell, Jennie. *One Woman's Work for Farm Women, The Story of Mary A. Mayo's Part in Rural Social Movements.* Boston: Whitcomb & Barrows, 1908.
Campbell, Wallace J. *The History of CARE: A Personal Account.* New York: Praeger, 1990.
Capper, Arthur. *The Agricultural Bloc.* New York: Harcourt, Brace and Company, 1922.
Cerney, George. "Cooperation in the Midwest in the Granger Era, 1869-1875." *Agricultural History 37* (October 1963): 187-205.
Darrow, J.W. *Origin and Early History of the Order of Patrons of Husbandry in the United States.* Chatham, N.Y.: Courier Printing House, 1904.
Davidson, Osha Gray. *Broken Heartland: The Rise of America's Rural Ghetto.* New York: Free Press, 1990.
Davis, C. Jerome. *Notes And Quotes on the Origin of the Ritual and Early Years of the Order of Patrons of Husbandry.* Privately printed, 1974.
-----. *Proud Heritage: The Early Years of the Order of the Patrons of Hus-*

bandry. Washington, D.C.: National Grange, 1987.

Dumenil, Lynn. *Freemasonry and American Culture, 1880-1930.* Princeton: Princeton University Press, 1984.

Dyson, Lowell K. *Farmers' Organizations.* New York: Greenwood Press, 1986.

Fite, Gilbert C. *American Farmers: The New Minority.* Bloomington: Indiana University Press, 1981.

-----. "The Pioneer Farmer: A View Over Three Centuries." *Agricultural History 50* (January 1976): 275-289.

Gardner, Charles M. *The Grange, Friend of the Farmer.* Washington, D.C.: National Grange, 1949.

-----. *Facing Grange Weaknesses.* Washington, D.C.: National Grange, 1950.

Gates, Warren J. "Moderinization as a Function of an Agricultural Fair: The Great Granger's Picnic Exhibition at Williams Grove, Pennsylvania, 1873-1916." *Agricultural History 58* (July 1984): 262-279.

Gist, Noel P. "Secret Societies: A Cultural Study of Fraternalism in the United States." *The University of Missouri Studies,* Vol. XV No. 4, (October 1, 1940): 1-184.

Gould, Joseph E. *The Chautauqua Movement.* New York: State University of New York, 1961.

Hassing, Jean. *The Bible in Grange Ritualism.* No publishing information given.

Higgs, Robert. "Railroad Rates and the Populist Uprising." *Agricultural History 44* (July 1970): 291-297.

Holbrook, Stewart H. *Lost Men of American History.* New York: Macmillan, 1946.

Howard, Robert West. *The Vanishing Land.* New York: Ballentine Books, 1986.

Irwin, Alfreda L. *Three Taps of the Gavel: Pledge to the Future (The Chautauqua Story).* Chautauqua: Chautauqua Institution, 1987.

Ivins, Lester S. *Fifty Famous Farmers.* New York: Macmillan, 1924.

Junkin, Elizabeth Darby. *Lands of Brighter Destiny: The Public Lands of the American West.* Golden, Colorado: Fulcrum, 1986.

Kelley, Oliver Hudson. *Origin and Progress of the Order of the Patrons of Husbandry in the United States; A History from 1866 to 1873.* Philadelphia: J.A. Wagenseller, 1875. (Reprinted by New York State Grange, 1987.)

Knapp, Joseph G. *Seeds That Grew: A History of the Cooperative Grange League Federation Exchange.* Hinsdale, N.Y.: Anderson House, 1960.

Latham, Frank B. *1872-1972, A Century of Serving Customers: The Story of Montgomery Ward.* Chicago: Montgomery Ward & Co., 1972.

LaPalombara, Joseph G. *The Initiative and Referendum in Oregon, 1930-1948.* Corvallis: Oregon State College Press, 1959.

Lynd, Robert, and Helen Lynd. *Middletown: A Study in Modern American*

Culture. New York: Harcourt, Brace & World, 1929.
——. *Middletown in Transition.* New York: Harcourt, Brace & World, 1937.
Marti, Donald B. *Women of the Grange: Mutuality and Sisterhood in Rural America, 1866-1920.* New York: Greenwood Press, 1991.
-----. "Woman's Work in the Grange: Mary Ann Mayo of Michigan, 1882-1903." *Agricultural History 56* (April 1982): 439-452.
-----. "Sisters of the Grange: Rural Feminism in the Late Nineteenth Century." *Agricultural History 58* (July 1984): 247-261.
McWilliams, Wilson Carey. *The Idea of Fraternity in America.* Berkeley: University of California Press, 1973.
Morrison, Theodore. *Chautauqua, A Center for Education, Religion, and the Arts in America.* Chicago: University of Chicago Press, 1974.
National Grange. *Barriers to Increased Consumption of Fluid Milk.* Washington, D.C.: National Grange, 1955.
-----. *Golden Jubilee of the National Grange P. of H.* (Program of anniversary exercises held.) Washington, D.C.: National Grange, 1916.
-----. *Journal of Proceedings.* 1873-1991.
-----. *Legal and Economic Influence of the Grange, 1867-1967.* Washington, D.C.: National Grange, 1967.
-----. *Manual of Subordinate Granges of the Patrons of Husbandry.* Washington, D.C.: National Grange, 1972.
-----. *National Grange Monthly, Grange Magazine, National Grange Newsletter, Washington Update, Grange Newsletter for Farm Broadcasters, View From the Hill, National Grange Legislative Policies.*
National Rural Electric Cooperative Association. *Rural Electric Sourcebook.* Washington, D.C.: NRECA, 1990.
Neely, Wayne Caldwell. *The Agricultural Fair.* New York: Columbia University Press, 1935.
Newlon, George, Kenneth King and Dorothy Mitchell. *As Others See Us.* Washington County (Indiana) Pomona Grange, 1962.
Noblin, Stuart. *Codification of Grange Policy.* Raleigh: North Carolina State College, 1961.
Nordin, Dennis Sven. *Rich Harvest: A History of the Grange, 1867-1900.* Jackson: University Press of Mississippi, 1974.
-----. *A Preliminary List of References for the History of the Granger Movement.* Davis, Calif.: Agricultural History Center, 1967.
-----. "A Revisionist Interpretation of the Patrons of Husbandry, 1867-1900." *Historian 32* (August 1970): 630-642.
Oregon State Grange. *Journal of Proceedings.* 1875.
Oregon Grange Bulletin. October 1948, May 1963.
Orr, James L. ed. *Grange Melodies.* Philadelphia: National Grange, 1913.
Partin, Robert. "Black's Bend Grange, 1873-77: A Case Study of a Subordinate Grange of the Deep South." *Agricultural History 31* (July 1957): 49-59.

Rawson, Deborah. *Without A Farmhouse Near.* New York: Ballantine Books, 1989.

Rickertsen, Leo N. *To Gather Together: CENEX, the First Fifty Years.* Minneapolis: Cooperative Printing Association, 1980.

Riggs, A.R., and Tom Velk, "Neglected Roosevelt Progressives: The Grange in National Politics, 1905-1912." Unpublished article.

Robbins, Roy M. *Our Landed Heritage, The Public Domain, 1776-1936.* Lincoln: University of Nebraska Press, 1962.

Robinson, W.L. *The Grange: First Century of Service and Evolution.* Washington, D.C.: National Grange, 1966.

Rudolph, Richard and Scott Ridley. *Power Struggle: The Hundred-Year War Over Electricity.* New York: Harper and Row, 1986.

Russell, Charles Edward. *The Story of the Nonpartisan League.* New York: Arno Press, 1975.

Schwantes, Carlos A. "Farmer-Labor Insurgency in Washington State." *Pacific Northwest Quarterly 76* (January 1985): 1-11

-----. "Making the World Unsafe for Democracy." *Montana, The Magazine of Western History 31* (September 1981): 18-29.

Stampp, Kenneth M. *The Era of Reconstruction, 1865-1877.* New York: Vintage Books, 1963.

Strange, Marty. *Family Farming, A New Economic Vision.* Lincoln: University of Nebraska Press, 1988.

The Grange News. Seattle: Washington State Grange.

Tollefson, Gene. *BPA and the Struggle for Power at Cost.* Portland: Bonneville Power Administration, 1987.

Tonz, Robert L. "Memberships of General Farmer's Organizations, 1874-1960." *Agricultural History 38* (July 1964): 143-156.

Trelease, Allen W. *Reconstruction, The Great Experiment.* New York: Harper & Row, 1971.

True, Alfred Charles. *A History of Agricultural Education in the United States, 1785-1925.* Washington, D.C.: U.S. Department of Agriculture, 1929.

Tyrrell, Ian R. *Woman's World / Woman's Empire: The Woman's Christian Temperance Union in International Perspective, 1800-1930.* Chapel Hill: University of North Carolina Press, 1991.

Wallace, Henry A. *New Frontiers.* New York: Reynal & Hitchcock, 1934.

Warner, William Lloyd. *Americn Life: Dream And Reality.* Chicago: University of Chicago Press, 1962.

Weydemeyer, Winton. *A Grange Master's America.* Smithtown, N.Y.: Exposition Press, 1981.

Williams, Robert C. *Fordson, Farmall, and Poppin' Johnny.* Urbana: University of Illinois Press, 1987.

Woodell, Marshall E. *Grange Influence on Direct Legislation in Oregon, 1902-1934.* Master's thesis, University of Oregon, 1936.

Woods, Thomas A. *Knights of the Plow: Oliver H. Kelley and the Origins of the Grange in Republican Ideology.* Ames: Iowa State University Press, 1991.

State Histories

Over the years there have been numerous books written to record activities of the Grange on a state level. Many were issued in the 1970s to commemorate the centennials of state Granges.

While several of these histories could be called outstanding—most notably Brenkman, Norwood and Barns—many consist primarily of lists of important members and annual summaries of activities abridged from journals of proceedings.

The listing below is by no means complete; it represents those volumes that have been helpful in preparation of this study. It was initially hoped that more state Grange accomplishments could be woven into *People, Pride and Progress,* but space limitations prohibited it. It should be said that much of the Grange's best work is achieved by leaders on the local and state levels. Those accomplishments deserve more intensive treatment.

Alexander, L. Ray. *100 Year History of the New York State Grange, 1961-1973.* Courtland, N.Y.: New York State Grange, 1973. (Includes Allen, Leonard L. *History of the New York State Grange, 1873-1933.* Watertown: Hungerford-Holbrook Co., 1934. Also includes Arthur, Elizabeth L. *History of the New York State Grange 1934-1960.* No publishing information given.)

Barns, William D. *The West Virginia State Grange: The First Century, 1873-1973.* Morgantown: Morgantown Printing and Binding Co., 1973.

-----. "The Influence of the West Virginia Grange Upon Public Agricultural Education of Less Than College Grade, 1873-1914." *West Virginia History,* Vol. X, No. 1 (October 1948): 5-24.

-----. *The Granger and Populist Movements in West Virginia.* Privately published, 1959.

Brenckman, Fred. *History of the Pennsylvania State Grange.* Harrisburg: Pennsylvania State Grange, 1949.

Colorado State Grange. *Colorado State Grange History, 1874-1975.* Denver: Colorado State Grange, 1975.

Crawford, Harriet Ann. *The Washington State Grange, A Romance of Democracy, 1889-1924.* Portland: Binfords & Mort, 1940.

Dowler, John F. ed. *Ohio State Grange, Centennial History.* Columbus: Ohio State Grange, 1973.

Geil, John J. *Florida State Grange: 1873-1976.* No publishing information given.

Jenkins, Mary and Eben. *The First Hundred Years: Maryland State Grange, 1874-1974.* Maryland State Grange, 1974.

Malone, Max E. *The Grange in Nebraska, 1872-1987.* Privately printed, 1987.

Marquart, LaVerne H. *Wisconsin's Agricultural Heritage: The Grange, 1871-1971.* Lake Mills, Wisc.: Rural Life Publishing, 1972.

Massachusetts State Grange. *Massachusetts State Grange, P. of H. Inc., A Century of Community Service and Accomplishment.* No publishing information given.

Norwood, Gus. *Washington Grangers Celebrate a Century.* Seattle: Washington State Grange, 1988.

Ohio State Grange. *Centennial History, The Junior Grange in Ohio.* Salem, Ohio: Lyle Printing and Publishing, 1988.

Passmore, Joanne. *History of the Delaware State Grange, 1875-1975.* Delaware State Grange, 1975.

Pennsylvania State Grange. *Pennsylvania Grange History.* Harrisburg: Pennsylvania State Grange, 1973.

Saturley, John L. *The Grange: A Century of Service in New Hampshire.* Privately printed.

-----. *The Grange, Fifteen Years in the Second Century in New Hampshire.* Chichester, N.H.: Country Road Press, no date.

Trump, Fred. *The Grange in Michigan.* Privately printed, 1963.

Valentine, John A. *Indiana State Grange History.* Privately printed, 1988.

Index

About the Author

David H. Howard is uniquely qualified to tell the story of the Grange. A member himself since 1976, with his wife Georgetta, of Fairmount Grange No. 252 in Albany, Oregon, he has a long record of service to the organization. He also has the distinction of having immediate family members who were active and held office in Oregon Granges dating from the late nineteenth century.

Born and raised in Albany, he earned a bachelor's degree in journalism from Whitworth College, Spokane, Washington. After graduate study at San Diego State University, he was involved in the National Teacher Corps in southern California and a classroom teacher in eastern Washington. Following several years' work as a social worker and labor union organizer, he returned to the Willamette Valley where he and his wife still reside on their 45-acre cattle and Douglas fir farm near Lebanon.

Grange activity in Oregon included service as master of Fairmount Grange and county deputy for the Oregon State Grange. In 1982 he was hired as information director for the Washington State Grange and editor of their monthly member newspaper, *The Grange News.* While in that position he wrote *News Handbook for Granges,* a guide used by Granges nationwide. He was with the Washington State Grange nearly seven years.

Besides free-lance writing, Howard also is the moderator of a monthly television agriculture and rural affairs program, *The Farm-City Forum.* The half-hour telecast originates in Tacoma and is seen throughout the Pacific Northwest. The Howards have three grown sons.